INTELLECTUAL PROPERTY IN THE 21ST CENTURY

U.S. PATENT SYSTEM REFORM, ABUSE AND DISPUTES

INTELLECTUAL PROPERTY IN THE 21ST CENTURY

Additional books in this series can be found on Nova's website under the Series tab.

Additional E-books in this series can be found on Nova's website under the E-books tab.

CONGRESSIONAL POLICIES, PRACTICES AND PROCEDURES

Additional books in this series can be found on Nova's website under the Series tab.

Additional E-books in this series can be found on Nova's website under the E-books tab.

Intellectual Property in the 21st Century

U.S. Patent System Reform, Abuse and Disputes

Frances Parker
and
Marlena Lopez
Editors

Nova Science Publishers, Inc.
New York

Copyright © 2011 by Nova Science Publishers, Inc.

All rights reserved. No part of this book may be reproduced, stored in a retrieval system or transmitted in any form or by any means: electronic, electrostatic, magnetic, tape, mechanical photocopying, recording or otherwise without the written permission of the Publisher.

For permission to use material from this book please contact us:
Telephone 631-231-7269; Fax 631-231-8175
Web Site: http://www.novapublishers.com

NOTICE TO THE READER

The Publisher has taken reasonable care in the preparation of this book, but makes no expressed or implied warranty of any kind and assumes no responsibility for any errors or omissions. No liability is assumed for incidental or consequential damages in connection with or arising out of information contained in this book. The Publisher shall not be liable for any special, consequential, or exemplary damages resulting, in whole or in part, from the readers' use of, or reliance upon, this material. Any parts of this book based on government reports are so indicated and copyright is claimed for those parts to the extent applicable to compilations of such works.

Independent verification should be sought for any data, advice or recommendations contained in this book. In addition, no responsibility is assumed by the publisher for any injury and/or damage to persons or property arising from any methods, products, instructions, ideas or otherwise contained in this publication.

This publication is designed to provide accurate and authoritative information with regard to the subject matter covered herein. It is sold with the clear understanding that the Publisher is not engaged in rendering legal or any other professional services. If legal or any other expert assistance is required, the services of a competent person should be sought. FROM A DECLARATION OF PARTICIPANTS JOINTLY ADOPTED BY A COMMITTEE OF THE AMERICAN BAR ASSOCIATION AND A COMMITTEE OF PUBLISHERS.

Additional color graphics may be available in the e-book version of this book.

Library of Congress Cataloging-in-Publication Data

U.S. patent system reform, abuse and disputes / editors, Frances Parker and Marlena Lopez.
    p. cm.
  Includes index.
  CRS report for Congress prepared for members and committees of Congress.
  ISBN 978-1-61470-528-4 (hardcover)
  1. Patent laws and legislation--United States. 2. Law reform--United States. I. Parker, Frances, 1970- II. Lopez, Marlena. III. Library of Congress. Congressional Research Service. IV. Title: United States patent system reform, abuse and disputes.
  KF3100.6.U15 2011
  346.7304'86--dc23
                2011024676

Published by Nova Science Publishers, Inc. † New York

CONTENTS

Preface		**vii**
Chapter 1	Patent Reform in the 112th Congress: Innovation Issues *Wendy H. Schacht and John R. Thomas*	**1**
Chapter 2	Patent Reform: Judicial Developments in Areas of Legislative Interest *John R. Thomas*	**49**
Chapter 3	Patent Reform: Issues in the Biomedical and Software Industries *Wendy H. Schacht*	**73**
Chapter 4	Deferred Examination of Patent Applications: Implications for Innovation Policy *John R. Thomas*	**91**
Chapter 5	False Patent Marking: Litigation and Legislation *Brian T. Yeh*	**111**
Chapter 6	The Design and Implementation of Patent Revocation Proceedings: Innovation Issues *John R. Thomas*	**123**
Chapter 7	Current Issues in Patentable Subject Matter: Business Methods, Tax Planning Methods, and Genetic Materials *John R. Thomas*	**149**

Chapter 8	Gene Patents: A Brief Overview of Intellectual Property Issues *Wendy H. Schacht*	**173**
Chapter Sources		**181**
Index		**183**

PREFACE

This book provides an overview of current patent reform issues including a summary of the structure of the current patent system and the role of patents in innovation policy. Also discussed are patent quality, the high costs of patent litigation, international harmonization, and speculation in patents, which have motivated the reform proposals

Chapter 1 - Congressional interest in patent reform has increased as the patent system becomes more significant to U.S. industry. Patent ownership is perceived as an incentive to the technological advancement that leads to economic growth. Yet, this augmented attention to patents has been accompanied by persistent concerns about the fairness and effectiveness of the current system. Several studies, including those by the National Academy of Sciences and the Federal Trade Commission, recommended reform of the patent system to address perceived deficiencies in the operation of the patent regime. Other experts maintain that major alterations in existing law are unnecessary and that the patent process can adapt, and is adapting, to technological progress.

Chapter 2 - Legislative interest in the patent system has been evidenced by the introduction of reform legislation in the 111th and predecessor Congresses. These bills would have amended existing patent law in numerous respects. Although none of these bills were enacted, discussion of patent reform may continue in the 112th Congress.

Chapter 3 - Congress has shown recurring interest in reform of the existing patent system. This attention to patent policy reflects a recognition of the increasing importance of intellectual property to U.S. innovation. Patent ownership is perceived as an incentive to the technological advancement that leads to economic growth. As such, the number of patent applications and grants has grown significantly, as have the type and breadth of inventions that can be patented.

Chapter 4 - Recent congressional interest in the patent system has in part focused upon the capabilities of the U.S. Patent and Trademark Office (USPTO). Many experts have expressed concern that the USPTO lacks the capacity to process the large number of patent applications that it receives. The USPTO's growing inventory of filed, but unexamined applications could potentially lead to longer delays in the USPTO patent-granting process.

Chapter 5 - A patent holder that manufactures or sells a patented product will usually mark it with the patent number or other words that provide notice to the public that the article is patented. Such marking also permits the patent holder to recover an increased amount of damages in patent infringement lawsuits. However, marking a product with an expired patent number or inapplicable patent number is a violation of the false marking statute, Section 292 of the Patent Act. Section 292 provides that anyone who *falsely* marks an *unpatented* product with either a patent number, the words "patent," "patent pending," or any other words or numbers implying that the product is protected by a current or pending patent when, in fact, it is not, *and* does so with the intent of deceiving the public, shall "be fined not more than $500 for every such offense."

Chapter 6 - Congressional recognition of the role patents play in promoting innovation and economic growth has resulted in the introduction of legislation proposing changes to the patent system. Among other goals, these changes would potentially decrease the cost of resolving disputes concerning patents, increase commercial certainty regarding the validity of particular patents, address potential abuses committed by speculators, and account for the particular needs of individual inventors, universities, and small firms with respect to the patent system.

Chapter 7 - Congressional interest in the patent system has grown in recent years, tracking increasing recognition of the importance of intellectual property to innovative U.S. industries. One of the areas of interest is the topic of patentable subject matter—that is, the sorts of inventions for which patents may be obtained. In particular, patents on business methods, tax planning methods, and genetic materials have proven controversial. Legislation introduced in recent sessions of Congress would restrict the availability of patents in these fields. None of these bills has been enacted.

Chapter 8 - The courts have upheld gene patents that meet the criteria of patentability defined by the Patent Act However, the practice of awarding patents on genes has come under scrutiny by some scientists, legal scholars, politicians, and other experts. Gene patenting may raise ethical, legal, and economic issues; a short discussion of these issues follows.

In: U.S. Patent System Reform ...
Editors: F. Parker and M. Lopez

ISBN: 978-1-61470-528-4
© 2011 Nova Science Publishers, Inc.

Chapter 1

PATENT REFORM IN THE 112TH CONGRESS: INNOVATION ISSUES

Wendy H. Schacht and John R. Thomas

SUMMARY

Congressional interest in patent reform has increased as the patent system becomes more significant to U.S. industry. Patent ownership is perceived as an incentive to the technological advancement that leads to economic growth. Yet, this augmented attention to patents has been accompanied by persistent concerns about the fairness and effectiveness of the current system. Several studies, including those by the National Academy of Sciences and the Federal Trade Commission, recommended reform of the patent system to address perceived deficiencies in the operation of the patent regime. Other experts maintain that major alterations in existing law are unnecessary and that the patent process can adapt, and is adapting, to technological progress.

Two omnibus patent reform bills introduced in the 112th Congress, each titled the America Invents Act, would make significant changes to the patent system. Both S. 23 and H.R. 1249 would adopt a first-inventor-to-file priority system, allow assignee filing, establish USPTO fee-setting authority, provide for post-issuance review proceedings at the USPTO, and introduce other reforms. Several of these proposals have been the subject of discussion within the patent community for many years, but others present more novel propositions.

Although S. 23 and H.R. 1249 have many similarities, the two bills differ in some respects. For example, S. 23 would address the residency requirement of judges serving on the U.S. Court of Appeals for the Federal Circuit, while H.R. 1249 would not. Unlike S. 23, H.R. 1249 would significantly broaden patent law's first inventor defense. Other distinctions with respect to USPTO post-issuance review proceedings and other topics exist as well.

While the provisions of the proposed legislation would arguably institute the most sweeping reforms to the U.S. patent system since the nineteenth century, many of these proposals, such as pre-issuance publication and prior user rights, have already been implemented in U.S. law to a more limited extent. These and other reforms, such as the first-inventor-to-file priority system and post-grant review proceedings, also reflect the decades-old patent practices of Europe, Japan, and our other leading trading partners.

Some observers are nonetheless concerned that certain of these provisions would weaken patent rights, thereby diminishing incentives for innovation. Other experts believe that changes of this magnitude, occurring at the same time, do not present the most prudent course for the patent system. Patent reform therefore confronts Congress with difficult legal, practical, and policy issues, but also with apparent possibilities for altering and possibly improving the legal regime that has long been recognized as an engine of innovation within the U.S. economy.

INTRODUCTION

Congressional interest in patent reform is evidenced by sustained legislative activity over the last four congresses.[1] There is broad agreement that more patents are sought and enforced than ever before; that the attention paid to patents in business transactions and corporate boardrooms has dramatically increased; and that the commercial and social significance of patent grants, licenses, judgments, and settlements are at an all-time high.[2] As the United States becomes even more of a high-technology, knowledge-based economy, the importance of patents may grow even further in the future.

Expanded attention to patents has been accompanied by persistent concerns about the fairness and effectiveness of the current system. The American Inventors Protection Act, passed in the 106th Congress, mandated

Patent Reform in the 112th Congress: Innovation Issues 3

several changes to the patent laws, including U.S. Patent and Trademark Office (USPTO) publication of certain patent applications prior to grant and patent term restoration for delays caused by the USPTO during grant proceedings.[3] Several studies completed since the enactment of that legislation, including those by the National Academy of Sciences and the Federal Trade Commission, have recommended additional legal reforms to address perceived deficiencies in the operation of the patent regime.[4] Other experts maintain that major alterations in existing law are unnecessary and that the patent process can adapt, and is adapting, to technological progress.

Legislation introduced in the 112th Congress attempts to respond to current concerns about the functioning of the patent process. S. 23, originally titled the Patent Reform Act of 2011, now the America Invents Act, was introduced on January 25, 2011. S. 23 was reported, amended, from the Senate Committee on the Judiciary on February 3, 2011. Consideration of the bill on the Senate floor commenced on February 28, 2011; S. 23 passed the Senate, as amended, on March 8, 2011. H.R. 1249, also titled the American Invents Act, was introduced on March 30, 2011. It was ordered reported from the House Committee on the Judiciary on April 14, 2011.

S. 23 and H.R. 1249 have many provisions that are worded similarly or identically. Both S. 23 and H.R. 1249 would adopt a first-inventor-to-file priority system, allow assignee filing, establish USPTO fee-setting authority, provide for post-issuance review proceedings at the USPTO, and introduce other reforms. However, the bills differ in some respects. For example, S. 23 would address the residency requirement of judges serving on the U.S. Court of Appeals for the Federal Circuit, while H.R. 1249 would not. Unlike S. 23, H.R. 1249 would significantly broaden patent law's first inventor defense. Other distinctions with respect to USPTO post-issuance review proceedings and other topics exist as well.

Two additional bills in the 112th Congress are directed to a single topic that is addressed within the more comprehensive provisions of S. 23 and H.R. 1249. The Patent Lawsuit Reform Act of 2011, H.R. 243, would also limit the currently available cause of action for false patent marking. As well, S. 139 (not yet titled) would place restrictions upon the availability of patents on tax strategies and is comparable to section 14 of S. 23. Appropriate sections of this report review H.R. 243 and S. 139. In the event additional patent reform bills are introduced, this report will be updated to address them.

This study provides an overview of current patent reform issues. It begins by offering a summary of the structure of the current patent system and the role of patents in innovation policy. The specific components of this legislation are then identified and reviewed in greater detail. The report closes with a review of some of the broader issues and concerns, including patent quality, the high costs of patent litigation, international harmonization, and speculation in patents, which have motivated these diverse legislative reform proposals.

PATENTS AND INNOVATION POLICY

The Mechanics of the Patent System

The patent system is grounded in Article I, Section 8, Clause 8 of the U.S. Constitution, which states that "The Congress Shall Have Power ... To promote the Progress of Science and useful Arts, by securing for limited Times to Authors and Inventors the exclusive Right to their respective Writings and Discoveries.... " As mandated by the Patent Act of 1952,[5] U.S. patent rights do not arise automatically. Inventors must prepare and submit applications to the U.S. Patent and Trademark Office (USPTO) if they wish to obtain patent protection.[6] USPTO officials known as examiners then assess whether the application merits the award of a patent.[7] The patent acquisition process is commonly known as "prosecution."[8]

In deciding whether to approve a patent application, a USPTO examiner will consider whether the submitted application fully discloses and distinctly claims the invention.[9] In addition, the application must disclose the "best mode," or preferred way, that the applicant knows to practice the invention.[10] The examiner will also determine whether the invention itself fulfills certain substantive standards set by the patent statute. To be patentable, an invention must consist of a process, machine, manufacture, or composition of matter that is useful, novel and nonobvious.

The requirement of usefulness, or utility, is satisfied if the invention is operable and provides a tangible benefit.[11] To be judged novel, the invention must not be fully anticipated by a prior patent, publication or other state-of-the-art knowledge that is collectively termed the "prior art."[12] A nonobvious invention must not have been readily within the ordinary skills of a competent artisan at the time the invention was made.[13]

If the USPTO allows the patent to issue, the patent proprietor obtains the right to exclude others from making, using, selling, offering to sell or importing into the United States the patented invention.[14] Those who engage in

Patent Reform in the 112th Congress: Innovation Issues

these acts without the permission of the patentee during the term of the patent can be held liable for infringement. Adjudicated infringers may be enjoined from further infringing acts.[15] The patent statute also provides for the award of damages "adequate to compensate for the infringement, but in no event less than a reasonable royalty for the use made of the invention by the infringer."[16]

The maximum term of patent protection is ordinarily set at 20 years from the date the application is filed.[17] At the end of that period, others may employ that invention without regard to the expired patent.

Patent rights are not self-enforcing. Patentees who wish to compel others to observe their rights must commence enforcement proceedings, which most commonly consist of litigation in the federal courts. Although issued patents enjoy a presumption of validity, accused infringers may assert that a patent is invalid or unenforceable on a number of grounds.[18] The U.S. Court of Appeals for the Federal Circuit (Federal Circuit) possesses national jurisdiction over most patent appeals from the district courts.[19] The U.S. Supreme Court enjoys discretionary authority to review cases decided by the Federal Circuit.[20]

Innovation Policy

Most experts agree that patent ownership is an incentive to innovation, the basis for the technological advancement that contributes to economic growth. It is through the commercialization and use of new products and processes that productivity gains are made and the scope and quality of goods and services are expanded. Award of a patent is intended to stimulate the investment necessary to develop an idea and bring it to the marketplace embodied in a product or process. Patent title provides the recipient with a limited-time monopoly over the use of his discovery in exchange for the public dissemination of information contained in the patent application. This is intended to permit the inventor to receive a return on the expenditure of resources leading to the discovery but does not guarantee that the patent will generate commercial benefits. The requirement for publication of the patent is expected to stimulate additional innovation and other creative means to meet similar and expanded demands in the marketplace.

Innovation produces new knowledge. One characteristic of this knowledge is that it is a "public good," a good that is not consumed when it is used. This "public good" concept underlies the U.S. patent system. Absent a patent system, "free riders" could easily duplicate and exploit the inventions of others. Further, because they incurred no cost to develop and perfect the technology involved, copyists could undersell the original inventor. The resulting inability of inventors to capitalize on their inventions would lead to an environment where too few inventions are made.[21] The patent system corrects this market failure problem by providing innovators with an exclusive interest in their inventions for a period of time, thereby allowing them to capture the innovation's marketplace value.

The regime of patents purportedly serves other goals as well. The patent system encourages the disclosure of products and processes, for each issued patent must include a description sufficient to enable skilled artisans to practice the patented invention.[22] At the close of the patent's 20-year term,[23] others may practice the claimed invention without regard to the expired patent. In this manner the patent system ultimately contributes to the growth of the public domain.

Even during their term, issued patents may also encourage others to "invent around" the patentee's proprietary interest. A patentee may point the way to new products, markets, economies of production and even entire industries. Others can build upon the disclosure of a patent instrument to produce their own technologies that fall outside the exclusive rights associated with the patent.[24]

The patent system has also been identified by legal observers as a facilitator of markets. Absent patent rights, an inventor may have scant tangible assets to sell or license. In addition, an inventor might otherwise be unable to police the conduct of a contracting party. Any technology or know-how that has been disclosed to a prospective licensee might be appropriated without compensation to the inventor. The availability of patent protection decreases the ability of contracting parties to engage in opportunistic behavior. By lowering such transaction costs, the patent system may make technology-based transactions more feasible.[25]

Through these mechanisms, the patent system can provide more socially desirable results than its chief legal alternative, trade secret protection. Trade secrecy guards against the improper appropriation of valuable, commercially useful and secret information. In contrast to patenting, trade secret protection does not result in the disclosure of publicly valuable information. That is because an enterprise must take reasonable measures to keep secret the information for which trade secret protection is sought. Taking the steps necessary to maintain secrecy, such as implementing physical security measures, also imposes costs that may ultimately be unproductive for society.[26]

The patent system has long been subject to criticism, however. Some observers have asserted that the patent system is unnecessary due to market forces that already suffice to create an optimal level of innovation. From this perspective, the desire to obtain a lead time advantage over competitors, as well as the recognition that technologically backward firms lose out to their rivals, can provide sufficient inducement to invent without the need for further incentives.[27] Other commentators believe that the patent system encourages industry concentration and presents a barrier to entry in some markets.[28] Still other observers believe that the patent system too frequently attracts speculators who prefer to acquire and enforce patents rather than engage in socially productive activity.[29]

When analyzing the validity of these competing views, it is important to note the lack of rigorous analytical methods available for studying the effect of the patent law upon the U.S. economy as a whole. The relationship between innovation and patent rights remains poorly understood. As a result, current economic and policy tools do not allow us to calibrate the patent system precisely in order to produce an optimal level of investment in innovation. Thus, each of the arguments for and against the patent system remains open to challenge by those who are not persuaded by their internal logic.

PROPOSED LEGISLATIVE INITIATIVES

S. 23 and H.R. 1249 include numerous substantive, procedural, and technical amendments to the patent laws. The following table identifies and contrasts the principal provisions of the two bills.

First Inventor to File

In a significant change to the patent process, S. 23 and H.R. 1249 would shift the U.S. patent priority rule from the current "first-to-invent" principle to the "first-inventor-to-file" principle.[30] Within the patent law, the priority rule addresses the circumstance where two or more persons independently develop the identical or similar invention at approximately the same time. In such cases the patent law must establish a rule as to which of these inventors obtains entitlement to a patent.[31] Under current U.S. law, when more than one patent application is filed claiming the same invention, the patent will be awarded to the applicant who was the first inventor in fact. This conclusion holds even if the first inventor was not the first person to file a patent application directed towards that invention.[32] Within this "first-to-invent" system,[33] the timing of real-world events, such as the date a chemist conceived of a new compound or a machinist constructed a new engine, is of significance.

Table 1. Principal Provisions of S. 23 and H.R. 1249.

S. 23	H.R. 1249
First inventor to file, § 2	First inventor to file, § 2
False marking, § 2(k)	False marking, § 15(b)
Assignee filing, § 3	Assignee filing, § 3
First inventor defense (prior user rights), § 4(a)	First inventor defense (prior user rights), § 4
Virtual marking, § 4 (b)	Virtual making, § 15(a)
Willful infringement, § 4(c)	Willful infringement, § 16
Post-grant review proceedings, § 5	Post-grant review proceedings, § 5
Post-grant citation of prior art, § 5(g)	Post-grant citation of prior art, § 5(g)
Preissuance submissions, § 7	Preissuance submissions, § 7
Venue, § 8	Venue, § 8
USPTO fee setting authority, § 9	USPTO fee setting authority, § 9
Supplemental examination, § 10	Supplemental examination, § 11
Residency of federal circuit judges, § 11	
Tax strategies, § 14	Tax strategies, § 13
Best mode requirement, § 15	Best mode requirement, § 14
Clarification of jurisdiction, § 17	Clarification of jurisdiction, § 19
Transitional business method patent program, § 18	Transitional business method patent program, § 18
USPTO funding, § 20	USPTO funding, § 22
USPTO satellite offices, § 21	USPTO satellite offices, § 23
Small business ombudsman, § 22	Small business ombudsman, § 24
Priority examination, § 23	Priority examination, § 25
	Patent term extension filings, § 25

In every patent-issuing nation except the United States, priority of invention is established by the earliest effective filing date of a patent application disclosing the claiming invention.[34] Stated differently, the inventor

Patent Reform in the 112th Congress: Innovation Issues 9

who first filed an application at the patent office is presumptively entitled to the patent. Whether or not the first applicant was actually the first individual to complete the invention in the field is irrelevant. This priority system follows the "first-inventor-to file" principle.

A simple example illustrates the distinction between these priority rules. Suppose that Inventor A synthesizes a new chemical compound on August 1, 2010, and files a patent application on November 1, 2010, claiming that compound. Suppose further that Inventor B independently invents the same compound on September 1, 2010, and files a patent application on October 1, 2010. Inventor A would be awarded the patent under the first-to-invent rule, while Inventor B would obtain the patent under the first-inventor-to-file principle.

Under the current U.S. first-to-invent rule, priority disputes may be resolved via "interference" proceedings conducted at the USPTO.[35] An interference is a complex administrative proceeding that may result in the award of priority to one of its participants. These proceedings are not especially common. One estimate concludes that less than one-quarter of one percent of patents are subject to an interference.[36] This statistic may mislead, however, because the expense of interference cases may result in their use only for the most commercially significant inventions. A shift to a first-inventor-to-file priority rule would eliminate the need for interference proceedings. Instead, the applicant with the earliest filing date, rather than the first individual to have created the invention, would be eligible for the patent.

The relative merits of the first-to-invent and first-inventor-to-file priority principles have been the subject of a lengthy debate within the patent community. Supporters of the current first-to-invent principle in part assert that the first-inventor-to-file system would create inequities by sponsoring a "race to the Patent Office." They are also concerned that the first-to-file system would encourage premature and sketchy technological disclosures in hastily-filed patent applications.[37]

Supporters of the first-inventor-to-file principle in part argue that it provides a definite, readily determined and fixed date of priority of invention, which would lead to greater legal certainty within innovative industries. They also contend that the first-inventor-to-file principle would decrease the complexity, length, and expense associated with current USPTO interference proceedings. Rather than being caught up in lengthy interference proceedings in an attempt to prove dates of inventive activity that occurred many years previously, they assert, inventors could continue to go about the process of innovation. Supporters also observe that informed U.S. firms already organize their affairs on a first-inventor-to-file basis in order to avoid forfeiture of patent rights abroad.[38]

The debate over a shift to the first-inventor-to-file rule and its impact on individual inventors, small firms, and universities is contentious. Some observers state that such entities often possess fewer resources and wherewithal than their larger competitors, and thus are less able to prepare and file patent applications quickly. Others disagree, stating that smaller concerns are more nimble than larger ones and thus better able to submit applications promptly. They also point to the availability of provisional applications,[39] asserting that such applications allow small entities to secure priority rights readily without a significant expenditure of resources. A quantitative study of interference proceedings by Gerald Mossinghoff, a former Commissioner of the USPTO, also suggested that the first-to-invent rule neither advantaged nor disadvantaged small entities vis-à-vis larger enterprises.[40]

Notably, a first-inventor-to-file priority rule does not permit one individual to copy another's invention and then, by virtue of being the first to file a patent application, be entitled to a patent. All patent applicants must have originated the invention themselves, rather than derived it from another.[41] In order to police this requirement, S. 23 and H.R. 1249 would provide for "derivation proceedings" that would allow the USPTO to determine which applicant is entitled to a patent on a particular invention.[42]

Grace Period

Current U.S. patent law essentially provides inventors with a one-year period to decide whether patent protection is desirable, and, if so, to prepare an application. Specified activities that occur before the "critical date"—patent parlance for the day one year before the application was filed—will prevent a patent from issuing.[43] If, for example, an entrepreneur first discloses an invention by publishing an article in a scientific journal, she knows that she has one year from the publication date in which to file a patent application. Importantly, uses, sales, and other technical disclosures by third parties will also start the one-year clock running. As a result, inventors have a broader range of concerns than merely their own activities.[44]

Suppose, for example, that an electrical engineer files a patent application claiming a new capacitor on February 1, 2010. While reviewing the application, a USPTO examiner discovers an October 1, 2008, journal article by any author disclosing the identical capacitor. Because the article was

Patent Reform in the 112th Congress: Innovation Issues 11

published prior to the critical date of February 1, 2009, that publication will prevent or "bar" the issuance of a patent on that capacitor.

If a relevant reference is first publicly disclosed during the one-year grace period—that is to say, after the critical date but prior to the filing date—the legal situation is more complex. Under current law, patent applicants may "antedate" such a reference by demonstrating that they had actually invented the subject matter of their application prior to the date of the reference. If the applicant can make such a showing, then the reference cannot ordinarily be used to defeat the patentability of the invention.

As an illustration of this procedure, suppose that an inventor files a patent application directed to a polymer on February 1, 2008. Suppose further that the USPTO examiner discovers that a textbook published on January 1, 2008, describes the same polymer that is claimed in the application.[45] Because the textbook was published subsequent to the critical date of February 1, 2007, it does not absolutely bar the application. In order to obtain a patent, however, the applicant must nonetheless demonstrate that he invented the polymer prior to January 1, 2008, the date the textbook was published. The applicant might submit copies of his laboratory notebook, for example, or submit a sworn declaration in order to make this showing.[46]

S. 23 and H.R. 1249 would modify the current grace period by causing it only to apply to patent applicants themselves.[47] Under this proposal, a disclosure "made by the inventor or joint inventor or by another who obtained the subject matter disclosed directly or indirectly from the inventor or a joint inventor" would not be patent-defeating, provided it was made "1 year or less before the effective filing date of a claimed invention." In contrast, disclosures qualify as prior art, and are therefore potentially patent-defeating, if they were made either by (1) the inventors and their associates more than one year before the patent application's filing date; or (2) anyone else prior to the filing date, provided that such a disclosure occurred prior to the inventor's own disclosure. These amendments would, in essence, protect the patent positions of individuals who disclosed their inventions up to one year before they filed a patent application. The grace period would no longer shield inventors from earlier disclosures made by unrelated individuals, however.

Marking

The Patent Act encourages patent proprietors that manufacture their patented inventions to notify the public of their patent rights.[48] Section 287(a) provides that patent owners should place the word "patent," or the abbreviation "pat.," along with the number of the patent, on patented goods. If the nature of the article does not allow this notice to be placed directly upon it, then a label may be placed on the article or its packaging. This practice is commonly termed "marking."[49]

There is no absolute duty to mark. If a patent proprietor fails to mark in the specified manner, however, then it may receive damages only for infringing acts that occur after the infringer receives actual notice of infringement.[50] Filing an infringement lawsuit is considered to provide such actual notice. Less severely, a patent owner may issue a specific charge of infringement, commonly by sending a cease and desist letter to the infringer. The marking statute is said "to give patentees the proper incentive to mark their products and thus place the world on notice of the existence of the patent."[51]

The marking statute does not apply in some situations. Obviously, if the patent owner does not sell products that embody the patented invention, then there is no obligation to mark. In addition, "[t]he law is clear that the notice provisions of section 287 do not apply where the patent is directed to a process or method."[52] Because these types of patent concern inchoate behavior, rather than a discrete physical product, the courts have reasoned that there is no tangible item on which to place a patent marking.[53]

The Patent Act also addresses the issue of "false marking." Section 292 prohibits marking a product with the number of another's patent, the name of another patent owner, or a patent or application number where no such patent or application exists. Prohibited marks also include the number of expired patents and patents that do not cover the marked product, provided such marks were affixed for the "purpose of deceiving the public."

The Patent Act mandates a maximum fine of $500 for "every such" offense. According to the statute, "any person may sue for the penalty, in which event one-half shall go to the person suing and the other to the use of the United States."[54] In its decision in *The Forest Group, Inc. v. Bon Tool Co.*,[55] the Federal Circuit construed that provision to require imposition of that fine with respect to each item that was falsely marked. In so doing the Court of Appeals specifically rejected an interpretation that would assess the fine on the basis of the offender's single decision to mark an entire line of products. A false patent marking on one million identical products would therefore generate a maximum fine of not $500, but rather $500 million. Although the Federal Circuit acknowledged that "interpreting the fine of § 292 to apply on a per article basis would encourage 'a new cottage industry' of false marking litigation by plaintiffs who have not suffered any direct harm," the court explained "that in the case of inexpensive mass-produced articles, a court has the discretion to determine that a fraction of a penny per article is a proper penalty."[56]

S. 23 and H.R. 1249 propose to alter the Patent Act's false marking provision by stipulating that the statute may only be privately enforced by a "person who has suffered a competitive injury as a result of the violation...."[57] Damages in such cases would also be limited to those "adequate to compensate for the injury." This amendment would change current law, which allows any private person to bring a civil action for false marking, whether or not they have been negatively affected. These provisions do not apply to the U.S. government. Under the provisions of S. 23 and H.R. 1249, the U.S. government would continue to bring false marking suits without regard to competitive injury, and also would retain the ability to recover a maximum fine of $500 per falsely marked article.

In addition, H.R. 1249 would stipulate that no liability shall attach to false marking for activity during the three-year period beginning on the date the patent expires. H.R. 1249 would also allow manufacturers to avoid liability if they place the word "expired" next to a patent marking following that three-year period. S. 23 does not include analogous provisions with respect to this grace period and use of the word "expired."

S. 23 and H.R. 1249 would also allow for "virtual marking." Under this proposal, the marking standard would be fulfilled if the product or its packaging included the word "patent" or the abbreviation "pat.," together with an Internet address that provided the number of the patent associated with the patented article.[58]

A stand-alone bill, H.R. 243, also addresses false marking. Titled the Patent Lawsuit Reform Act of 2011, this legislation would also limit entitlement to bring suit to those who have suffered direct economic harm as a result of the false marking.[59] In addition, H.R. 243 would limit the damages available for false marking violations to a single fine, in the aggregate, of not more than $500.[60]

First Inventor Defense (Prior User Rights)

The two bills each address the "first inventor defense" established by the American Inventors Protection Act of 1999. As currently found at 35 U.S.C. § 273, an earlier inventor of a "method of doing or conducting business" that was later patented by another may claim a defense to patent infringement in certain circumstances. Both S. 23 and H.R. 1249 would expand the range of individuals who may assert the first inventor defense in court. H.R. 1249 would go further, eliminating the current restriction of the first inventor to business method patents. Under H.R. 1249, a patent claiming any sort of invention may be subject to the first inventor defense.

The current "first inventor defense" accounts for the complex relationship between the law of trade secrets and the patent system. Trade secrecy protects individuals from misappropriation of valuable information that is useful in commerce. One reason an inventor might maintain the invention as a trade secret rather than seek patent protection is that the subject matter of the invention may not be regarded as patentable. Such inventions as customer lists or data compilations have traditionally been regarded as amenable to trade secret protection but not to patenting.[61] Inventors might also maintain trade secret protection due to ignorance of the patent system or because they believe they can keep their invention as a secret longer than the period of exclusivity granted through the patent system.[62]

The patent law does not favor trade secret holders, however. Well-established patent law provides that an inventor who makes a secret, commercial use of an invention for more than one year prior to filing a patent application at the USPTO forfeits his own right to a patent.[63] This policy is based principally upon the desire to maintain the integrity of the statutorily prescribed patent term. The patent law grants patents a term of twenty years, commencing from the date a patent application is filed.[64] If the trade secret holder could make commercial use of an invention for many years before choosing to file a patent application, he could disrupt this regime by delaying the expiration date of his patent.

On the other hand, settled patent law principles established that prior secret uses would not defeat the patents of later inventors.[65] If an earlier inventor made secret commercial use of an invention, and another person independently invented the same technology later and obtained patent protection, then the trade secret holder could face liability for patent infringement. This policy is based upon the reasoning that once issued, published patent instruments fully inform the public about the invention, while trade secrets do not. Between a subsequent inventor who patented the invention, and thus had disclosed the invention to the public, and an earlier trade secret holder who had not, the law favored the patent holder.

An example may clarify this rather complex legal situation. Suppose that Inventor A develops and makes commercial use of a new manufacturing

Patent Reform in the 112th Congress: Innovation Issues   15

process. Inventor A chooses not to obtain patent protection, but rather maintains that process as a trade secret. Many years later, Inventor B independently develops the same manufacturing process and promptly files a patent application claiming that invention. In such circumstances, Inventor A's earlier, trade secret use does not prevent Inventor B from procuring a patent. Furthermore, if the USPTO approves the patent application, then Inventor A faces infringement liability should Inventor B file suit against him.

The American Inventors Protection Act of 1999 somewhat modified this principle. That statute in part provided an infringement defense for an earlier inventor of a "method of doing or conducting business" that was later patented by another. By limiting this defense to patented methods of doing business, Congress responded to the 1998 Federal Circuit opinion in *State Street Bank and Trust Co. v. Signature Financial Group*.[66] That judicial opinion recognized that business methods could be subject to patenting, potentially exposing individuals who had maintained business methods as trade secrets to liability for patent infringement.

Again, an example may aid understanding of the first inventor defense. Suppose that Inventor X develops and exploits commercially a new method of doing business. Inventor X maintains his business method as a trade secret. Many years later, Inventor Y independently develops the same business method and promptly files a patent application claiming that invention. Even following the enactment of the American Inventors Protection Act, Inventor X's earlier, trade secret use would not prevent Inventor Y from procuring a patent. However, should the USPTO approve Inventor Y's patent application, and should Inventor Y sue Inventor X for patent infringement, then Inventor X may potentially claim the benefit of the first inventor defense. If successful,[67] Inventor X would enjoy a complete defense to infringement of Inventor Y's patent.

Under current law, the first inventor defense "may be asserted only by the person who performed the acts necessary to establish the defense...." Both S. 23 and H.R. 1249 would also allow the defense to be asserted by "any other entity that controls, is controlled by, or is under common control with such person...." H.R. 1249 additionally eliminates the restriction of the first inventor defense to business method patents. Under the House bill, any sort of patented invention would be subject to the first inventor defense. H.R. 1249 would therefore establish a system of "prior user rights" found in many other patent-issuing states. H.R. 1249 also stipulates that the first inventor defense is not available if "the subject matter of the patent on which the defense is based was developed pursuant to a funding agreement under chapter 18 of this title [the University and Small Business Patent Procedures Act of 1980, commonly known as the Bayh-Dole Act] or by a nonprofit institution of higher education, or a technology transfer organization affiliated with such an institution, that did not receive funding from a private business enterprise in support of that development."

Inventor's Oath and Assignee Filing

Under current U.S. law, a patent application must be filed by the inventor—that is, the natural person or persons who developed the invention.[68] This rule applies even where the invention was developed by individuals in their capacity as employees. Even though rights to the invention have usually been contractually assigned to an employer, for example, the actual inventor, rather than the employer, must be the one that applies for the patent. In particular, Section 115 of the Patent Act obliges each applicant must also submit an oath or declaration stating that he believes himself to be the "original and first inventor" of the subject matter for which he seeks a patent. Section 118 of the Patent Act allows a few exceptions to this general rule. If an inventor cannot be located, or refuses to perform his contractual obligation to assign an invention to his employer, then the employer may file the patent application in place of the inventor.

S. 23 and H.R. 1249 would modify these rules by incorporating the exceptions found in current Section 118 into Section 115 of the Patent Act.[69] This proposal appears to be primarily technical in nature, although a few differences between the proposed statute and present law exist. First, S. 23 and H.R. 1249 require inventors to declare only that they are the "original inventor"—rather than the "original and first inventor"—in keeping with the proposed shift to a first-inventor-to-file priority system. Second, S. 23 and H.R. 1249 allow an "individual who is under an obligation of assignment for patent [to] include the required statements ... in the assignment executed by the individual, in lieu of filing such statements separately." This provision comports with the allowance of the filing of patent applications by employers and other assignees of patent rights.

The two bills further stipulate that a "person to whom the inventor has assigned or is under an obligation to assign the invention may make an application for patent." Individuals who otherwise make a showing of a "sufficient proprietary interest in the matter" may also apply for a patent on behalf of the inventor upon a sufficient show of proof of the pertinent facts.

Under S. 23 and H.R. 1249, if the USPTO "Director grants a patent on an application filed under this section by a person other than the inventor, the patent shall be granted to the real party in interest and upon such notice to the inventor as the Director considers to be sufficient."

Legal reforms allowing assignee filing of patent applications have been discussed for many years. Two well-known commissions encouraged this shift, albeit some years ago. A 1966 Report of the President's Commission on the Patent System recommended the allowance of assignee filing as a way to simplify formalities of application filing and to avoid delays caused by the need to identify and obtain signatures from each inventor.[70] The 1992 Advisory Commission on Patent Law Reform was also in favor of this change. The 1992 Commission observed that the United States was "the only country which does not permit the assignee of an invention to file a patent application in its own name."[71] In the opinion of the 1992 Commission, assignee filing would appropriately accompany a U.S. shift to a first-inventor-to-file priority system, as the reduction of formalities would allow innovative enterprises to file patent applications more promptly.

The 1992 Commission also explained that adoption of assignee filing may have some negative consequences. The Commission noted that patent applications filed by assignees may lack the actual inventor's personal guarantee that the application was properly prepared. In addition, assignee filing might derogate the right of natural persons to their inventions. In the opinion of the Commission, however, the advantages of assignee filing outweighed the disadvantages.[72]

Willful Infringement

The patent statute currently provides that a court "may increase the damages up to three times the amount found or assessed."[73] An award of enhanced damages, as well as the amount by which the damages will be increased, is committed to the discretion of the trial court. Although the statute does not specify the circumstances in which enhanced damages are appropriate, the Federal Circuit recently explained that "a patentee must show by clear and convincing evidence that the infringer acted despite an objectively high likelihood that its actions constituted infringement of a valid patent."[74] This circumstance is termed "willful infringement."[75]

Courts will not ordinarily enhance damages due to willful infringement if the adjudicated infringer did not know of the patent until charged with infringement in court, or if the infringer acted with the reasonable belief that the patent was not infringed or that it was invalid. Prior to the 2007 decision in *In re Seagate Technology*, Federal Circuit decisions emphasized the duty of someone with actual notice of a competitor's patent to exercise due care in determining if his acts will infringe that patent.[76] In *Seagate Technology*, however, the Federal Circuit opted to "abandon the affirmative duty of due care."[77] The court of appeals instead explained that "proof of willful infringement permitting enhanced damages requires at least a showing of objective recklessness."[78]

Prior to 2004, the Federal Circuit held that when an accused infringer invoked the attorney-client or work-product privilege, courts should be free to reach an adverse inference that either (1) no opinion had been obtained or (2) an opinion had been obtained and was contrary to the infringer's desire to continue practicing the patented invention.[79] However, in its decision in *Knorr-Bremse Systeme fuer Nutzfahrzeuge GmbH v. Dana Corp.*,[80] the Federal Circuit expressly overturned this principle. The Court of Appeals further stressed that the failure to obtain legal advice did not occasion an adverse inference with respect to willful infringement either. Following the *Knorr-Bremse* opinion, willful infringement determinations are based upon "the totality of circumstances, but without the evidentiary contribution or presumptive weight of an adverse inference that any opinion of counsel was or would have been unfavorable."[81]

Patent law's willful infringement doctrine has proven controversial. Some observers believe that this doctrine ensures that patent rights will be respected in the marketplace. Critics of the policy believe that the possibility of trebled damages discourages individuals from reviewing issued patents. Out of fear that their inquisitiveness will result in multiple damages, innovators may simply avoid looking at patents until they are sued for infringement. To the extent this observation is correct, the law of willful infringement discourages the dissemination of technical knowledge, thereby thwarting one of the principal goals of the patent system. Fear of increased liability for willful infringement may also discourage firms from challenging patents of dubious validity. Consequently some have argued that the patent system should shift to a "no-fault" regime of strictly compensatory damages, without regard to the state of mind of the adjudicated infringer.[82]

The original version of S. 23 would have added several clarifications and changes to the law of willful infringement. The bill stipulated that infringement was not willful unless "the claimant proves by clear and convincing evidence that the accused infringer's conduct with respect to the patent was objectively reckless." Knowledge of the patent, by itself, would not have constituted willful infringement. Further, damages were not to be increased if there is a close case as to infringement, validity, or enforceability. These provisions were removed in the amended version of S. 23 reported from the Senate Committee on the Judiciary, and are not included in the bill passed by the Senate.

However, both S. 23 (as passed by the Senate) and H.R. 1249 include language specifying that the "failure of an infringer to obtain the advice of counsel ... may not be used to prove that the accused infringer willfully infringed the patent...."[83] This provision appears essentially to codify the holding of *Knorr-Bremse* described above.

Inter Partes **and Post-Grant Reviews**

S. 23 and H.R. 1249 mandate changes to the options available for post-grant USPTO review proceedings by (1) replacing the existing *inter partes* reexamination system with *inter partes* review proceedings;[84] and (2) introducing a new proceeding titled "post-grant review."[85] Both *inter partes* and post-grant reviews are patent revocation proceedings administered by the USPTO. They would operate similarly to the existing reexamination system, which has been part of U.S. law since 1981. The USPTO currently administers two types of reexamination proceedings, termed *ex parte* and *inter partes*.

Under the reexamination statute, any individual, including the patentee, a competitor, and even the USPTO Director, may cite a prior art patent or printed publication to the USPTO. If the USPTO determines that this reference raises a "substantial new question of patentability" with respect to an issued patent, then it will essentially reopen prosecution of the issued patent. Traditional reexamination proceedings are conducted in an accelerated fashion on an *ex parte* basis—that is to say, as a dialogue between applicant and examiner without extended participation by others. Following the American Inventors Protection Act of 1999,[86] an *inter partes* reexamination allows the requester to participate more fully in the proceedings through the submission of arguments and the filing of appeals. Either sort of reexamination may result in a certificate confirming the patentability of the original claims, an amended patent with narrower claims, or a declaration of patent invalidity.

Congress intended reexamination proceedings to serve as an inexpensive alternative to judicial determinations of patent validity.[87] Reexamination also allows further access to the legal and technical expertise of the USPTO after a patent has issued.[88] However, some commentators believe that reexamination proceedings have been employed only sparingly and question their effectiveness.[89]

Both S. 23 and H.R. 1249 would establish a new proceeding termed a "post-grant review." Unlike current reexamination proceedings, petitioners may challenge validity based upon on any ground of patentability in a post-grant review. Under S. 23, a post-grant review must be filed within 9 months of the date of patent grant; that time limit is 12 months in H.R. 1249. To initiate a post-grant review, the petitioner must present information that, if not rebutted, would demonstrate that it is more likely than not that at least one of the claims is unpatentable. A post-grant review must be completed within one year of its commencement, with an extension of six months possible for good cause shown. As well, the individual who commenced the proceeding, along with his privies, are barred in the future from raising issues that were "raised or reasonably could have been raised" during the post-grant review.

The two bills also replace existing *inter partes* reexamination proceedings with a similar system termed "*inter partes* review." A notable difference between the existing and proposed proceedings is that the USPTO would be required to complete the proceeding within one year of its commencement, with an extension of six months possible for good cause shown. In broad outline, the bill would allow a person who is not the patent owner to file a petition requesting *inter partes* review nine months after a patent issues or reissues, or the conclusion of any post-grant review, whichever occurs later. In contrast to the proposed post-grant review, the basis for requesting an *inter partes* review is restricted to patents or printed publications. As a result, patent challenges under *inter partes* review are limited to the patentability issues of novelty and nonobviousness.[90] Post-grant reviews would allow a patent challenger to raise additional patentability issues, such as unpatentable subject matter or lack of enablement, that are not based upon a patent or printed publication.

S. 23 and H.R. 1249 differ on the evidentiary threshold required for the USPTO to commence an *inter partes* review. Under S. 23, the petitioner must demonstrate that there is a "reasonable likelihood" that he would prevail with respect to at least one claim in order for the *inter partes* proceeding to begin. H.R. 1249 requires that petitioner's evidence and arguments raise "a substantial new question of patentability"—the current standard for *inter partes* reexamination—in order to provoke *inter partes* review.

Under the time frames established by S. 23, the effective result is that a patent may be challenged at the USPTO on any basis of any patentability issue

Patent Reform in the 112th Congress: Innovation Issues 21

within nine months from the date it issued (via post-grant review). Thereafter, and throughout its entire term, the patent may be challenged at the USPTO on the grounds of novelty and nonobviousness (via *inter partes* review). H.R. 1249 operates similarly, except that post-grant review may be brought up to 12 months after patent issuance.

Under S. 23 and H.R. 1249, an accused infringer may not seek *inter partes* review if he has already filed a lawsuit challenging the patent or more than six months have passed since the date the accused infringer was served with a complaint alleging infringement of that patent. The bills afford the patent proprietor a single opportunity to amend its patent during the proceeding, with further opportunities available with good cause shown. Should the patent survive the *inter partes* review proceeding, the individual who commenced the proceeding, along with his privies, are barred in the future from raising issues that were "raised or reasonably could have been raised."

Many observers have called for the United States to adopt a more effective post-grant administrative revocation system in order to provide timelier, lower cost, and more efficient review of issued patents.[91] Such a system could potentially improve the quality of issued patents by weeding out invalid claims. It might also encourage innovative firms to review issued patents soon after they are granted, thereby increasing the opportunity for technology spillovers.[92] However, concerns have arisen over oppositions because they too may be costly, complex, and prone to abuse as a means for harassing patent owners.[93] A successful post-grant review proceeding will require a balancing of these issues.

Post-Grant Citation of Prior Art

Under current law, any person may at any time cite to the USPTO "patents or printed publications" believed to "have a bearing on the patentability of any claim of a particular patent."[94] That person may also include a written statement explaining the relevance of the cited document to the patent. This sort of "prior art citation" does not provoke any sort of administrative proceeding. However, the USPTO will place these submissions within the official file of the relevant patent, where they are accessible to the public. Prior art that potentially has a negative impact upon the patent's validity may be of considerable interest to the patent owner, its customers and competitors, and possibly others. The name of the person who files a prior art citation may be kept confidential by request.

The ability of members of the public to cite to the USPTO information that may be pertinent to the validity of a granted patent would be augmented under the provisions of S. 23 and H.R. 1249. The bills would also allow the citation of written statements that the patent owner has filed before a federal court or the USPTO regarding the scope of the patent's claims. [95]

Preissuance Submissions

The ability of members of the public to submit information to the USPTO that is pertinent to pending applications would be increased under S. 23 and H.R. 1249.[96] Under current law, interested individuals may enter a protest against a patent application. The protest must specifically identify the application and be served upon the applicant. The protest must also include a copy and, if necessary, an English translation, of any patent, publication, or other information relied upon. The protester also must explain the relevance of each item.[97]

Protest proceedings have traditionally played a small role in U.S. patent practice. Until Congress enacted the American Inventors Protection Act of 1999, the USPTO maintained applications in secrecy. Therefore, the circumstances in which members of the public would learn of the precise contents of a pending patent application were relatively limited. With the USPTO commencing publication of some pending patent applications, protests would seem far more likely. Seemingly aware of this possibility, the 1999 Act provided that the USPTO shall "ensure that no protest or other form of pre-issuance opposition ... may be initiated after publication of the application without the express written consent of the applicant."[98] Of course, the effect of this provision is to eliminate the possibility of protest in exactly that class of cases where the public is most likely to learn of the contents of a pending application.

Through rulemaking, the USPTO has nonetheless established a limited mechanism for members of the public to submit information they believe is pertinent to a pending, published application. The submitted information must consist of either a patent or printed publication, and it must be submitted within two months of the date the USPTO published the pending application. Nondocumentary information that may be relevant to the patentability determination, such as sales or public use of the invention, will not be considered.[99] In addition, because Congress stipulated that no protest or pre-grant opposition may occur absent the consent of the patent holder, the

Patent Reform in the 112th Congress: Innovation Issues 23

USPTO has explained that it will not accept *comments* or *explanations* concerning the submitted patents or printed publications. If such comments are attached, USPTO staff will redact them before the submitted documents are forwarded to the examiner.[100]

The possibility for preissuance submissions would be expanded by S. 23 and H.R. 1249. Under the bill, any person may submit patent documents and other printed publications to the USPTO for review. Such prior art must be submitted within the later date of either (1) the date the USPTO issues a notice of allowance to the patent applicant; or (2) either six months after the date of pre-grant publication of the application, or the date of the first rejection of any claim by the USPTO examiner. Such a submission must include "a concise description of the asserted relevance of each submitted document."

Most observers agree that ideally, the USPTO should have access to all pertinent information when making patentability determinations. A more expansive pre-issuance submission policy may allow members of the public to disclose relevant patents and other documents that the USPTO's own searchers may not have revealed, thereby leading to more accurate USPTO decision making. On the other hand, lengthy pre-issuance submissions may merely be repetitive of the USPTO's own search results, but still require extensive periods of examiner review that might ultimately delay examination. The proposals attempted to balance these concerns by expanding existing opportunities for post-publication submissions, but limiting the timing and nature of those submissions so as to prevent undue burdens upon the USPTO and patent applicants.

Venue

Both S. 23 and H.R. 1249 alter the venue provisions that apply to suits where the USPTO is a party—for example, appeals from inventors whose patent applications have been rejected.[101] Such cases are currently heard by the District Court for the District of Columbia. Under the bills, the District Court for the Eastern District of Virginia would hear such cases. This change in venue may reflect the fact that the headquarters of the USPTO is no longer located within Washington, DC, but rather in Alexandria, VA.

In addition, H.R. 1249 requires that a lawsuit charging infringement of a "covered business method patent" may be brought only where the defendant has its principal place of business or is incorporated, where the defendant has committed acts of infringement and has a regular and established place of business, or where the defendant has consented to be sued. A "covered business method patent" is defined to include patents that claim "a method or corresponding apparatus for performing data processing operations utilized in the practice, administration, or management of a financial product or service, except that the term shall not include patents for technological inventions." S. 23 does not address this issue.

USPTO Fee-Setting Authority

The USPTO enjoys certain rulemaking authority provided by law. The USPTO may establish regulations that "govern the conduct of proceedings" before it, for example, as well as regulations that "govern the recognition and conduct" of patent attorneys.[102] However, the fees charged by the USTPO currently are determined by Congress.

S. 23 and H.R. 1249 propose that the USPTO be granted the additional authority "to set or adjust by rule any fee established or charged by the Office" under certain provisions of the patent and trademark laws.[103] This proposal appears to provide the USPTO with greater flexibility to adjust its fee schedule absent congressional intervention. S. 23 and H.R. 1249 would require that "patent and trademark fee amounts are in the aggregate set to recover the estimated cost to the Office for processing, activities, services and materials relating to patents and trademarks, respectively, including proportionate shares of the administrative costs of the Office." Under H.R. 1249, USPTO authority to set fees terminates six years following the enactment of the statute; S. 23 does not include a sunset provision.

H.R. 1249 additionally stipulates fees for patent services provided by the USPTO.[104] In general, the House bill raises the fees slightly. For example, the current fees for filing a patent application and for the issuance of an approved application are $300 and $1,400 respectively; H.R. 1249 changes the fees to $330 and $1,510. As previously discussed, each of these fees would then presumably be subject to adjustment by the USPTO. The Senate bill does not include analogous provisions.

Both S. 23 and H.R. 1249 also establish within the Treasury of the United States a "United States Patent and Trademark Office Public Enterprise Fund."[105] Most fees collected by the USPTO would be placed into this Fund. The USPTO would then be allowed to access this Fund to cover its administrative and operating expenses without fiscal year limitation. Not later than 60 days after the end of each fiscal year, the USPTO would be required to

Patent Reform in the 112th Congress: Innovation Issues   25

submit a report to Congress that summarizes previous operations and provides a detailed plan for the upcoming fiscal year.

Under current law, patent applicants that qualify as "small entities"[106] are entitled to a 50% discount of many USPTO fees. S. 23 and H.R. 1249 establish a new "micro entity" category of applicants.[107] A micro entity must make a certification that it qualifies as a small entity, has not been named on five previously filed patent applications, does not have a gross income exceeding three times the average gross income, and has not conveyed an interest in the application to another entity with an income exceeding that threshold. The Senate-passed bill also includes any employee of a "State public institution of higher education" within the definition of a micro entity (without having to make the preceding certifications). Micro entities would be entitled to a 75% discount of many USPTO fees. The USPTO Director is given authority to limit those who qualify as a micro entity if such limitations "are reasonably necessary to avoid an undue impact on other patent applicants or owners and are otherwise reasonably necessary and appropriate." The USPTO must inform Congress at least three months in advance of imposing such limitations.

Supplemental Examination

S. 23 and H.R. 1249 establish a new post-issuance administrative proceeding termed "supplemental examination."[108] With respect to S. 23, this proceeding appears to be based upon a need to address concerns over the legal doctrine of inequitable conduct, a topic that bears some explanation. The administrative process of obtaining a patent from the USPTO has traditionally been conducted as an *ex parte* procedure. Stated differently, patent prosecution involves only the applicant and the USPTO. Members of the public, and in particular the patent applicant's marketplace competitors, do not participate in patent acquisition procedures.[109] As a result, the patent system relies to a great extent upon the applicant's observance of a duty of candor and truthfulness towards the USPTO.

An applicant's obligation to proceed in good faith may be undermined, however, by the great incentive applicants might possess not to disclose, or to misrepresent, information that might deleteriously impact their prospective patent rights. The patent law therefore penalizes those who stray from honest and forthright dealings with the USPTO. Under the doctrine of "inequitable conduct," if an applicant intentionally misrepresents a material fact or fails to disclose material information, then the resulting patent will be declared unenforceable.[110] Two elements must exist before a court will decide that the applicant has engaged in inequitable conduct. First, the patentee must have misrepresented or failed to disclose material information to the USPTO in the prosecution of the patent.[111] Second, such nondisclosure or misrepresentation must have been intentional.[112]

During patent infringement litigation, an accused infringer has the option of asserting that the plaintiff's patent is unenforceable because it was procured through inequitable conduct. Some observers have expressed concerns that charges of inequitable conduct have become routine in patent cases. As one commentator explains:

> The strategic and technical advantages that the inequitable conduct defense offers the accused infringer make it almost too attractive to ignore. In addition to the potential effect on the outcome of the litigation, injecting the inequitable conduct issue into patent litigation wreaks havoc in the patentee's camp. The inequitable conduct defense places the patentee on the defensive, subjects the motives and conduct of the patentee's personnel to intense scrutiny, and provides an avenue for discovery of attorney-client and work product documents....[113]

The Federal Circuit has stated that "the habit of charging inequitable conduct in almost every major patent case has become an absolute plague."[114] Other observers believe that because inequitable conduct requires an analysis of the knowledge and intentions of the patent applicants, the doctrine may also be contributing disproportionately to the time and expense of patent litigation.[115]

Due to these perceived burdens upon patent litigation, some experts have proposed that the inequitable conduct defense be eliminated.[116] Others believe that inequitable conduct is necessary to ensure the proper functioning of the patent system. As the Advisory Commission on Patent Law Reform explained in its 1992 report:

> Some mechanism to ensure fair dealing between the patentee, public, and the Federal Government has been part of the patent system for over 200 years. In its modern form, the unenforceability defense provides a necessary incentive for patent applicants to engage in fair and open dealing with the [USPTO] during the ex parte prosecution of patent applications, by imposing the penalty of forfeiture of patent rights for failure to so deal. The defense is also considered to be an essential safeguard against truly fraudulent conduct before the [USPTO]. Finally, the defense provides a means for encouraging complete disclosure of

Patent Reform in the 112th Congress: Innovation Issues 27

information relevant to a particular patent application.... Thus, from a policy perspective, the defense of unenforceability based upon inequitable conduct is desirable and should be retained.[117]

S. 23 would permit patent owners to request a "supplemental examination" in order to "consider, reconsider, or correct information believed to be relevant to the patent." If the USPTO Director believes that this information raises a substantial new question of patentability, then a reexamination will be ordered. S. 23 provides that a "patent shall not be held unenforceable ... on the basis of conduct relating to information that had not been considered, was inadequately considered, or was incorrect in a prior examination of the patent if the information was considered, reconsidered, or corrected during a supplemental examination of the patent." The supplemental examination request and resulting reexamination must be concluded prior to the start of litigation for the patent to obtain this benefit.

The proposed supplemental examination serves a similar goal as the existing reissue procedure—correction of an issued patent that may be inoperative or invalid.[118] A significant distinction between supplemental examination and reissue is that the latter proceeding only applies to patents that are defective due to an "error without any deceptive intention." As a result, patent proprietors must identify an error, such as the existence of a highly relevant journal article that qualifies as prior art, in order to reissue a patent. In addition, reissue may not be used to rehabilitate a patent that was procured through inequitable conduct.[119] In contrast, supplemental examination is not limited to situations where an error occurred. The proposed proceeding would also allow a patent that had been acquired through inequitable conduct to be rendered enforceable under the stipulated conditions.

The supplemental examination proceeding set out in H.R. 1249 operates similarly to that of S. 23, but with one notable distinction. H.R. 1249 stipulates that "[n]o supplemental examination shall be commenced [or continued concerning] an application or patent in connection with which fraud on the Office was practiced or attempted." This provision appears to eliminate the possibility of employing supplemental examination as a mechanism for addressing issues of inequitable conduct.

Residency of Federal Circuit Judges

Under current law, each Federal Circuit jurist must "reside within fifty miles of the District of Columbia" while in active service.[120] S. 23 would eliminate this requirement.[121] H.R. 1249 does not address this issue.

Liberalization of the residency requirement would potentially broaden the pool of individuals eligible for service on the Federal Circuit. This reform may also be appropriate for a court that enjoys jurisdiction over patent appeals that arise across the United States.[122] No other federal appellate court is subject to a similar residency requirement.[123] On the other hand, because the Federal Circuit courthouse is located in Washington, DC, the current residency rule might promote greater interaction among its jurists.

Tax Strategy Patents

In recent years, the USPTO has issued patents on financial, investment, and other methods that individuals might use in order to minimize their tax obligations.[124] The so-called "SOGRAT" patent, U.S. Patent No. 6,567,790, has been identified as one such "tax planning method" patent. The SOGRAT patent is titled "[e]stablishing and managing grantor retained annuity trusts funded by nonqualified stock options." The patent's abstract explains that it concerns:

> An estate planning method for minimizing transfer tax liability with respect to the transfer of the value of stock options from a holder of stock options to a family member of the holder.
> The method comprises establishing a Grantor Retained Annuity Trust (GRAT) funded with nonqualified stock options. The method maximizes the transfer of wealth from the grantor of the GRAT to a family member by minimizing the amount of estate and gift taxes paid. By placing the options outside the grantor's estate, the method takes advantage of the appreciation of the options in said GRAT.

Tax planning method patents have been the subject of a spirited debate.[125] Some observers believe that such patents negatively impact social welfare. According to some experts, tax planning method patents may limit the ability of taxpayers to utilize provisions of the tax code, interfering with congressional intent and leading to distortions in tax obligations.[126] Others assert that tax planning method patents potentially complicate legal compliance by tax professionals and taxpayers alike.[127] Still others believe that the patent system should not provide incentives for individuals to develop new ways to reduce their tax liability.[128]

On the other hand, some commentators explain that patents concerning the broader category of "business methods" have been obtained and enforced for many years.[129] Legislation enacted in 1999 that accounted expressly for patents claiming "a method of doing or conducting business" arguably approved of such patents.[130] Some observers believe that tax planning method patents present a positive development offering taxpayers access to a variety of legal tax minimizing strategies. In addition, these patents may potentially improve the public disclosure of tax shelters for the attention of Congress and federal tax authorities.[131] Other experts assert that many kinds of patents, on subject matter ranging from automobile seat belts to airplane navigation systems, potentially involve legal compliance.[132]

Under S. 23 and H.R. 1249, for purpose of evaluating whether an invention meets the requirements of novelty and nonobviousness, "any strategy for reducing, avoiding, or deferring tax liability, whether known or unknown at the time of the invention or application for patent, shall be deemed insufficient to differentiate a claimed invention from the prior art."[133] Under this rule, unless a tax strategy patent claimed an additional component that met the novelty and nonobviousness requirements—such as new computer hardware—then the invention could not be patented. S. 23 and H.R. 1249 stipulate that this provision does not apply to that part of an invention "used solely for preparing a tax or information return or other tax filing...." A standalone bill, S. 139, would act similarly.

H.R. 1249 includes additional provisions not found in the Senate bills. First, the House bill stipulates that the tax strategy patent provision does not apply to "a method, apparatus, technology, computer program product, or system used solely for financial management, to the extent it is severable from any tax strategy or does not limit the use of any tax strategy by any taxpayer or tax adviser." H.R. 1249 also includes language stating that "[n]othing in this section shall be construed to imply that other business methods are patentable or that other business-method patents are valid."

Best Mode

Currently, inventors are required to "set forth the best mode contemplated by the inventor of carrying out his invention."[134] Failure to disclose the best mode known to the inventor is a ground for invalidating an issued patent. The courts have established a two-part standard for analyzing whether an inventor disclosed her best mode in a particular patent. The first inquiry was whether the inventor knew of a way of practicing the claimed invention that she considered superior to any other. If so, then the patent instrument must identify, and disclose sufficient information to enable persons of skill in the art to practice that best mode.[135]

Proponents of the best mode requirement have asserted that it allows the public to receive the most advantageous implementation of the technology known to the inventor. This disclosure becomes part of the patent literature and may be freely reviewed by those who wish to design around the patented invention. Absent a best mode requirement, some observers say, patent proprietors may be able to maintain the preferred way of practicing their inventions as a trade secret. Members of the public are also said to be better able to compete with the patentee on equal footing after the patent expires.[136]

The best mode requirement has been the subject of ongoing discussion in recent years, however.[137] For example, a 1992 Presidential Commission recommended that Congress eliminate the best mode requirement. The Commission reasoned that patents also are statutorily required to disclose "the manner and process of making and using [the invention], in such full, clear, concise, and exact terms as to enable any person skilled in the art ... to make and use the same."[138] This "enablement" requirement was believed to provide sufficient information to achieve the patent law's policy goals.[139]

The Commission further stated that the best mode requirement leads to increases in the costs and complexity of patent litigation. As the Commission explained:

> The disturbing rise in the number of best mode challenges over the past 20 years may serve as an indicator that the best mode defense is being used primarily as a procedural tactic. A party currently can assert failure to satisfy the best mode requirement without any significant burden. This assertion also entitles the party to seek discovery on the "subjective beliefs" of the inventors prior to the filing date of the patent application. This broad authority provides ample opportunity for discovery abuse. Given the fluidity by which the requirement is evaluated (e.g., even accidental failure to disclose any superior element, setting, or step can negate the validity of the patent), and the wide ranging opportunities for discovery, it is almost certain that a best mode challenge will survive at least initial judicial scrutiny.[140]

The Commission further reasoned that the best mode at the time of filing is unlikely to remain the best mode when the patent expires many years later.[141] Because many foreign patent laws include no analog to the best mode requirement, inventors based overseas have also questioned the desirability of the best mode requirement in U.S. law.

S. 23 and H.R. 1249 would continue to apply the best mode requirement to all patents. However, violation of the best mode requirement would no longer form the basis for a defense to a charge of patent infringement during enforcement litigation or post-grant review proceedings.[142] Compliance with the best mode requirement would remain subject to review by USPTO examiners during the initial prosecution of a patent, although USPTO rejection of applications based upon failure to comply with the best mode requirement is reportedly a rare circumstance.[143]

Clarification of Jurisdiction

The two bills also include provisions governing which courts may hear patent cases.[144] S. 23 and H.R. 1249 confirm that state courts do not possess jurisdiction to hear claims for relief under the patent, plant variety protection, and copyright laws. The bills further provide that the Federal Circuit possesses jurisdiction over appeals relating to patent and plant variety protection cases. In addition, cases are allowed to be removed from courts that do not possess jurisdiction and transferred to those that do.

Transitional Program for Covered Business-Method Patents

S. 23 and H.R. 1249 would create a transitional post-grant review proceeding for the review of the validity of certain business method patents.[145] This transitional proceeding would be limited to patents that claim "a method or corresponding apparatus for performing data processing operations utilized in the practice, administration, or management of a financial product or service, except that the term shall not include patents for technological inventions." Only individuals who have been either sued for infringement or charged with infringement of a business method patent may petition the USPTO to commence such a proceeding. The transitional program would apply to all business method patents issued before, on, or after the date of enactment of the legislation. S. 23 and H.R. 1249 stipulate that a party may seek a stay of litigation related to the transitional proceeding, and that the district court's decision may be subject to an immediate interlocutory appeal to the Federal Circuit. This transitional program is subject to a sunset provision that would repeal the program after four years.

H.R. 1249 creates additional limitations upon enforcement of covered business method patents through infringement litigation. First, such suits may be brought only where the defendant has its principal place of business or is incorporated, where the defendant has committed acts of infringement and has a regular and established place of business, or where the defendant has consented to be sued. Second, the prevailing party in such litigation is entitled to the payment of its reasonable attorney's fees and costs from the losing party. Third, if a party seeks a stay of litigation relating to the transitional proceeding, any party may take an immediate interlocutory appeal from that decision to the Federal Circuit.

H.R. 1249 further provides that its business method patent provisions shall not be construed as amending or interpreting categories of patent-eligible subject matter.

USPTO Satellite Offices

Under current law, the USPTO is required to maintain its principal office in the metropolitan Washington, DC, area. Current law further allows the USPTO to "establish satellite offices in such other places in the United States as it considers necessary and appropriate in the conduct of its business."[146] The USPTO recently announced it would open its first satellite office in Detroit, Michigan.[147]

S. 23 and H.R. 1249 would mandate the USPTO to establish three or more satellite offices in the United States subject to available resources.[148] The bills that the satellite offices are intended to increase inventor outreach activities, enhance patent examiner retention, improve recruitment of patent examiners, decrease the number of unexamined patent applications, and improve the quality of patent examination. The USPTO is required to ensure the geographic diversity of its satellite offices. S. 23 would also designate the Detroit, Michigan satellite office as the "Elijah J. McCoy United States Patent and Trademark Office."[149]

Other USPTO Programs

S. 23 and H.R. 1249 would provide for other reforms relating to the USPTO. Among them is the creation of a patent ombudsman program for small business concerns, subject to available resources.[150] In addition, the legislation would allow the USPTO to prioritize examination of patent applications relating to technologies that are "important to the national economy or national competitiveness."[151]

Patent Term Extension Filings

The Drug Price Competition and Patent Term Restoration Act of 1984, commonly known as the Hatch-Waxman Act, provides patent holders on pharmaceuticals and other regulated products with an extended term of protection to compensate for delays experienced in obtaining marketing approval. Under current law, a petition to receive such term extension "may only be submitted [to the USPTO] within the sixty-day period beginning on the date the product received permission under the provision of law under which the applicable regulatory review period occurred...."[152] H.R. 1249 stipulates that if regulatory approval is transmitted after 4:30 PM Eastern time on a business day, or is transmitted on a day that is not a business day, then the product shall be deemed to have received such permission on the next business day. No analogous provision appears in S. 23.

CURRENT ISSUES AND CONCERNS

A number of changes to diverse aspects of the patent system are proposed in S. 23 and H.R. 1249. Although these reforms were undoubtedly motivated by a range of concerns, a discrete number of issues have been the subject of persistent discussion in the patent community over a period of many years. Among these issues are concern for the quality of issued patents, the expense and complexity of patent litigation, harmonization of U.S. patent law with the laws of our leading trading partners, potential abuses committed by patent speculators, and the special needs of individual inventors, universities, and small firms with respect to the patent system. In addition, although the patent statute in large measure applies the same basic rules to different sorts of inventions, regardless of the technological field of that invention, the patent system is widely believed to impact different industries in varying ways.[153] As a result, different industries can be expected to espouse dissimilar views of certain patent reform proposals. Before turning to a more specific analysis of individual legislative proposals, this report reviews the proposed legislation's broader themes with regard to these issues and concerns.

Patent Quality

Government, industry, academia and the patent bar alike have long insisted that the USPTO approve only those patent applications that describe and claim a patentable advance.[154] Because they meet all the requirements imposed by the patent laws, quality patents may be dependably enforced in court and employed as a technology transfer tool. Such patents are said to confirm private rights by making their proprietary uses, and therefore their value, more predictable.

Quality patents also may clarify the extent that others may approach the protected invention without infringing. These traits in turn should strengthen the incentives of private actors to engage in value-maximizing activities such as innovation or commercial transactions.[155]

In contrast, poor patent quality is said to create deleterious consequences. Large numbers of inappropriately granted patents may negatively impact entrepreneurs. For example, innovative firms may be approached by an individual with a low quality patent that appears to cover the product they are marketing. The innovative firm may recognize that the cost of challenging a patent even of dubious validity may be considerable. Therefore, the firm may choose to make payments under licensing arrangements, or perhaps decide not to market its product at all, rather than contest the patent proprietor's claims.[156]

Poor patent quality may also encourage opportunistic behavior. Perhaps attracted by large damages awards and a potentially porous USPTO, rent-seeking entrepreneurs may be attracted to form speculative patent acquisition and enforcement ventures. Industry participants may also be forced to expend considerable sums on patent acquisition and enforcement.[157] The net results would be reduced rates of innovation, decreased patent-based transactions, and higher prices for goods and services.

Although low patent quality appears to affect both investors and competitors of a patentee, patent proprietors themselves may also be negatively impacted. Patent owners may make managerial decisions, such as

Patent Reform in the 112th Congress: Innovation Issues   35

whether to build production facilities or sell a product, based upon their expectation of exclusive rights in a particular invention. If their patent is declared invalid by the USPTO or a court, patentees will be stripped of exclusive rights without compensation. The issuance of large numbers of invalid patents would increase the possibility that the investment-backed expectations of patentees would be disappointed.[158]

The notion that high patent quality is socially desirable has been challenged, however. Some commentators believe that market forces will efficiently assign patent rights no matter what their quality. Others observe that few issued patents are the subject of litigation and further estimate that only a minority of patents are licensed or sold. Because many patented inventions are not used in a way that calls their validity into question, some observers maintain, society may be better off making a detailed review into the patentability of an invention only in those few cases where that invention is of commercial significance.[159]

S. 23 and H.R. 1249 address the patent quality issue in part by allowing for increased public participation in USPTO decision-making through a pre-issuance submission procedure. This bill also permits post-issuance review proceedings, which would potentially allow interested parties to "weed out" invalid patents before they are the subject of licensing or infringement litigation.

Litigation Costs

Patent enforcement is often expensive. The complex legal and technological issues, extensive discovery proceedings, expert witnesses, and specially qualified attorneys associated with patent trials can lead to high costs.[160] One study published in 2000 concluded that the average cost of patent enforcement was $1.2 million.[161] These expenses appear to be increasing, with one more recent commentator describing an "industry rule of thumb" whereby "any patent infringement lawsuit will easily cost $1.5 million in legal fees alone to defend."[162] Higher stakes litigation is even more costly according to a 2008 American Intellectual Property Law Association study: for patent suits involving damages claims of more than $25 million, expenses reportedly increased in 2007 to $5 million.[163]

For innovative firms that are not infrequently charged with patent infringement, or that bring claims of patent infringement themselves, the annual expenses associated with patent litigation can be very dear. The

Microsoft Corporation reportedly defends an average of 35 to 40 patent lawsuits annually at a cost of almost $100 million.[164] The Intel Corporation has recently been estimated to spend $20 million a year on patent litigation.[165]

The high costs of litigation may discourage patent proprietors from bringing meritorious claims against infringers. They may also encourage firms to license patents of dubious merit rather than contest them in court. S. 23 and H.R. 1249 endeavor to make patent litigation less costly and complex through adoption of an administrative post-issuance review proceeding that could serve as a less expensive alternative to litigation, the introduction of supplemental examination, and modification of the best mode requirement.

International Harmonization

In the increasingly globalized, high-technology economy, patent protection in a single jurisdiction is often ineffective to protect the interests of inventors. As a result, U.S. inventors commonly seek patent protection abroad. Doing so can be a costly, time-consuming, and difficult process. There is no global patent system. Inventors who desire intellectual property protection in a particular country must therefore take specific steps to procure a patent within that jurisdiction.[166]

Differences in national laws are among the difficulties faced by U.S. inventors seeking patent rights overseas. Although the world's patent laws have undergone considerable harmonization in recent years, several notable distinctions between U.S. patent law and those of our leading trading partners persist. S. 23 and H.R. 1249 address some of these differences by modifying U.S. patent law in order to comport with international standards. Among these proposed reforms are adoption of a first-inventor-to-file priority system, a more robust post-issuance review system, and assignee filing.

Potential Abuses by Patent Speculators

Some commentators believe that the patent system too frequently attracts speculators who prefer to acquire and enforce patents rather than engage in research, development, manufacturing, or other socially productive activity.[167] Patent speculators are sometimes termed "trolls," after creatures from folklore that would emerge from under a bridge in order to waylay travelers.[168] The late Jerome C. Lemelson, a prolific inventor who owned hundreds of patents and launched numerous charges of patent infringement, has sometimes been mentioned in this context. The total revenue of the Lemelson estate's patent licensing program has been reported as in excess of $1.5 billion.[169] But as explained by journalist Michael Ravnitzky, "critics charge that many Lemelson patents are so-called submarine patents, overly broad applications that took so long to issue or were so general in nature that their owners could unfairly claim broad infringement across entire industry sectors."[170] Of such patent ventures, patent attorney James Pooley observes:

> Of course there is nothing inherently wrong with charging someone rent to use your property, including intellectual property like patents. But it's useful to keep in mind—especially when listening to prattle about losing American jobs to foreign competition—that these patent mills produce no products. Their only output is paper, of a highly threatening sort.[171]

Patent enforcement suits brought by patent speculators appear to present special concerns for manufacturers and service providers. If one manufacturer or service provider commences litigation against another, the defendant can often assert its own claims of patent infringement against the plaintiff. Because patent speculators do not otherwise participate in the marketplace, however, the defendant is unable to counter with its own patent infringement charges. This asymmetry in litigation positions reportedly reduces the bargaining power of manufacturers and service providers, potentially exposing them to harassment.[172]

Observers hasten to note, however, that not every patent proprietor who does not commercialize the patented invention should properly be considered an opportunistic "troll." A nonmanufacturing patentee may lack the expertise or resources to produce a patented product, prefer to commit itself to further innovation, or otherwise have legitimate reasons for its behavior.[173] Universities and small biotechnology companies often fit into this category. Further, whether classified as a "troll" or not, each patent owner has presumptively fulfilled all of the relevant statutory requirements. Among these obligations is a thorough disclosure of a novel, nonobvious invention to the public.[174]

Concerns over "trolling" are addressed in S. 23 and H.R. 1249 by the introduction of post-issuance review procedures.

The Role of Individuals, Universities, and Small Entities

Entrepreneurs and small, innovative firms play a role in the technological advancement and economic growth of the United States.[175] Several studies commissioned by U.S. federal agencies have concluded that individuals and small entities constitute a significant source of innovative products and services.[176] Studies have also indicated that entrepreneurs and small, innovative firms rely more heavily upon the patent system than larger enterprises. Larger companies are said to possess alternative means for achieving a proprietary or property-like interest in a particular technology. For example, trade secrecy, ready access to markets, trademark rights, speed of development, and consumer goodwill may to some degree act as substitutes to the patent system.[177] However, individual inventors and small firms often do not have these mechanisms at their disposal. As a result, the patent system may enjoy heightened importance with respect to these enterprises.[178]

In recent years, universities have also become more full-fledged participants in the patent system. This trend has been attributed to the Bayh-Dole Act,[179] a federal statute that allowed universities and other government contractors to retain patent title to inventions developed with the benefit of federal funding.[180] In recent years there has reportedly "been a dramatic increase in academic institutions' investments in technology licensing activities."[181] This increase has been reflected in the growth in the number of patents held by universities, the number of universities with technology transfer offices, and the amount of patent-based licensing revenues that these offices have raised.[182]

The U.S. patent system has long acknowledged the role, and particular needs, of independent inventors, small firms, and universities. For example, the patent statute calls for each of these entities to receive a 50% discount on many USPTO fees.[183] As the USPTO is currently entirely funded by the fees it charges its users,[184] this provision effectively calls for larger institutions to subsidize the patent expenditures of their smaller competitors.

Beyond potentially diminished financial resources vis-à-vis larger concerns, however, observers have disagreed over whether independent inventors, small firms, and universities have particular needs with respect to the patent system, and if so whether those needs should be reflected in patent law doctrines. For example, with respect to the proposed system of "prior user rights,"[185] some observers state that such rights would particularly benefit small entities, which may often lack a sophisticated knowledge of the patent system.[186] Others disagree, stating that smaller concerns rely heavily on the exclusivity of the patent right, and that the adoption of prior user rights would advantage large enterprises.[187] Similar debates have occurred with respect to other patent reform proposals, perhaps reflecting the fact that the community of independent inventors, small firms, and universities is itself a diverse one.

A number of provisions in S. 23 and H.R. 1249 appear to be of particular interest to independent inventors, universities, and small businesses, including a shift to a first-inventor-to-file priority system, post-grant review procedures, the creation of a patent ombudsman program for small business concerns, and reduced fees for "micro entities."

Differing Patent Values in Distinct Industries

To a large extent, the patent statute subjects all inventions to the same standards, regardless of the field in which those inventions arose. Whether the invention is an automobile engine, semiconductor, or a pharmaceutical, it is for the most part subject to the same patentability requirements, scope of rights, and term of protection. Both experience and economic research suggest that distinct industries encounter the patent system in different ways, however. As a result, it can be expected that particular industries will react differently to the various patent reform proposals currently before Congress.[188]

Studies suggest that different industries attach widely varying values to patents. For example, one analysis of the aircraft and semiconductor industries suggested that lead time and the strength of the learning curve were superior to patents in capturing the value of investments.[189] In contrast, members of the drug and chemical industries attach a higher value to patents where patents are considered the most effective method to protect inventions, particularly when biotechnology is included.[190] Among the reasons for these divergent assessments are "the cost of research and development (especially in relation to imitation costs), the technological risk associated with such research, and the availability of effective non-patent means of protection."[191]

Although broad generalizations should be drawn with care, two industries widely perceived as using the patent system in different ways are the pharmaceutical and software sectors. Within the pharmaceutical industry, individual patents are perceived as critical to a business model that provides life-saving and life-enhancing medical innovations, but eventually allows members of the public access to medicines at low cost. In particular, often only a handful, and sometimes only one or two patents cover a particular drug product, therefore "the relative value per patent is much higher in the life sciences."[192] Patents are also judged to be crucial to the pharmaceutical sector because of the large R&D investments associated with bringing a drug to market, as well as the relative ease of replicating the finished product. For example, while it is expensive, complicated, and time consuming to duplicate an airplane, it is relatively simple to perform a chemical analysis of a pill and reproduce it.[193]

In contrast to the pharmaceutical field, the nature of software development is such that innovations are typically cumulative and new products often embody numerous patentable inventions. This environment has led to what has been described as a

> poor match between patents and products in the [software] industry: it is difficult to patent an entire product in the software industry because any particular product is likely to include dozens if not hundreds of separate technological ideas.[194]

This situation may be augmented by the multiplicity of patents often associated with a finished computer product that uses the software. It is not uncommon for thousands of different patents (relating to hardware and software) to be embodied in one single computer. In addition, ownership of these patents may well be fractured among hundreds or thousands of different individuals and firms.

In general, the patent laws provide a "one size fits all" system, where all inventions are subject to the same requirements of patentability and scope of protection, regardless of the technical field in which they arose. Innovators in different fields nonetheless have varying experiences with the patent system. The differing valuation of patents among sectors leads to the expectation that distinct industries may react differently to the various patent reform proposals presently being considered by Congress, particularly the assessment of damages.

CONCLUDING OBSERVATIONS

As introduced in the 112th Congress, S. 23 and H.R. 1249 arguably would work the most sweeping reforms to the U.S. patent system since the nineteenth century. However, many of the provisions in the bill, such as preissuance submissions and post-issuance proceedings, have already been implemented in U.S. law to a more limited extent. These and other proposed modifications,

Patent Reform in the 112th Congress: Innovation Issues   41

such as the first-inventor-to-file priority system and assignee filing, also reflect the decades-old patent practices of Europe, Japan, and our other leading trading partners. As well, many of the suggested changes enjoy the support of diverse institutions, including the Federal Trade Commission, National Academies, economists, industry representatives, attorneys, and legal academics.

Other knowledgeable observers are nonetheless concerned that certain of these proposals would weaken the patent right, thereby diminishing needed incentives for innovation. Some experts also believe that changes of this magnitude, occurring at the same time, do not present the most prudent course for the patent system. Patent reform therefore confronts Congress with difficult legal, practical, and policy issues, but also with the apparent possibility for altering and potentially improving the legal regime that has long been recognized as an engine of innovation within the U.S. economy.

ACKNOWLEDGMENTS

This report was funded in part by a grant from the John D. and Catherine T. MacArthur Foundation.

End Notes

[1] This report is based substantially on three predecessor reports on patent reform issues in the 111th, 110th, and 109th Congresses: CRS Report R40481, *Patent Reform in the 111th Congress: Innovation Issues*, by Wendy H. Schacht and John R. Thomas; CRS Report RL33996, *Patent Reform in the 110th Congress: Innovation Issues*, by John R. Thomas and Wendy H. Schacht; and CRS Report RL32996, *Patent Reform: Innovation Issues*, by John R. Thomas and Wendy H. Schacht.

[2] Statistics from the United States Patent and Trademark Office (USPTO) support this account. In 1980, 104,329 utility patent applications were received at the U.S. Patent and Trademark Office (USPTO); by 2009, this number had more than quadrupled to 456,106 applications. During the same time period, the number of U.S. utility patents granted grew from 61,819 to 167,349. U.S. Patent and Trademark Office, *U.S. Patent Statistics, Calendar Years 1963-2009*, available at http://www.uspto.gov/web/offices/ac/ido/oeip/taf/us_stat.pdf.

[3] The American Inventors Protection Act of 1999, P.L. 106-113, was part of the Intellectual Property and Communications Omnibus Reform Act of 1999, attached by reference to the Consolidated Appropriations Act for Fiscal Year 2000. President Clinton signed this bill on November 29, 1999.

[4] National Research Council, National Academy of Sciences, *A Patent System for the 21st Century* [Washington, National Academies Press, 2004] and Federal Trade Commission, *To Promote Innovation: The Proper Balance of Competition and Patent Law and Policy*, October 2003, available at http://www.ftc.gov.

[5] P.L. 82-593, 66 Stat. 792 (codified at Title 35 United States Code).

[6] 35 U.S.C. § 111.

[7] 35 U.S.C. § 131.

[8] John R. Thomas, "On Preparatory Texts and Proprietary Technologies: The Place of Prosecution Histories in Patent Claim Interpretation," 47 *UCLA Law Review* (1999), 183.

[9] 35 U.S.C. § 112.

[10] *Ibid.*

[11] 35 U.S.C. § 101.

[12] 35 U.S.C. § 102.

[13] 35 U.S.C. § 103.

[14] 35 U.S.C. § 271(a).

[15] 35 U.S.C. § 283.

[16] 35 U.S.C. § 284.

[17] 35 U.S.C. § 154(a)(2). Although patent term is based upon the filing date, the patentee gains no enforceable legal rights until the USPTO allows the application to issue as a granted patent. A number of Patent Act provisions may modify the basic 20-year term, including examination delays at the USPTO and delays in obtaining marketing approval for the patented invention from other federal agencies.

[18] 35 U.S.C. § 282.

[19] 28 U.S.C. § 1295(a)(1).

[20] 28 U.S.C. § 1254(1).

[21] *See* Rebecca S. Eisenberg, "Patents and the Progress of Science: Exclusive Rights and Experimental Use," 56 *University of Chicago Law Review* 1017 (1989).

[22] 35 U.S.C. § 112.

[23] 35 U.S.C. § 154.

[24] Eisenberg, *supra,* at 1017.

[25] Robert P. Merges, "Intellectual Property and the Costs of Commercial Exchange: A Review Essay," 93 *Michigan Law Review* (1995), 1570.

[26] David D. Friedman *et al.,* "Some Economics of Trade Secret Law," 5 *Journal of Economic Perspectives* (1991), 61.

[27] *See* Jonathan M. Barnett, "Private Protection of Patentable Goods," 25 *Cardozo Law Review* (2004), 1251.

[28] *See* John R. Thomas, "Collusion and Collective Action in the Patent System: A Proposal for Patent Bounties," *University of Illinois Law Review* (2001), 305.

[29] *Ibid.*

[30] S. 23 at § 2(b); H.R. 1249 at § 2(b).

[31] *See* Roger E. Schechter & John R. Thomas, *Principles of Patent Law* § 1.2.5 (2d ed. 2004).

[32] In addition, the party that was the first to invent must not have abandoned, suppressed or concealed the invention. 35 U.S.C. § 102(g)(2).

[33] *See* Charles E. Gholz, "First-to-File or First-to-Invent?," 82 *Journal of the Patent and Trademark Office Society* (2000), 891.

[34] *See* Peter A. Jackman, "Adoption of a First-to-File System: A Proposal," 26 *University of Baltimore Law Review* (1997), 67.

[35] 35 U.S.C. § 135.

[36] *See* Clifford A. Ulrich, "The Patent Systems Harmonization Act of 1992: Conformity at What Price?," 16 *New York Law School Journal of International and Comparative Law* (1996), 405.

[37] *See* Brad Pedersen & Vadim Braginsky, "The Rush to First-to-File Patent System in the United States: Is a Globally Standardized Patent Reward System Really Beneficial to Patent Quality and Administrative Efficiency?," 7 *Minnesota Journal of Law, Science & Technology* (2006), 757.

Patent Reform in the 112th Congress: Innovation Issues   43

[38] *See* Whitney E. Fraser Tiedemann, "First-to-File: Promoting the Goals of the United States Patent System as Demonstrated Through the Biotechnology Industry," 41 *University of San Francisco Law Review* (2007), 477.

[39] 35 U.S.C. § 111(b).

[40] Gerald J. Mossinghoff, "The U.S. First-to-Invent System Has Provided No Advantage to Small Entities," 84 *Journal of the Patent and Trademark Office Society* (2002), 425.

[41] 35 U.S.C. § 101.

[42] S. 23 at § 2(h); H.R. 1249 at § 2(h).

[43] 35 U.S.C. § 102(b).

[44] Schechter & Thomas, *supra*, at § 4.3.1.

[45] In addition, the textbook must be attributable to someone other than the patent applicant. *See* 35 U.S.C. § 102(a).

[46] 37 C.F.R. § 1.131.

[47] S. 23 at § 2(b); H.R. 1249 at § 2(b).

[48] For further discussion of current patent marking issues and proposed legislation, see CRS Report R41418, *False Patent Marking: Litigation and Legislation*, by Brian T. Yeh.

[49] *See* Schechter & Thomas, *supra*, at § 9.2.3.

[50] It should be further appreciated that under 35 U.S.C. § 286, "no recovery shall be had for any infringement committed more than six years prior to the filing of the complaint or counterclaim for infringement in the action."

[51] Laitram Corp. v. Hewlett-Packard Co., 806 F. Supp. 1294, 1296 (E.D. La. 1992).

[52] American Med. Sys., Inc. v. Medical Eng'g Corp., 6 F.3d 1523, 1538 (Fed. Cir. 1993).

[53] *See* State Contracting & Eng'g Corp. v. Condotte Am., Inc., 346 F.3d 1057, 1074 (Fed. Cir. 2003).

[54] 35 U.S.C. § 292(b). This sort of proceeding is termed a *qui tam* action.

[55] 590 F.3d 1295 (Fed. Cir. 2009).

[56] *Ibid.* at 1303-04.

[57] S. 23 at § 2(k); H.R. 1249 at § 15(b).

[58] S. 23 at § 4(b); H.R. 1249 at § 15(a).

[59] H.R. 243, § 2(a)(2).

[60] *Id.* at § 2(a)(1)(C).

[61] Restatement of Unfair Competition § 39.

[62] David D. Friedman, "Some Economics of Trade Secret Law," 5 *Journal of Economic Perspectives* (1991), 61, 64.

[63] 35 U.S.C. § 102(b). *See* Metallizing Engineering Co. v. Kenyon Bearing & Auto Parts, 153 F.2d 516 (2d Cir. 1946).

[64] 35 U.S.C. § 154.

[65] W.L. Gore & Associates v. Garlock, Inc., 721 F.2d 1540 (Fed. Cir. 1983).

[66] 149 F.3d 1368 (Fed. Cir. 1998).

[67] As presently codified at 35 U.S.C. § 273, the first inventor defense is subject to a number of additional qualifications. First, the defendant must have reduced the infringing subject matter to practice at least one year before the effective filing date of the application. Second, the defendant must have commercially used the infringing subject matter prior to the effective filing date of the patent. Finally, any reduction to practice or use must have been made in good faith, without derivation from the patentee or persons in privity with the patentee.

[68] 35 U.S.C. § 111.

[69] S. 23 at § 3; H.R. 1249 at § 3.

[70] President's Commission on the Patent System, *"To Promote the Progress of... Useful Arts" in an Age of Exploding Technology* (1966).

[71] Advisory Commission on Patent Reform, *A Report to the Secretary of Commerce* (August 1992), 179.

[72] *Id.*

[73] 35 U.S.C. § 284.

[74] *In re Seagate Technology*, 497 F.3d 1360 (Fed. Cir. 2007) (in banc).

[75] *See* Beatrice Foods Co. v. New England Printing & Lithographing Co., 923 F.2d 1576, 1578 (Fed. Cir. 1991).

[76] *See, e.g.,* Jon E. Wright, "Willful Patent Infringement and Enhanced Damages—Evolution and Analysis," 10 *George Mason Law Review* (2001), 97.

[77] *Seagate Technologies, supra.*

[78] *Id.*

[79] *See, e.g.,* Fromson v. Western Litho Plate & Supply Co., 853 F.2d 1568, 1572 (Fed. Cir. 1988).

[80] 383 F.3d 1337 (Fed. Cir. 2004).

[81] *Ibid* at 1341.

[82] *See generally* Schechter & Thomas, *supra*, at § 9.2.5.

[83] S. 23 at § 4(c); H.R. 1249 at § 16.

[84] S. 23 at § 5(a); H.R. 1249 at § 5(a).

[85] S. 23 at § 5(d); H.R. 1249 at § 5(d).

[86] The American Inventors Protection Act of 1999, P.L. 106-113, was part of the Intellectual Property and Communications Omnibus Reform Act of 1999, attached by reference to the Consolidated Appropriations Act for Fiscal Year 2000. President Clinton signed this bill on November 29, 1999.

[87] Mark D. Janis, "Inter Partes Reexamination," 10 *Fordham Intellectual Property, Media & Entertainment Law Journal* (2000), 481.

[88] Craig Allen Nard, "Certainty, Fence Building and the Useful Arts," 74 *Indiana Law Journal* (1999), 759.

[89] *See* Schechter & Thomas, *supra*, at § 7.5.4.

[90] Notably, the proposed restriction of *inter partes* review to patents and printed publications limits the grounds on which a patent challenger may request such a review. Once a patent is subject to *inter partes* review, the USPTO may potentially consider other pertinent patentability issues, such as claim definiteness.

[91] *See* National Research Council of the National Academies, *A Patent System for the 21st Century* (2004), 96.

[92] *Ibid.* at 103.

[93] *See* Mark D. Janis, "Rethinking Reexamination: Toward a Viable Administrative Revocation System for U.S. Patent Law," 11 *Harvard Journal of Law and Technology* (1997), 1.

[94] 35 U.S.C. § 301.

[95] S. 23 at § 5(g); H.R. 1249 at § 5(g)

[96] S. 23 at § 7; H.R. 1249 at § 7.

[97] 37 C.F.R. § 1.291.

[98] 35 U.S.C. § 122(c).

[99] 37 C.F.R. § 1.99.

[100] U.S. Dept. of Commerce, U.S. Patent & Trademark Off., Manual of Patent Examining Procedure § 1134.01 (8th ed. July 2008).

[101] S. 23 at § 8; H.R. 1249 at § 8.

[102] 35 U.S.C. § 2(b)(2). It should be appreciated that "Congress has not vested the [USPTO] with any general substantive rulemaking power.... " Cybor Corp. v. FAS Techs, Inc., 138 F.3d 1448, 1479 (Fed. Cir. 1998) (en banc) (Newman, J., additional views).

[103] S. 23 at § 9; H.R. 1249 at § 9.

[104] H.R. 1249 at § 10.

[105] S. 23 at § 20; H.R. 1249 at § 22.

[106] "Small entities" consist of "with respect to their application to any small business concern as defined under section 3 of the Small Business Act, and to any independent inventor or nonprofit organization as defined in regulations issued by the Director." 35 U.S.C. § 41(h).

[107] S. 23 at § 12; H.R. 1249 at § 9(g)

[108] S. 23 at § 10; H.R. 1249 at § 11.

[109] 35 U.S.C. § 122(a) (stating the general rule that "applications for patents shall be kept in confidence by the Patent and Trademark Office and no information concerning the same given without authority of the applicant.... ").

[110] Glaverbel Societe Anonyme v. Northlake Mktg. & Supply Inc., 45 F.3d 1550 (Fed. Cir. 1995).

[111] Heidelberger Druckmaschinen AG v. Hantscho Comm'l Prods., Inc., 21 F.3d 1068 (Fed. Cir. 1993).

[112] Jazz Photo Corp. v. U.S. Int'l Trade Comm'n, 264 F.3d 1094 (Fed. Cir. 2001).

[113] John F. Lynch, "An Argument for Eliminating the Defense of Patent Unenforceability Based on Inequitable Conduct," 16 *American Intellectual Property Law Association Quarterly Journal* (1988), 7.

[114] Burlington Indus., Inc. v. Dayco Corp., 849 F.2d 1418 (Fed. Cir. 1988).

[115] *See, e.g.,* Scott D. Anderson, "Inequitable Conduct: Persistent Problems and Recommended Resolutions," 82 *Marquette Law Review* (1999), 845.

[116] Lynch, *supra*, at 7.

[117] 1992 Advisory Commission, *supra*, at 114.

[118] *See* 35 U.S.C. §§ 251-252.

[119] Aventis Pharma S.A. v. Amphastar Pharmaceuticals, Inc., 525 F.3d 1334, 1341 n.6 (Fed. Cir. 2008).

[120] 28 U.S.C. § 44(c).

[121] S. 23 at § 11.

[122] 28 U.S.C. § 1295(a)(1).

[123] Marcia Coyle, "Court's Residency Rule May Fall: Federal Circuit Rule Limits Bench Talent," 29 *National Law Journal* no. 44 (July 9, 2007), 1.

[124] *See* CRS Report RL34221, *Patents on Tax Strategies: Issues in Intellectual Property and Innovation*, by John R. Thomas.

[125] *See, e.g.,* Jo-el J. Meyer, "Proliferation of Retirement Plan Patents Poses Problems for Practitioners," *Patent, Trademark, & Copyright Journal* (BNA June 8, 2007), 186; Wealth Transfer Group LLC v. Rowe, D. Conn., No. 3:06cv00024 (AWT), filed January 6, 2006.

[126] *See* Letter from Jeffrey R. Hoops, Chair, American Institute of Certified Public Accountants Tax Executive Committee, to Members of Congress (February 28, 2007) (available at http://www.macpa.org/content/Public/ Documents/PDF/aicpa_tax030607.pdf).

[127] *See* Letter from Kimberly S. Blanchard, Chair, New York State Bar Association Tax Section, to Members of Congress (August 17, 2006) (available at http://www.nysba.org/ Content/ContentGroups/Section_Information1/ Tax_Section_Reports/1115rpt.PDF).

[128] *See* William A. Drennan, "The Patented Loophole: How Should Congress Respond to This Judicial Invention?," 59 *Florida Law Review* (2007), 229.

[129] *See* Andrew F. Palmieri & Corinne Marie Pouliquen, "A Primer on Business Method Patents: What You Need to Know for Your Real Estate Practice," 21 *Probate and Property* (May/June 2007), 26.

[130] First Inventor Defense Act of 1999, P.L. 106-113, § 4302, 113 Stat. 1501 (codified at 35 U.S.C. § 273 (2006)).

[131] Drennan, *supra*, at 328 (noting this argument).

[132] Stephen T. Schreiner & George Y. Wang, "Discussions on Tax Patents Have Lost Focus," *IP Law 360* (available at http://www.hunton.com).

[133] S. 23 at § 14; H.R. 1249 at § 13.

[134] 35 U.S.C. § 112.

[135] *See, e.g.,* Chemcast Corp. v. Arco Industries Corp. 913 F.2d 923 (Fed. Cir. 1990).

[136] *See* Dale L. Carlson *et al.*, "Patent Linchpin for the 21st Century? Best Mode Revisited," 87 *Journal of the Patent and Trademark Office Society* (2005), 89.

[137] *See, e.g.,* Steven B. Walmsley, "Best Mode: A Plea to Repair or Sacrifice This Broken Requirement of United States Patent Law," 9 *Michigan Telecommunications and Technology Law Review* (2002), 125.

[138] 35 U.S.C. § 101.

[139] 1992 Advisory Commission Report, *supra,* at 102-03.

[140] *Id.* at 101.

[141] *Id.* at 102-03.

[142] S. 23 at § 17; H.R. 1249 at § 19.

[143] Jerry R. Selinger, "In Defense of "Best Mode": Preserving the Benefit of the Bargain for the Public, 43 *Catholic University Law Review* (1994), 1099 ("Failure to comply with best mode ... is not something an examiner normally can evaluate when reviewing the application.... ").

[144] S. 23 at § 2(b); H.R. 1249 at § 2(b).

[145] S. 23 at § 18; H.R. 1249 at § 18.

[146] 35 U.S.C. §1(b).

[147] U.S. Patent and Trademark Office, Press Release, *USPTO to Open First Ever Satellite Office in Detroit* (Dec. 16, 2010), available at http://www.uspto.gov/news/pr/2010/10_65.jsp.

[148] S. 23 at § 21; H.R. 1249 at § 23.

[149] S. 23 at § 24; H.R. 1249 at § 26.

[150] S. 23 at § 22; H.R. 1249 at § 24.

[151] S. 23 at § 23; H.R. 1249 at § 25.

[152] 35 U.S.C. § 156(d)(1).

[153] *See* Dan L. Burk & Mark A. Lemley, "Is Patent Law Technology-Specific?," 17 *Berkeley Technology Law Journal* (2002), 1155. *See also* CRS Report RL33367, *Patent Reform: Issues in the Biomedical and Software Industries*, by Wendy H. Schacht.

[154] CRS Report RL31281, *Patent Quality and Public Policy: Issues for Innovative Firms in Domestic Markets*, by John R. Thomas.

[155] *See* Joseph Farrell & Robert P. Merges, "Incentives to Challenge and Defend Patents: Why Litigation Won't Reliably Fix Patent Office Errors and Why Administrative Patent Review Might Help," 19 *Berkeley Technology Law Journal* (2004), 943.

[156] *See* Bronwyn H. Hall & Dietmar Harhoff, "Post-Grant Reviews in the U.S. Patent System— Design Choices and Expected Impact," 19 *Berkeley Technology Law Journal* (2004), 989.

[157] *See* Robert P. Merges, "As Many As Six Impossible Patents Before Breakfast: Property Rights for Business Concepts and Patent System Reform," 14 *Berkeley Technology Law Journal* (1999), 577.

[158] *See* Craig Allen Nard, "Certainty, Fence Building and the Useful Arts," 74 *Indiana Law Journal* (1999), 759.

[159] Mark A. Lemley, "Rational Ignorance at the Patent Office," 95 *Northwestern University Law Review* (2001), 1495.

[160] Steven J. Elleman, "Problems in Patent Litigation: Mandatory Mediation May Provide Settlement and Solutions," 12 *Ohio State Journal on Dispute Resolution* (1997), 759.

[161] Dee Gill, "Defending Your Rights: Protecting Intellectual Property is Expensive," *Wall Street Journal* (September 25, 2000), 6.

[162] Mark H. Webbink, "A New Paradigm for Intellectual Property Rights in Software," 2005 *Duke Law and Technology Review* (May 1, 2005), 15.

[163] *See* Bart Showalter, *Cost of Patent Litigation*, AIPLA Mid-Winter Conference, January 25, 2008, available at http://www.aipla.org/Content/ContentGroups/Speaker_Papers/Mid-Winter1/20083/Showalter-slides.pdf.

[164] "Microsoft Advocates for Patent Reform," *eWEEK* (March 10, 2005).

[165] Stirland, *supra,* at 613.

[166] CRS Report RL31132, *Multinational Patent Acquisition and Enforcement: Public Policy Challenges and Opportunities for Innovative Firms*, by John R. Thomas.

[167] *See* Elizabeth D. Ferrill, "Patent Investment Trusts: Let's Build a Pit to Catch the Patent Trolls," 6 *North Carolina Journal of Law and Technology* (2005), 367.

[168] *See* Lorraine Woellert, "A Patent War Is Breaking Out on the Hill," *BusinessWeek* 45 (July 4, 2005).

[169] Nicholas Varchaver, "The Patent King," *Fortune* (May 14, 2001), 202.

Patent Reform in the 112th Congress: Innovation Issues 47

[170] Michael Ravnitzky, "More Lemelson Suits," *The National Law Journal* (December 17, 2001), B9.

[171] James Pooley, "Opinion: U.S. Patent Reform—A Good Invention," *Electronic Business* (January 1, 2000), 72.

[172] *See* Ronald J. Mann, "Do Patents Facilitate Financing in the Software Industry?," 83 *Texas Law Review* (2005), 961.

[173] *See* David G. Barker, "Troll or No Troll? Policing Patent Usage with An Open Post-Grant Review," 2005 *Duke Law and Technology Review* (April 15, 2005), 11.

[174] 35 U.S.C. § 112.

[175] CHI Research Inc., *Small Firms and Technology: Acquisitions, Inventor Movement, and Technology Transfer*, report for the Office of Advocacy, U.S. Small Business Administration, January 2004, 2-3, available at http://www.sba.gov/advo/research/rs233tot.pdf. *See also* CRS Report RL30216, *Small, High Tech Companies and Their Role in the Economy: Issues in the Reauthorization of the Small Business Innovation Research (SBIR) Program*, by Wendy H. Schacht.

[176] For example, the National Academy of Engineering concluded that "small high-tech companies play a critical and diverse role in creating new products and services, in developing new industries, and in driving technological change and growth in the U.S. economy." National Academy of Engineering, *Risk & Innovation: The Role and Importance of Small High-Tech Companies in the U.S. Economy* (Washington: National Academy Press, 1995), 37. This assessment was founded on the ability of small firms to develop markets rapidly, generate new goods and services, and offer diverse products. The study also concluded that small businesses were less risk adverse than larger, established corporations and were often better positioned to exploit market opportunities quickly.

[177] *See* Barnett, *supra*.

[178] J. Douglas Hawkins, "Importance and Access of International Patent Protection for the Independent Inventor," 3 *University of Baltimore Intellectual Property Journal* (1995), 145.

[179] P.L. 96-517, 94 Stat. 2311 (codified at 35 U.S.C. §§ 200-212).

[180] CRS Report RL32076, *The Bayh-Dole Act: Selected Issues in Patent Policy and the Commercialization of Technology*, by Wendy H. Schacht.

[181] Josh Lerner, "Patent Policy Innovations: A Clinical Examination," 53 *Vanderbilt Law Review* (2000), 1841.

[182] *See* Arti K. Rai & Rebecca S. Eisenberg, "Bayh-Dole Reform and the Progress of Biomedicine," 66 *Law and Contemporary Problems* (Winter/Spring 2003), 289.

[183] 35 U.S.C. § 41(g).

[184] CRS Report RS20906, *U.S. Patent and Trademark Office Appropriations Process: A Brief Explanation*, by Wendy H. Schacht.

[185] Under a rule of "prior user rights," when a conflict exists between an issued patent and an earlier user of the patented technology, the validity of the patent is upheld but the prior user is exempted from infringement. *See* Pierre Jean Hubert, "The Prior User Right of H.R. 400: A Careful Balancing of Competing Interests," 14 *Santa Clara Computer and High Technology Law Journal* (1998), 189. Prior user rights are discussed further in this report below.

[186] *See* Gary L. Griswold & F. Andrew Ubel, "Prior User Rights—A Necessary Part of a First-to-File System," 26 *John Marshall Law Review* (1993), 567.

[187] *See* David H. Hollander, Jr., "The First Inventor Defense: A Limited Prior User Right Finds Its Way Into U.S. Patent Law," 30 *American Intellectual Property Law Association Quarterly Journal* (2002), 37 (noting the perception that prior user rights favor large, well-financed corporations).

[188] For additional discussion on this issue see CRS Report RL33367, *Patent Reform: Issues in the Biomedical and Software Industries*, by Wendy H. Schacht.

[189] Richard C. Levin, Alvin K. Klevorick, Richard R. Nelson, and Sidney G. Winter, "Appropriating the Returns for Industrial Research and Development," Brookings Papers on

Economic Activity, 1987, in *The Economics of Technical Change*, eds. Edwin Mansfield and Elizabeth Mansfield (Vermont, Edward Elgar Publishing Co., 1993), 254.

[190] Wesley M. Cohen, Richard R. Nelson, and John P. Walsh, *Protecting Their Intellectual Assets: Appropriability Conditions and Why U.S. Manufacturing Firms Patent (or Not)*, NBER Working Paper 7552, Cambridge, National Bureau of Economic Research, February 2000, available at http://www.nber.org/papers/w7552.

[191] *See* Peter S. Menell, "A Method for Reforming the Patent System," 13 *Michigan Telecommunications & Technology Law Review* (2007), 487.

[192] California Healthcare Institute, *Impact of Patent Law Changes on Biomedical Investment and Innovation*, available at http://www.chi.org/uploadedFiles/CHI%20Patent%20Law%20changes%20paper.pdf.

[193] Federic M. Scherer, "The Economics of Human Gene Patents," 77 *Academic Medicine* (December 2002), 1350.

[194] Mann, *supra*, at 979.

In: U.S. Patent System Reform ...
Editors: F. Parker and M. Lopez

ISBN: 978-1-61470-528-4
© 2011 Nova Science Publishers, Inc.

Chapter 2

PATENT REFORM:
JUDICIAL DEVELOPMENTS IN AREAS
OF LEGISLATIVE INTEREST

John R. Thomas

SUMMARY

Legislative interest in the patent system has been evidenced by the introduction of reform legislation in the 111th and predecessor Congresses. These bills would have amended existing patent law in numerous respects. Although none of these bills were enacted, discussion of patent reform may continue in the 112th Congress.

Although the patent system has been the subject of congressional interest over the past few years, the courts have also been active in making changes to important patent law principles. Many changes introduced by the judiciary have concerned topics that are also the subject of congressional consideration. In particular:

- The Supreme Court issued an important decision in 2007 concerning the availability of injunctive relief against adjudicated patent infringers in *eBay v. MercExchange.*

- In 2008, the Court of Appeals for the Federal Circuit ("Federal Circuit") reached its ruling in *In re TS Tech* concerning the standards for deciding which venue is appropriate for conducting a patent trial.
- In 2009, the Federal Circuit handed down its opinion in *Lucent Technologies. v. Gateway* with respect to the assessment of damages in patent infringement cases.
- The Federal Circuit issued a decision in 2007 concerning the availability of enhanced damages for willful patent infringers in *In re Seagate Technology*.
- The 2007 Supreme Court opinion in *Microsoft v. AT&T* addressed the scope of extraterritorial protection afforded to U.S. patents.
- The 2010 Supreme Court opinion in *Bilski v. Kappos* concerned the issue of patentable subject matter.

Some observers believe that several of these opinions have addressed the very concerns that had motivated legislative reform proposals, thereby obviating or reducing the need for congressional action. However, other commentators believe that these decisions have not fully addressed perceived problems with principles of patent law.

INTRODUCTION

Legislative interest in the patent system was evidenced by the introduction of reform legislation in earlier sessions of Congress.[1] In the 111th Congress, bills would have amended existing patent law in numerous respects, including changes to the right of a patent owner to obtain compensatory damages,[2] the standard for judicial award of enhanced damages for willful infringement,[3] the ability of patent owners to select the court in which they will bring suit,[4] and the willingness of courts to accept appeals of orders interpreting a patent.[5] Patent reform legislation introduced in earlier Congresses would have made additional changes, including modifications to the doctrine of inequitable conduct. Discussion of these issues may potentially continue in the 112th Congress.[6]

Although the patent system has been the subject of congressional scrutiny over the past few years, the courts have also been active in making changes to important patent law principles. Many changes introduced by the judiciary have concerned topics that are also the subject of congressional consideration.

For example, the Supreme Court issued an important decision concerning injunctive relief in *eBay Inc. v. MercExchange, L.L.C.*[7] at the same time legislation before Congress would have addressed that issue.[8] Some experts believe that as a result of the *eBay* decision, legislative reform of the principles of injunctive relief in patent law became unnecessary.[9] Indeed, the patent reform bills placed before Congress subsequent to *eBay* have not addressed this issue.

Review of pertinent judicial developments relating to selected patent law topics is timely for several reasons. First, an awareness of recent judicial opinions may assist understanding of the context of current legislative reform proposals. Second, some observers believe that several of these opinions have addressed the very concerns that had motivated legislative reform proposals, thereby obviating or reducing the need for congressional action.[10] Third, a review of legislative and judicial developments provides an instructive historical narrative and allows for a comparison of relative institutional capabilities of these two branches of government.

This report reviews the relationship between Congress and the courts in patent reform. It begins by offering a summary of the patent system. The report then discusses a number of topics that have been the subject of both judicial and legislative consideration. The current state of the law is then contrasted with legislative reform proposals before previous Congresses. The report closes with observations concerning the subtle interaction between legislative, administrative, and judicial actors within the patent system and their impact upon the U.S. innovation environment.

PATENT FUNDAMENTALS

The U.S. Constitution confers upon Congress the power "To promote the Progress of ... useful Arts, by securing for limited Times to ... Inventors the exclusive Right to their ... Discoveries...."[11] In accordance with the Patent Act of 1952,[12] an inventor may seek the grant of a patent by preparing and submitting an application to the U.S. Patent & Trademark Office (USPTO). USPTO officials known as examiners then determine whether the invention disclosed in the application merits the award of a patent.[13]

USPTO procedures require examiners to determine whether the invention fulfills certain substantive standards set by the patent statute. To be patentable, an invention that constitutes a "process, machine, manufacture, or composition of matter" may be patented.[14] It must also be novel, or different, from subject matter disclosed by an earlier patent, publication, or other state-of-the-art knowledge.[15] In addition, an invention is not patentable if "the subject matter as a whole would have been obvious at the time the invention was made to a person having ordinary skill in the art to which said subject matter pertains."[16] This requirement of "nonobviousness" prevents the issuance of patents claiming subject matter that a skilled artisan would have been able to implement in view of the knowledge of the state of the art.[17] The invention must also be useful, a requirement that is satisfied if the invention is operable and provides a tangible benefit.[18]

In addition to these substantive requirements, the USPTO examiner will consider whether the submitted application fully discloses and distinctly claims the invention.[19] In particular, the application must enable persons skilled in the art to make and use the invention without undue experimentation.[20] In addition, the application must disclose the "best mode," or preferred way, that the applicant knows to practice the invention.[21]

If the USPTO allows the patent to issue, its owner obtains the right to exclude others from making, using, selling, offering to sell or importing into the United States the patented invention.[22] Those who engage in those acts without the permission of the patentee during the term of the patent can be held liable for infringement. Adjudicated infringers may be enjoined from further infringing acts.[23] The patent statute also provides for an award of damages "adequate to compensate for the infringement, but in no event less than a reasonable royalty for the use made of the invention by the infringer."[24]

The maximum term of patent protection is ordinarily set at 20 years from the date the application is filed.[25] At the end of that period, others may employ that invention without regard to the expired patent.

Patent rights do not enforce themselves. Patent owners who wish to compel others to respect their rights must commence enforcement proceedings, which most commonly consist of litigation in the federal courts. Although issued patents enjoy a presumption of validity, accused infringers may assert that a patent is invalid or unenforceable on a number of grounds. The Court of Appeals for the Federal Circuit (Federal Circuit) possesses nationwide jurisdiction over most patent appeals from the district courts.[26] The Supreme Court enjoys discretionary authority to review cases decided by the Federal Circuit.[27]

PATENT REFORM LEGISLATION

Since 2005, a number of bills titled "The Patent Reform Act" have been introduced before Congress. To varying degrees, each of the bills would work substantial changes to the current patent system. The bills have differed in the specific reforms that they have proposed. The many proposed reforms have included a shift to a first-inventor-to-file priority system, allowance of assignee filing, changes to the law of patent damages, introduction of post-grant opposition proceedings, and modifications to the principle of venue as it applies to patent cases.[28]None of this legislation has yet been enacted.[29]

Even as Congress has contemplated patent reform legislation, the courts also have been active in issuing patent decisions. Many of these rulings relate to the same legal topics that proposed legislation would address, and several made significant changes to existing law. As attorneys Bill Rooklidge and Alyson Barker observe, "through a variety of important decisions, the courts have embarked on their own patent reform."[30] This paper next reviews a common phenomenon in patent reform: Judicial changes to legal doctrines that are the subject of pending congressional legislation.

JUDICIAL REFORMS TO PATENT DOCTRINE

Numerous patent substantive and procedural doctrines have fallen under legislative scrutiny in recent years. A recent, recurring trend is that the courts have contemporaneously reviewed a number of the same principles. Among them are the availability of injunctions in patent cases, selection of the appropriate venue for trying a patent case, the assessment of damages against adjudicated infringers, the standards governing determinations of willful infringement, extraterritorial patent enforcement, and the availability of patents for tax planning methods. This report reviews each of these episodes in turn.

Injunctions

Section 283 of the Patent Act allows courts to "grant injunctions in accordance with the principles of equity to prevent the violation of any right secured by patent, on such terms as the court deems reasonable."[31] In practice, for much of its history the Federal Circuit routinely granted injunctions to patent owners that prevailed in infringement litigation. Only in rare instances, when the patented invention pertained to an important public need, would an injunction be denied.[32] An injunction prevents the adjudicated infringer from practicing the patented invention until the patent expires.[33]

Some observers criticized injunction practice as encouraging speculation by entities that do not engage in research, development, or manufacturing, but rather acquire and enforce patents against companies with commercialized products.[34] These speculators were sometimes termed "patent trolls," an arguably pejorative term that referred to creatures from folklore that would emerge from under a bridge in order to waylay travelers.[35] Some manufacturers were concerned that the Federal Circuit's injunction practice provided non-manufacturing entities with too much leverage during patent licensing negotiations.

In view of industry concerns, the 109th Congress contemplated amending section 283 of the Patent Act. Under a proposal included within H.R. 2795, the Patent Reform Act of 2005, courts would have been required to "consider the fairness of the remedy in light of all the facts and the relevant interests of the parties associated with the invention." This legislation was not enacted.

As discussion of legislative proposals with respect to injunctions continued, the judiciary reached a number of rulings on this topic. One of them resulted from the well-known patent litigation concerning the BlackBerry handheld device and communication service. In that litigation, a federal district court ruled that the BlackBerry infringed patents held by New Technology Products, Inc. (NTP).[36] When the Federal Circuit affirmed this judgment,[37] many BlackBerry subscribers faced the unsettling prospect of an immediate interruption of service due to a court-ordered injunction. A subsequent settlement between the litigants ensured that an injunction would never come into effect.[38] The BlackBerry patent litigation led to increasing discussion over the availability of injunctions in patent cases, perhaps in part because NTP did not commercialize the patented invention itself.

Shortly after the BlackBerry litigation concluded, the Supreme Court issued an important decision concerning injunctive relief in *eBay Inc. v. MercExchange, L.L.C.*[39] The patent at issue in the *eBay* case concerned "a system for selling goods through an 'electronic network of consignment stores.'"[40] The district court explained that the patent proprietor, MercExchange, "does not practice its inventions and exists merely to license its patented technology to others."[41] Although a jury concluded that eBay infringed the MercExchange patent, the district court refused to issue an

Patent Reform

55

injunction. The district court in part reasoned that MercExchange had licensed its patents to others, did not practice its invention, and had made comments to the media that it desired to obtain royalties from eBay rather than obtain an injunction.

On appeal, the Federal Circuit rejected the district court's reasoning and ruled that MercExchange was entitled to an injunction. The appellate court explained that "[b]ecause the right to exclude recognized in a patent is but the essence of the concept of property, the general rule is that a permanent injunction will issue once infringement and validity have been adjudged."[42] The Federal Circuit did recognize that in rare cases a court should decline to issue an injunction, such as "when a patentee's failure to practice the patented invention frustrates an important public need for the invention."[43] In this case, however, the Federal Circuit concluded that the district court had not offered "any persuasive reason to believe this case is sufficiently exceptional to justify the denial of a permanent injunction."[44]

The Supreme Court subsequently granted *certiorari* and issued an opinion vacating the Federal Circuit's judgment. According to Justice Thomas, the author of the unanimous opinion of the Court, neither lower court had followed the correct rules in deciding whether to issue an injunction or not. The Supreme Court explained that the district court had incorrectly reasoned that injunctive relief was unavailable where patent proprietors chose to license their patents rather than commercialize the patented invention themselves. Justice Thomas further explained that although the Patent Act requires that injunctions issue "in accordance with the principles of equity," the Federal Circuit had ignored long-established equitable standards in following a "general rule" that injunctions issue.[45]

The Supreme Court directed lower courts to consider four traditional factors for deciding whether an injunction should issue or not in patent infringement cases. Those factors are:

> (1) whether the patent owner would face irreparable injury if the injunction did not issue; (2) whether the patent owner possesses an adequate legal remedy, such as monetary damages; (3) whether granting the injunction would be in the public interest; and (4) whether the balance of hardships tips in the patent owner's favor.[46]

Expressing no opinion about how these factors applied to the dispute between the litigants, the Supreme Court then remanded the case to the district court.[47] In the wake of *eBay*, some courts have declined to issue injunctions against adjudicated infringers of valid and enforceable patents.[48]

Opinions upon the impact of the *eBay* ruling upon legislative reform of patent injunctions have varied. Some observers believed that "the Supreme Court failed to meaningfully restructure the injunctive grant process in its *eBay* rejection of the automatic injunction rule" and opined that "the need for legislation ... is renewed rather than removed."[49] Others viewed the Supreme Court's ruling more favorably. For example, attorneys Bill Rooklidge and Alyson Barker describe *eBay* as a "solution to the perceived injunction problem" that satisfied the concerns of different constituents in the patent filed in an "elegant" manner. [50] The latter view appears to have prevailed, however, as no subsequent versions of the Patent Reform Act have incorporated proposed reforms to injunction practice. Rooklidge and Barker have therefore concluded that the "legislative effort to reform injunctions is finished, at least for the foreseeable future."[51]

Venue

Patent reform legislation also has proposed changes to the rules governing the doctrine of venue in patent litigation. Venue principles decide which court, out of those that possess personal and subject matter jurisdiction, may most conveniently hear a particular lawsuit.[52] Patent cases are governed by a specialized venue statute codified at 28 U.S.C. § 1400(b). That statute provides that in patent litigation, venue is proper either: (1) in the judicial district where the defendant resides, or (2) where the defendant has committed acts of infringement and has a regular and established place of business.

An important question under this provision is where a corporation is deemed to "reside." Prior to 1988, a corporation was viewed as residing in its state of its incorporation.[53] In 1988, Congress adopted a new definition of "reside" as it applies to venue for corporate defendants.[54] Under the new definition, a corporation is presumed to reside in any judicial district to which it could be subject to personal jurisdiction at the time the litigation commences. Congress codified this change in a separate provision found at 28 U.S.C. § 1391. Although Congress arguably did not contemplate that these reforms would hold consequences for the specialized patent venue statute, the Federal Circuit nonetheless held that this amendment should also be read into § 1400(b).[55]

The result of the 1988 amendments has been significant for corporate defendants, which constitute the majority of defendants in patent litigation. Although § 1400(b) still governs venue in patent cases, few, if any plaintiffs rely upon the restrictive second prong of that section. Instead they base venue upon the "residence" requirement of the first prong—which now is entirely conterminous with personal jurisdiction, and which for larger corporations is likely to include every federal district in the country. For corporate defendants, then, the venue statute has essentially become superfluous, for the same standards governing personal jurisdiction also dictate whether a court may provide an appropriate venue or not.

Some observers allege that the liberal venue statute promotes forum shopping, allowing patent proprietors to bring suit in courts that they believe favor patent owners over accused infringers. One such "magnet jurisdiction" is said to be the rural Eastern District of Texas, and in particular the Marshall, Texas, federal court. According to one account, many observers "wonder how a East Texas town of 25,000—even if it was named after Supreme Court Justice John Marshall—came to harbor an oversized share of intellectual property disputes."[56] In addition, reportedly "many of the local lawyers who once specialized in personal injury cases are turning their attention to intellectual property law."[57] Others believe that the existence of a single appellate court for patent cases, the Federal Circuit, minimizes forum shopping concerns, and that certain district courts attract patent cases due to their expertise and timeliness, rather than an inherent favoritism for patent holders.[58]

While the 110th Congress was considering legislative changes, the Federal Circuit also addressed the venue laws. In its December 29, 2008, decision in *In re TS Tech USA Corp.*,[59] the Federal Circuit held that the District Court for the Eastern District of Texas abused its discretion in denying a motion to transfer to another venue. Some observers believe that the *TS Tech* decision eliminated the need for legislative intervention,[60] while others suggest that one current congressional proposal would codify its holding.[61]

In *TS Tech*, Lear Corporation brought a patent infringement suit in the Eastern District of Texas against TS Tech, which operated principal places of business in Ohio, Michigan, and Canada. The district court denied TS Tech's request for transfer to Ohio, in part reasoning that the Eastern District of Texas possessed a local interest in resolving patent infringement disputes involving products sold there. The district court also held that the district presumptively was convenient for one of the litigants because Lear had chosen to file suit there.[62]

In its review of the issue, the Federal Circuit granted TS Tech's petition to transfer the litigation to Ohio. Several factors were central to the Federal Circuit's holding. The appellate court reasoned that the district court had given too much weight to Lear's choice of venue.[63] It further explained that the district court had not given sufficient weight to the cost of attendance for witnesses, as well as the inconvenience associated with physical and documentary evidence located distant from Texas.[64] Finally, the Federal Circuit observed that the alleged infringing products were sold throughout the United States. As a result, the Eastern District of Texas had no greater connection to the dispute than any other venue.[65] Some observers believe that these factors are present in many patent cases brought before the Eastern District of Texas, and possibly other magnet jurisdictions. As a result, *TS Tech* may mean that motions to transfer venue will be granted with greater frequency.[66] Other observers are less impressed, believing that *TS Tech* did not work a "sea change" in transfer motion practice and observing that the patent dockets of the Eastern District of Texas remain active.[67]

Subsequent to *TS Tech*, several different versions of the Patent Reform Act have proposed changes to the venue provisions governing patent cases. In the 111th Congress, three bills titled "The Patent Reform Act of 2009" considered this issue. They were H.R. 1260, introduced on March 3, 2009, by Representative Conyers; S. 515, introduced on March 3, 2009, by Senators Hatch and Leahy; and S. 610, introduced by Senator Kyl on March 17, 2009. On April 2, 2009, the Senate Judiciary Committee voted 15-4 to bring S. 515 before the full Senate. None of this legislation was enacted.

In the 111th Congress, H.R. 1260 and S. 610 generally called for venue to exist (1) where the defendant has its principal place of business, (2) where the defendant has committed a substantial portion of its acts of infringement and has an established physical facility, (3) if the plaintiff is an institution of higher education, individual, or small business, the plaintiff's residence, or (4) the place of the plaintiff's established physical facility devoted to research, development, or manufacturing. In addition, H.R. 1260 stipulated that "a party shall not manufacture venue by assignment, incorporation, or otherwise to invoke the venue of a specific district court."

In contrast, S. 515 did not present new substantive rules for venue for patent cases. Rather, it succinctly provided that "[f]or the convenience of parties and witnesses, in the interest of justice, a district court shall transfer any civil action arising under any Act of Congress relating to patents upon a showing that the transferee venue is clearly more convenient than the venue in

Patent Reform 59

which the civil action is pending." Some observers believed that S. 515 would essentially have codified the holding in the *TS Tech* case.[68]

Assessment of Damages

Commencing with the introduction of the Patent Reform Act of 2005 in the 109th Congress,[69] each version of omnibus reform legislation has proposed amendments to the damages provisions of the Patent Act. These proposals have been, in the eyes of some observers, the most contentious issue within the debate over the modern patent system.[70] This difference in views may arise from divergent conceptions over the fairness of damages awards levied against infringers.

Some commentators believe that current damages standards have resulted in the systemic overcompensation of patent owners. Such overcompensation may place unreasonable royalty burdens upon producers of high technology products, ultimately impeding the process of technological innovation and dissemination that the patent system is meant to foster.[71] Others believe that current case law appropriately assesses damages for patent infringement. These observers are concerned that this reform might overly restrict damages in patent cases, thereby discouraging voluntary licensing and promoting infringement of patent rights. Limited damage awards for patent infringement might prevent innovators from realizing the value of their inventive contributions, a principal goal of the patent system.[72]

This debate, at least in part, is fueled by the fact that marketplace circumstances often make the determination of an appropriate damages award in patent litigation very difficult. In some cases, the product or process that is found to infringe may incorporate numerous additional elements beyond the patented invention. For example, the asserted patent may relate to a single component of an audio speaker, while the accused product consists of the entire stereo system. In such circumstances, a court may apply "the entire market value rule," which "permits recovery of damages based upon the entire apparatus containing several features, where the patent-related feature is the basis for consumer demand."[73] On the other hand, if the court determines that the infringing sales were due to many factors beyond the use of the patented invention, the court may apply principles of "apportionment" to measure damages based upon the value of the patented feature alone.[74]

As discussion of damages reform has proceeded before Congress, the courts have also been active. One of the more notable cases on patent damages principles arose from the efforts of Lucent Technologies, Inc., to enforce its so-called "Day patent," which related to a method of entering information into fields on a computer screen without using a keyboard.[75] In 2002, Lucent brought an infringement suit against computer manufacturer Gateway, Inc. Lucent asserted that Gateway infringed the Day patent because certain software developed by Microsoft Corporation—Microsoft Money, Microsoft Outlook, and Windows Mobile—were pre-installed in Gateway computers. More particularly, Lucent asserted that the software infringed because it enables the user to select a series of numbers corresponding to a day, month, and year using graphical controls. Microsoft subsequently intervened in order to defend the "date-picker tool" found in its software.[76]

At trial, the jury found the Day patent not invalid and infringed. Lucent sought damages of $561.9 million based on 8% of Microsoft's infringing sales, while Microsoft asserted "that a lump-sum payment of $6.5 million would have been the correct amount for licensing the protected technology." The jury then awarded Lucent a single lump-sum amount of $357,693,056.18 for all three Microsoft products. Microsoft subsequently pursued an appeal.[77]

The litigation in *Lucent Technologies, Inc. v. Gateway, Inc.* captured the attention of many observers. In a March 3, 2009, letter addressed to Senator Patrick Leahy, Chairman of the Judiciary Committee, Senator Arlen Specter requested a delay in Senate action on the Patent Reform Act of 2009 until the Federal Circuit heard oral argument in the case.[78] Observing a "symbiotic relationship between the judicial and legislative branches with regard to changes to the patent system," Senator Specter believed that "oral argument has the potential to facilitate a compromise or clarify the applicability of damages theories in various contexts."[79]

The Federal Circuit heard oral argument in the *Lucent* appeal on June 2, 2009, and issued its opinion on September 11, 2009.[80] In its decision, the Federal Circuit upheld the lower court's determination that the Day patent was not invalid and infringed. In the most anticipated portion of the opinion, the appellate court also struck down the jury's damages award as not supported by substantial evidence.[81] A lengthy portion of the *Lucent* opinion undertook a detailed review of the numerous elements—the so-called *Georgia-Pacific* factors—that were before the lower court when it reached its damages determination. The Federal Circuit ultimately concluded that the "evidence does not sustain a finding that, at the time of infringement, Microsoft and Lucent would have agreed to a lumpsum royalty payment subsequently amounting to approximately 8% of Microsoft's revenues for the sale of Outlook (and necessarily a larger percentage of Outlook's profits)."[82]

Some observers believe that the Federal Circuit has placed renewed emphasis upon the use of reliable evidence of damages in patent trials. For example, patent attorney Johnathan Tropp reportedly viewed *Lucent* as "an important signal to district courts that they have a responsibility to ... ensure that damages verdicts are appropriate and based on substantial evidence."[83] In addition, *Lucent* discussed the controversial issue of apportionment. Under the facts of the case, the Federal Circuit concluded that the entire market value rule did not apply:

[T]he only reasonable conclusion supported by the evidence is that the infringing use of the datepicker tool in Outlook is but a very small component of a much larger software program. The vast majority of the features, when used, do not infringe. The date-picker tool's minor role in the overall program is further confirmed when one considers the relative importance of certain other features, e.g., email. Consistent with this description of Outlook, Lucent did not carry its evidentiary burden of proving that anyone purchased Outlook because of the patented method.[84]

The Federal Circuit went on to speak in a more general way:
Although our law states certain mandatory conditions for applying the entire market value rule ... the base used in a running royalty calculation can always be the value of the entire commercial embodiment, as long as the magnitude of the rate is within an acceptable range.... [E]ven when the patented invention is a small component of a much larger commercial product, awarding a reasonable royalty based on either sale price or number of units sold can be economically justified.[85]

Some disagreement has reportedly resulted from this language. As legal journalist Steven Seidenberg explains:

Some say the ruling allows damages to be calculated based on an infringing product's entire market value, provided the calculation realistically reflects the patent's importance in the infringing product. Others assert that entire market value can be used only when a plaintiff's patented feature drives consumer demand for the infringing product, and that any damage calculations must reflect the relative importance of the infringing product.[86]

Each of the three patent reform bills in the 111th Congress was introduced prior to the issuance of the *Lucent* opinion. At least one observer, patent lawyer Kevin McCabe, reportedly opined that "the *Lucent* decision is the Federal Circuit's way of showing Congress that damage reform is unnecessary."[87] In any event, in the 111th Congress, H.R. 1260, S. 515, and S. 610 each addressed monetary remedies in patent cases. In brief, both H.R. 1260 and S. 515 called for a court to select one of the following methods for determining a "reasonable royalty" as the measure of damages: (1) the economic value that is properly attributable to the patented invention's specific contribution over the prior art, (2) the entire market value rule, or (3) other factors, such as terms of the nonexclusive marketplace licensing of the invention. Both bills also stipulated that courts may receive expert testimony as an aid to the determination of the appropriate royalty.

In contrast, S. 610 did not expressly address apportionment and the entire market value rule. It instead allowed courts to "consider any factors that are relevant to the determination of a reasonable royalty." However, S. 610 stipulated that the amount of royalties paid for patents other than the patent subject to litigation may only be considered in particular circumstances, and further that the financial condition of the infringer is not relevant to the reasonable royalty determination. S. 610 also required damages experts who intend to present testimony to provide data and other information from which they draw their conclusions, and also mandated that trial judges determine whether such testimony is based upon legally sufficient evidence before allowing it to be considered by a jury.

Willful Infringement

The patent statute currently provides that the court "may increase the damages up to three times the amount found or assessed."[88] An award of enhanced damages, as well as the amount by which the damages will be increased, falls within the discretion of the trial court. Although the statute does not specify the circumstances in which enhanced damages are appropriate, the Federal Circuit has limited such awards to cases of "willful infringement." The appellate court has explained that willful infringement occurs when "the infringer acted in wanton disregard of the patentee's patent rights" based upon such circumstances as copying, closeness of the case, the infringer's concealment of its conduct, and the infringer's motivations.[89] In its 1992 opinion in *Read Corp. v. Portec, Inc.*,[90] the Federal Circuit explained that:

> Willfulness is a determination as to a state of mind. One who has actual notice of another's patent rights has an affirmative duty to respect those

Patent Reform

63

rights. That affirmative duty normally entails obtaining advice of legal counsel although the absence of such advice does not mandate a finding of willfulness.[91]

As framed in *Read v. Portec* and numerous other judicial opinions issued prior to 2007, the willful infringement doctrine has proved controversial. Some observers believe that this doctrine ensured that patent rights will be respected in the marketplace. Critics of willful infringement believed that the possibility of trebled damages discourages individuals from reviewing issued patents. Out of fear that their inquisitiveness will result in multiple damages, innovators might simply avoid looking at patents until they are sued for infringement. To the extent this observation was correct, the law of willful infringement discouraged the dissemination of technical knowledge, thereby thwarting one of the principal goals of the patent system. Fear of increased liability for willful infringement might have also discouraged firms from challenging patents of dubious validity.

In view of these critiques, Congress considered legislative amendments to the law of willful infringement as early as 2005.[92] However, in its 2007 decision in *In re Seagate Technology*,[93] the Federal Circuit made significant changes to the law of willful infringement itself. The appellate court overturned two decades of its precedent by opting to "abandon the affirmative duty of due care."[94] The Federal Circuit instead explained that accused infringers possessed no obligation to obtain an opinion of counsel.[95] Rather, "proof of willful infringement permitting enhanced damages requires at least a showing of objective recklessness."[96] Under this view, the "state of mind of the accused infringer is not relevant to this objective inquiry."[97]

Many observers believe that *Seagate* significantly limited the circumstances under which courts will conclude that an infringer acted willfully.[98] Due to the *Seagate* opinion, some commentators believe that congressional reform of willful infringement principles is not needed at this time.[99] Others are more skeptical, believing that the "new objective recklessness standard will result in little practical change because potential infringers will likely continue to seek opinions of competent counsel to protect against a charge of willful infringement."[100]

In the 111th Congress, H.R. 1260 and S. 515 included identical language that would add several clarifications and changes to the law of willful infringement. First, a finding of willful infringement would be appropriate only where (1) the infringer received specific written notice from the patentee and continued to infringe after a reasonable opportunity to investigate; (2) the infringer intentionally copied from the patentee with knowledge of the patent; or (3) the infringer continued to infringe after an adverse court ruling. Second, willful infringement cannot be found where the infringer possessed an informed, good faith belief that its conduct was not infringing. Finally, a court may not determine willful infringement before the date on which the court determines that the patent is not invalid, enforceable, and infringed. No comparable language appeared in S. 610.

Extraterritorial Patent Protection

U.S. patents are generally effective only in the United States. They normally do not provide protection against acts that occur in other nations. However, one provision of the Patent Act, 35 U.S.C. § 271(f), provides U.S. patent owners with a limited measure of extraterritorial protection. Specifically, § 271(f) prohibits "supplying" a "component" of a patented invention abroad knowing that such components would be combined in a manner that would infringe the patent if such combination occurred within the United States. Congress enacted § 271(f) in order to prevent individuals from avoiding infringement liability under U.S. law by manufacturing parts domestically before shipping them abroad to be assembled into a patented device.[101]

Some observers had expressed concerns that § 271(f) had been interpreted overly broadly. In particular, the Federal Circuit had ruled that software designed in the United States, and then transmitted abroad for copying and sale, fell within § 271(f).[102] Some commentators believed that this holding would "impose liability for software developed in America and sold overseas," with the result that "American software developers would have faced a competitive disadvantage vis-à-vis their foreign counterparts."[103]

Proposals before Congress would have addressed this concern. In the 109th Congress, S. 3818, titled the Patent Reform Act of 2006, would have repealed 35 U.S.C. § 271(f).[104] However, the courts were the first to address the controversy regarding extraterritorial patent protection. In 2007, the Supreme Court issued its opinion in *Microsoft Corp. v. AT&T Corp.*[105] The issue before the Court was whether § 271(f) applied to a "master disk" of software that Microsoft sent from the United States to a foreign manufacturer. The foreign manufacturer then used the disk to create multiple copies of the software that was then installed on computers that were made and sold abroad. The Supreme Court held that sending the master disk abroad did not constitute "supplying" a "component" of the foreign computers within the meaning of § 271(f).[106] This "narrowing reading of § 271(f)" limited the liability of software firms accused of patent infringement based upon overseas activity.[107]

Possibly as a result of *Microsoft v. AT&T*, proposals to eliminate § 271(f) did not reappear in subsequent versions of the Patent Reform Act. As Senator Patrick Leahy explained on April 18, 2007, shortly before *Microsoft v. AT&T* was decided:

> The Patent Reform Act of 2007 is also significant for what is not included.... [W]e do not inject Congress into the ongoing litigation over the extra-territorial provision, section 271(f). S. 3818 would have repealed the provision in its entirety; the Patent Reform Act of 2007 does not, while the interpretation of the provision is currently pending before the Supreme Court. If the Court does not resolve that issue, we will revisit it in the legislative process.[108]

Although debate has continued over the soundness of the *Microsoft v. AT&T* ruling,[109] the lack of legislative interest in amending or eliminating § 271(f) may suggest that concerned actors believe the Supreme Court addressed perceived problems with that statute.

Tax Planning Methods

Controversy over the newly recognized phenomenon of patents on tax planning methods resulted in proposals to limit or prohibit them. For example, in the 110th Congress, the Patent Reform Act of 2007 stipulated that a patent may not be obtained on a tax planning method, which was defined as "a plan, strategy, technique, or scheme that is designed to reduce, minimize, or defer, or has, when implemented, the effect of reducing, minimizing, or deferring, a taxpayer's tax liability, but does not include the use of tax preparation software or other tools used solely to perform or model mathematical calculations or prepare tax or information returns."[110]

A number of recent court decisions have explored the topic of patentable subject matter—that is to say, what sorts of advances are eligible for patenting.[111] Most notable is the 2010 decision of the U.S. Supreme Court in *Bilski v. Kappos*.[112] There the Supreme Court reviewed a lower court ruling holding that a patent on a particular "method of hedging risk in the field of commodities trading" was not eligible for patenting because the invention was neither (1) tied to a particular machine or apparatus nor (2) transformed a particular article into a different state or thing.[113] This "machine-or-transformation" standard was widely viewed as narrowing the range of patentable subject matter.[114]

In *Bilski v. Kappos*, the Supreme Court ruled that the risk hedging method at issue was unpatentable. However, the Supreme Court also rejected the holding that the "machine-or-transformation" test was a categorical rule that governed which inventions were patentable. The lower court's "machine-or-transformation" standard was instead a factor to be considered in assessing patentability, the Supreme Court reasoned, but not the sole one. By a 5-4 margin, the Supreme Court also rejected the argument that business methods were categorically unpatentable. The Supreme Court further declined to announce a new test of patentable subject matter, instead suggesting that the analysis must proceed on a case-by-case basis founded on existing case law that rejected patents on laws of nature, natural phenomena and abstract ideas.[115]

The impact of the Supreme Court's ruling may influence legislative involvement with respect to tax planning method patents. Prior to the issuance of the Supreme Court opinion, Linda Beale, a member of the faculty of the Wayne State University Law School, explained that "[w]hen the Supreme Court hears the case, it may reverse *Bilski* and leave Congress no choice but to enact legislative exclusions to the patent laws."[116] On the other hand, Congress may believe that the holding in *Bilski v. Kappos* appropriately resolves concerns pertaining to patent eligibility. The possibility of legislative intervention regarding tax planning method patents remains to be seen.

OBSERVATIONS

This discussion of injunctions, venue, damages, willful infringement, extraterritorial patent protection, and tax strategy patents suggests that the courts have modified a number of patent law doctrines that were previously subject to congressional consideration. Of course, many of these principles had been developed through judicial opinions. To that extent, congressional interest in patent reform was itself a reaction to earlier developments in the courts. This interaction between different branches of government has become a hallmark of the recent patent reform process.

Notably, the Supreme Court and Federal Circuit have not reacted to every proposal in the various Patent Reform Acts in this manner. For example,

Congress has considered legislation that would permit interlocutory appeals of claim construction rulings.[117] The Federal Circuit has not altered its general practice of disfavoring such appeals, however.[118]

It also should be appreciated that judicial opinions have worked significant changes to a number of patent principles that were not expressly the target of proposed legislative reforms. For example, some observers believe that the 2007 Supreme Court opinion in *KSR v. Teleflex*[119] resulted in significant changes to the law of nonobviousness.[120] Of course, judicial changes to one component of the patent system may have an impact upon other doctrines, including those subject to congressional scrutiny.

A number of reasons may explain this pattern of judicial involvement in areas of legislative interest. First, Congress considered the initial Patent Reform Act in 2005.[121] During the years that legislation has been pending, many patent infringement cases have been tried and appealed. The courts have therefore had many opportunities to address core patent doctrines.

Second, the Federal Circuit hears all appeals from district courts across the United States in both patent acquisition and infringement cases.[122] This concentration of appellate jurisdiction provides one court with the ability to change patent doctrine relatively quickly. Further, although the rulings of other federal courts of appeal bind only a limited portion of the country, Federal Circuit patent precedent has effect throughout the United States.[123]

Some additional factors suggest judicial interest in legislative scrutiny of the patent system. The Federal Circuit's location in Washington, DC,[124] may imply an awareness of legislative activity involving patents. That several Federal Circuit judges formerly served as members of congressional staff may also suggest interest in patent reform efforts on the Hill.[125]

Whatever the reasons for the persistent interaction between Congress and the courts in the patent reform process, these circumstances raise a number of issues pertaining to institutional competence. The longstanding debate over whether legislatures or courts comprise the most appropriate body to work particular legal reforms has been renewed in this setting. Law professors Dan Burk and Mark Lemley side with the courts, asserting that "Congress has spent the last four years, from 2005 to 2008, in an ultimately futile effort to reform the patent system."[126] They further contend that "[d]uring the period in which Congress tried and failed to reform the patent system, courts were actively involved in fixing many of the very same problems Congress was ultimately unable to resolve."[127] In their view the "fact that courts proved capable of solving many of the problems on which Congress ultimately foundered" indicates that the courts are the most appropriate institution for working needed reforms to the patent laws.[128]

On the other hand, legislatures are frequently seen as possessing superior resources to investigate and develop factual evidence. Compared to the courts, Congress possesses greater research capabilities and superior means for obtaining information from informed third parties. The legislative decision-making process may better reflect the views of a wide range of stakeholders and offers the advantage of superior democratic accountability.[129]

It should also be appreciated that the judiciary does not oversee a number of significant components of the patent system. For example, the courts cannot directly influence the budget or internal operations of the USPTO.[130] In contrast, Congress possesses authority to determine such matters as the scope of USPTO rule-making authority, the level of fees the USPTO may charge, and the agency's budget.[131]

CONCLUSION

Several previous Congresses have considered enacting a Patent Reform Act. To the extent legislative deliberations are believed to alert the courts to perceived problems with a particular doctrine, however, Congress may be seen as already having prompted a great deal of change to the patent system. Our recent experience highlighting the interaction between the different branches of government during the patent reform process suggests the importance of legislative awareness of judicial developments. It also reminds us that although courts often possess a range of options in interpreting statutory language that the legislature has chosen, authority to alter the Patent Act itself ultimately resides with Congress.

ACKNOWLEDGMENTS

This report was funded in part by a grant from the John D. and Catherine T. MacArthur Foundation.

Patent Reform 69

End Notes

[1] In the 111th Congress, H.R. 1260, S. 515, and S. 610 were each titled "The Patent Reform Act of 2009."

[2] H.R. 1260 at § 5; S. 515 at § 4; S. 610 at § 4.

[3] H.R. 1260 at § 5; S. 515 at § 4; S. 610 at § 4.

[4] H.R. 1260 at § 10; S. 515 at § 8; S. 610 at § 8 (pertaining to venue).

[5] H.R. 1260 at § 5; S. 515 at § 4 (pertaining to interlocutory appeals). S. 610 does not include a comparable provision.

[6] For example, in the 110th Congress, section 12 of H.R. 1908 included provisions directed towards the doctrine of inequitable conduct. H.R. 1908 passed the House on September 9, 2007, but was not enacted.

[7] 547 U.S. 388 (2006).

[8] *See* CRS Report RL33429, *Availability of Injunctive Relief in Patent Cases: eBay, Inc. v. MercExchange, L.L.C.*, by Brian T. Yeh (May 19, 2006).

[9] *See* William C. Rooklidge & Alyson G. Barker, "Reform of a Fast-Moving Target: The Development of Patent Law Since the 2004 National Academies Report," 91 *Journal of the Patent and Trademark Office Society* (2009), 153 ("The legislative effort to reform injunctions is finished, at least for the foreseeable future.").

[10] *See* F. Scott Kieff & Kevin Rivette, "Congress—Let U.S. patent law 'marinate' before taking action," *Great Falls Tribune* (March 31, 2009).

[11] Article I, Section 8, Clause 8.

[12] Pub. L. No. 82-593, 66 Stat. 792 (codified at Title 35 of the United States Code).

[13] 35 U.S.C. § 131 (2006).

[14] 35 U.S.C. § 101 (2006).

[15] 35 U.S.C. § 102 (2006).

[16] 35 U.S.C. § 103(a) (2006).

[17] *See* KSR International Co. v. Teleflex Inc., 550 U.S. 398 (2007).

[18] *See* In re Fischer, 421 F.3d 1365, 1371 (Fed. Cir. 2005).

[19] 35 U.S.C. § 112 (2006).

[20] *See* Invitrogen Corp. v. Clontech Labs., Inc., 429 F.3d 1052, 1070-71 (Fed. Cir. 2005).

[21] *See* High Concrete Structures, Inc. v. New Enterprise Stone and Lime Co., 377 F.3d 1379, 1382 (Fed. Cir. 2004).

[22] 35 U.S.C. § 271(a) (2006).

[23] 35 U.S.C. § 283 (2006). *See* eBay Inc. v. MercExchange L.L.C., 547 U.S. 388 (2006).

[24] 35 U.S.C. § 284 (2006).

[25] 35 U.S.C. § 154(a)(2) (2006). Although the patent term is based upon the filing date, the patentee obtains no enforceable legal rights until the USPTO allows the application to issue as a granted patent. A number of Patent Act provisions may modify the basic 20-year term, including examination delays at the USPTO and delays in obtaining marketing approval for the patented invention from other federal agencies.

[26] 28 U.S.C. § 1295(a)(1) (2006).

[27] 28 U.S.C. § 1254(1) (2006).

[28] *See* CRS Report R40481, *Patent Reform in the 111th Congress: Innovation Issues*, by Wendy H. Schacht and John R. Thomas.

[29] One of the bills in the 110th Congress, H.R. 1908, passed the House of Representatives on September 7, 2007, but did not advance in the Senate.

[30] Rooklidge & Barker, *supra*, at 155.

[31] 35 U.S.C. § 283 (2006).

[32] MercExchange, L.L.C. v. eBay, Inc., 401 F.3d 1323, 1328 (Fed. Cir. 2005).

[33] *See* Roger E. Schechter & John R. Thomas, *Principles of Patent Law* (2d ed. 2005), 330.

[34] See Elizabeth D. Ferrill, "Patent Investment Trusts: Let's Build a Pit to Catch the Patent Trolls," 6 *North Carolina Journal of Law and Technology* (2005), 367.

[35] See Lorraine Woellert, "A Patent War Is Breaking Out on the Hill," *BusinessWeek* 45 (July 4, 2005).

[36] NTP, Inc. v. Research in Motion, Ltd., 261 F. Supp. 2d 423 (E.D. Va. 2002).

[37] NTP, Inc. v. Research in Motion, Ltd., 418 F.3d 1282 (Fed. Cir. 2005).

[38] *See* CRS Report RL33429, *Availability of Injunctive Relief in Patent Cases: eBay, Inc. v. MercExchange, L.L.C.*, by Brian T. Yeh.

[39] 547 U.S. 388 (2006).

[40] MercExchange, L.L.C. v. eBay, Inc., 401 F.3d 1323, 1327 (Fed. Cir. 2005).

[41] MercExchange, L.L.C. v. eBay, Inc., 275 F. Supp. 695, 712 (E.D. Va. 2003).

[42] 401 F.3d at 1339.

[43] Id.

[44] Id.

[45] 547 U.S. at 392-94.

[46] Id. at 391.

[47] Chief Justice Roberts issued a concurring opinion observing that courts have granted injunctive relief to the patent proprietor in "the vast majority of patent cases" and opining that this historical practice should be maintained. Id. at 394. Justice Kennedy also issued a concurring opinion. According to Justice Kennedy, the emergence of non-practicing patent holders and the "suspect validity" of business method patents were appropriate considerations for courts to "bear in mind" when deciding whether to issue an injunction or not. Id. at 395.

[48] *See* Jaideep Venkatesan, "Compulsory Licensing of Nonpracticing Patentees After *EBay v. MercExchange*," 14 *Virginia Journal of Law and Technology* (2009), 26.

[49] Robin M. Davis, "Failed Attempts to Dwarf the Patent Trolls: Permanent Injunctions in Patent Infringement Cases Under the Proposed Patent Reform Act of 2005 and *EBay v. MercExchange*," 17 *Cornell Journal of Law and Public Policy* (2008), 431.

[50] Rooklidge & Barker, *supra*, at 160.

[51] *Id.*

[52] *See* Wachovia Bank v. Schmidt, 546 U.S. 303 (2006).

[53] *See* Fourco Glass Co. v. Transmirra Prods. Corp., 353 U.S. 222 (1957).

[54] Judicial Improvements and Access to Justice Act, P.L. 100-702, tit. X, § 1013(a), 102 Stat. 4642, 4669 (1988).

[55] VE Holding Corp. v. Johnson Gas Appliance Co., 917 F.2d 1574 (Fed. Cir. 1990).

[56] Allen Pusey, "Marshall Law: Patent Lawyers Flood to East Texas Court for Its Expertise and 'Rocket Docket'," *Dallas Morning News* (March 26, 2006), 1D.

[57] *Id.*

[58] *See* Xuan-Thao Nguyen, "Justice Scalia's 'Renegade Jurisdiction': Lessons for Patent Law Reform," 83 *Tulane Law Review* (2008), 111.

[59] 551 F.3d 1315 (Fed. Cir. 2008).

[60] Rooklidge & Barker, *supra*, at 185.

[61] *See* Intellectual Property Owners Association, "Patent Reform (111th Congress)" (May 4, 2009) (available at http://www.ipo.org).

[62] Lear Corp. v. TS Tech, No. 2:07-CV-406 (E.D.Tex. Sept. 10, 2008).

[63] 551 F.3d at 1320.

[64] *Id.* at 1320-21.

[65] *Id.* at 1321.

[66] *See* Douglas C. Muth *et al.*, "The Local Patent Rules Bandwagon," 21 *Intellectual Property & Technology Law Journal* (Aug. 2009), no. 8 at 19.

[67] *See* Elizabeth Durham, "Will All Roads Lead to the Eastern District of Texas? Transfer Practice After *Volkswagen* and *TS Tech*," 21 *Intellectual Property & Technology Law Journal* (July 2009), no. 7 at 12.

[68] *See* Intellectual Property Owners, *supra.*

[69] H.R. 2795, 109th Congress, § 6(a).

[70] *See* Rooklidge & Barker, *supra.*

[71] Amy L. Landers, "Let the Games Begin: Incentives to Innovation in the New Economy of Intellectual Property Law," 46 *Santa Clara Law Review* (2006), 364-65.

[72] William C. Rooklidge, "Reform of the Patent Laws: Forging Legislation Addressing Disparate Interests," 88 *Journal of the Patent and Trademark Office Society* (2006).

[73] State Indus., Inc. v. Mor-Flo Indus., Inc., 883 F.2d 1573, 1580 (Fed. Cir. 1989).

[74] Dowagiac Mfg. Co. v. Minn. Moline Plow Co., 235 U.S. 641 (1915).

[75] Lucent Technologies, Inc. v. Gateway, Inc., 580 F.3d 1301 (Fed. Cir. 2009).

[76] Id. at 1308.

[77] Id. at 1309.

[78] The letter is available at http://specter.senate.gov/public/index.cfm?FuseAction=NewsRoom. NewsReleases& ContentRecord_id=CE8F4C18-970E-54D1-84DD-1D25F0BE2FCB.

[79] *Id.*

[80] 580 F.3d at 1301.

[81] *Id.* at 1335.

[82] *Id.*

[83] Steven Seidenberg, "Into the Fray: *Lucent* Ruling Makes It Harder to Prove Patent Damages," *InsideCounsel* (Dec. 1, 2009).

[84] 580 F.3d at 1337.

[85] Id. at 1339.

[86] Seidenberg, *supra.*

[87] Id.

[88] 35 U.S.C. § 284.

[89] *See* Transclean Corp. v. Bridgewood Services, Inc., 290 F.3d 1364 (Fed. Cir. 2002).

[90] 970 F.2d 816 (Fed. Cir. 1992).

[91] *Id.* at 828.

[92] H.R. 2795, 109th Congress, at § 6(b).

[93] 497 F.3d 1360 (Fed. Cir. 2007) (en banc).

[94] *Id.* at 1371.

[95] *Id.*

[96] *Id.*

[97] *Id.*

[98] *See* Siraj Husain, "The Willfulness Pendulum Swings Back: How *Seagate* Helps Level the Playing Field," 28 *Loyola of Los Angeles Entertainment Law Review* (2007-2008), 239.

[99] *See* Rooklidge & Barker, *supra*, at 167; IPO, *supra.*

[100] Christopher C. Bolten, "*In re Seagate Tech., LL.C.*, Is the Objective Recklessness Standard a Practical Change?," 49 *Jurimetrics Journal* (Fall 2008), 90.

[101] *See* Dariush Keyhani, "Patent Law in the Global Economy: A Modest for Proposal for U.S. Patent Law and Infringement Without Borders," 54 *Villanova Law Review* (2009), 291.

[102] Eolas Techs. Inc. v. Microsoft Corp., 399 F.3d 1325 (Fed. Cir. 2005).

[103] Rachel Krevans & Daniel P. Muino, "Restoring the Balance: The Supreme Court Joins the Patent Reform Movement," 9 *Sedona Conference Journal* (2008), 15.

[104] S. 3818, §5(f).

[105] 550 U.S. 437 (2007). *See* CRS Report RS22670, *Exporting Software and the Extraterritorial Reach of U.S. Patent Law: Microsoft Corp. v. AT&T Corp.*, by Brian T. Yeh.

[106] *Id.* at 453.

[107] *See* James Ernstmeyer, "Does Strict Territoriality Toll the End of Software Patents?," 89 *Boston University Law Review* (2009), 1267.

[108] U.S. Senator Patrick Leahy, "Leahy, Hatch, Berman And Smith Introduce Bicameral, Bipartisan Patent Reform Legislation" (April 18, 2007) (available at http://leahy.senate.gov/ press/200704/041807a.html).

[109] *See* Ernstmeyer, *supra.*

[110] H.R. 1908, 110th Congress, § .

[111] *See* Judy Naamat, "The State of the Patent Street: Does Statutory 'Matter'," 91 *Journal of the Patent and Trademark Office Society* (2009), 229.

[112] 130 S.Ct. 3218 (2010).

[113] 549 F.3d 943 (Fed. Cir. 2008) (*en banc*). *See* CRS Report R40803, *Patent-Eligibility of Process Claims Under Section 101 of the Patent Act: Bilski v. Kappos*, by Brian T. Yeh, Patent-Eligibility of Process Claims Under the Patent Act: Bilski v. Kappos., by Brian T. Yeh (Sept. 9, 2009).

[114] *See* Linda M. Beale, "Is *Bilski* Likely the Final Word on Tax Strategy Patents? Coherence Matters," 9 *John Marshall Review of Intellectual Property Law* (Summer 2009), 110.

[115] *See generally* Stephen T. Schreiner & Noah M. Lerman, "Intellectual Property Update: Viability of Business Method Patents and Financial Method Patents After the Supreme Court's *Bilski* Opinion," 127 *Banking Law Journal* (2010), 986.

[116] Beale, *supra.*

[117] In the 111th Congress, see H.R. 1260, § 10 and S. 515, § 8. S. 610 does not address interlocutory appeals of claim construction rulings.

[118] *See* Kelly C. McKinney, "The Patent Reform Act of 2007 and International Patent Law Harmonization," 31 *Houston Journal of International Law* (2008), 125.

[119] 550 U.S. 398 (2007). *See* CRS Report RS22669, *The Obviousness Standard in Patent Law: KSR International Co. v. Teleflex Inc.*, by Brian T. Yeh.

[120] *See* Rebecca S. Eisenberg, "Pharma's Nonobvious Problem," 12 *Lewis & Clark Law Review* (2008), 375.

[121] H.R. 2795, 109th Congress (introduced on June 8, 2005).

[122] 28 U.S.C. § 1295(a) (2006).

[123] *See* Chris J. Katopis, "The Federal Circuit's Forgotten Lessons?: Annealing New Forms of Intellectual Property Through Consolidated Appellate Jurisdiction," 32 *John Marshall Law Review* (1999), 581.

[124] 28 U.S.C. § 48(a) (2006).

[125] *See* U.S. Court of Appeals for the Federal Circuit, *Judicial Biographies* (available at http://www.cafc.uscourts.gov/ judgbios.html).

[126] Dan L. Burk & Mark A. Lemley, *The Patent Crisis and How the Courts Can Solve It* (University of Chicago Press 2009), 100.

[127] Id. at 102.

[128] Id.

[129] *See generally* Robert B. Schapiro, "Judicial Deference and Interpretive Coordinacy in State and Federal Constitutional Law," 85 *Cornell Law Review* (2000), 656.

[130] Rooklidge & Barker, *supra.*

[131] *See generally* Arti K. Rai, "Growing Pains in the Administrative State: The Patent Office's Troubled Quest for Managerial Control," 157 *University of Pennsylvania Law Review* (2009), 2051.

In: U.S. Patent System Reform ...
Editors: F. Parker and M. Lopez

ISBN: 978-1-61470-528-4
© 2011 Nova Science Publishers, Inc.

Chapter 3

PATENT REFORM: ISSUES IN THE BIOMEDICAL AND SOFTWARE INDUSTRIES

Wendy H. Schacht

SUMMARY

Congress has shown recurring interest in reform of the existing patent system. This attention to patent policy reflects a recognition of the increasing importance of intellectual property to U.S. innovation. Patent ownership is perceived as an incentive to the technological advancement that leads to economic growth. As such, the number of patent applications and grants has grown significantly, as have the type and breadth of inventions that can be patented.

Along with the expansion in the number and range of patents, there are growing concerns over whether the current system is working efficiently and effectively. Several studies recommended patent reform and several bills have been introduced in recent congresses that would make significant alterations in current patent law. Other experts maintain that major changes in existing law are unnecessary and that, while not perfect, the patent process can, and is, adapting to technological progress.

At the present time, the patent laws provide a system under which all inventions are subject to the same requirements of patentability regardless of the technical field in which they arose. However, inventors and innovative companies in different industries often hold divergent views concerning the importance of patents, reflecting varying experiences with the patent system. Innovators in the biomedical sector tend to see patent protection as a critically important way to prohibit competitors from appropriating the results of a company's research and development efforts. Typically only a few, often one or two, patents cover a particular drug. In contrast, the nature of software development is such that inventions often are cumulative and new products generally embody numerous patentable inventions. As a result, distinct industries may react differently to patent reform proposals under consideration by Congress.

INTRODUCTION

Recent congressional interest in patent reform has been manifest in omnibus legislation considered in the past three Congresses. This attention to patent policy reflects a recognition of the increasing importance of intellectual property to U.S. innovation. Patent ownership is perceived as an incentive to the technological advancement that leads to economic growth. As such, the number of patent applications and grants have grown significantly as have the type and breath of inventions that can be patented. In 1980, 104,329 utility patent applications were received at the U.S. Patent and Trademark Office (USPTO); by 2009, this number had more than quadrupled to 456,106 applications. During the same time period, the number of U.S. utility patents granted grew from 61,819 to 167,349.[1]

Along with the expansion in the number and range of patents, there are growing concerns over whether the current system is working efficiently and effectively. Several recent studies (including those by the National Academy of Sciences and the Federal Trade Commission)[2] recommend patent reform. In response, a number of bills have been introduced in Congress that would make significant alterations in current patent law.[3] Other experts maintain that major alterations in existing law are unnecessary and that, while not perfect, the patent process can, and is, adapting to technological progress.

The discussion of patent reform has led to the emergence of several, often opposing, points of view. While the patent laws provide a system under which all inventions are treated the same regardless of the technical field, the varying experiences of companies in different industries often give rise to differing views concerning the importance and role of patents. Innovators in biomedical industries tend to see patent protection as critically important as a way to

Patent Reform: Issues in the Biomedical and Software Industries 75

prohibit competitors from appropriating the results of a company's research and development efforts. Typically only a few, often one or two, patents cover a particular drug. In contrast, the nature of software development is such that inventions tend to be cumulative and new products generally embody numerous patentable inventions. Acknowledging these differences, this report explores the relationships between patents and innovation and looks at the role of intellectual property in the biomedical and software industries, two sectors where U.S. investment in research and development (R&D) has led to market leadership, a strong export position, and contributed to the Nation's economic growth.

PATENTS AND INNOVATION

Patent law is based upon the Patent Act of 1952, codified in Title 35 of the United States Code. According to the statute, one who "invents or discovers any new and useful process, machine, manufacture, or any composition of matter, or any new and useful improvement thereof, may obtain a patent therefore, subject to the conditions and requirements of this title."[4] Patents are issued by the United States Patent and Trademark Office (USPTO), generally for a term of 20 years from the date of filing. The patent grants its owner the right to exclude others from making, using, selling, offering to sell, or importing into the United States the patented invention. To be afforded patent rights, an invention must be judged to consist of patentable subject matter, possess utility, and be novel and nonobvious. The application must fully disclose and distinctly claim the invention for which protection is sought.

The grant of a patent does not necessarily provide the owner with an affirmative right to market the patented invention. For example, pharmaceutical products are also subject to marketing approval by the Food and Drug Administration (FDA).[5] Federal laws typically require that pharmaceutical manufacturers demonstrate that their products are safe and effective in order to bring these drugs to the marketplace. USPTO issuance of a patent and FDA marketing consent are distinct events that depend upon different criteria.[6]

Patent ownership is perceived to be an incentive to innovation, the basis for the technological advancement that contributes to economic growth. Patent title provides the recipient with a limited-time monopoly over the use of his discovery in exchange for the public dissemination of information contained in the patent application. Award of a patent is intended to stimulate the investment necessary to develop an idea and bring it to the marketplace embodied in a product or process, although it does not guarantee that the patent will generate commercial benefits. The requirement for publication of the patent is expected to stimulate additional innovation and other creative means to meet similar and expanded demands in the marketplace.

Innovation produces new knowledge. However, innovation typically is costly and resource intensive. Studies demonstrate that the rate of return to society as a whole generated by investments in research and development leading to innovation is significantly larger than the benefits that can be captured by the person or organization financing the work.[7] Some estimate that the social rate of return on R&D spending is over twice that of the rate of return to the inventor. Ideas often are easily imitated as the knowledge associated with an innovation is dispersed and adapted to other products and processes that, in turn, stimulate growth in the economy. Patents permit novel concepts or discoveries to become "property" when reduced to practice and therefore allow for control over their use.

Issuance of a patent furnishes the inventor with a limited-time exclusive right, the benefits of which are mitigated by other factors, particularly the requirements for information disclosure, the length of the patent, and the scope of rights conferred. The process of obtaining a patent places the concept on which it is based in the public domain. In return for a monopoly right to the application of the knowledge generated, the inventor must publish the ideas covered in the patent. As a disclosure system, the patent can, and often does, stimulate other firms or individuals to invent "around" existing patents to provide for parallel technical developments or meet similar market needs.

Patents may also provide a more socially desirable outcome than its chief legal alternative, trade secret protection. Trade secrecy guards against the improper appropriation of valuable, commercially useful information that is the subject of reasonable measures to preserve its secrecy.[8] Taking the steps necessary to maintain secrecy, such as implementing physical security and enforcement, imposes costs that may ultimately be unproductive for society.[9] Also, while the patent law obliges inventors to disclose their inventions to the public,[10] trade secret protection requires firms to conceal them. The disclosure obligations of the patent system may better serve the objective of encouraging the diffusion of advanced technological knowledge. Patents may also prevent unproductive expenditures of time and money associated with R&D that duplicates other work.

Patent Reform: Issues in the Biomedical and Software Industries   77

The patent system thus has dual policy goals—providing incentives for inventors to invent and encouraging inventors to disclose technical information.[11] Disclosure requirements are factors in achieving a balance between current and future innovation through the patent process, as are limitations on scope, novelty mandates, and nonobviousness considerations.[12] Patents often give rise to an environment of competitiveness with multiple sources of innovation, which is viewed by some experts as the basis for technological progress. This is important because, as Professors Robert Merges and Richard Nelson found in their studies, in a situation where only "a few organizations controlled the development of a technology, technical advance appeared sluggish."[13]

Not everyone agrees that the patent system is a particularly effective means to stimulate innovation. Some observers believe that the patent system encourages industry concentration and presents a barrier to entry in some markets.[14] They suggest that the patent system often converts pioneering inventors into technological suppressors, who use their patents to block subsequent improvements and thereby impede technological progress.[15] Others believe that the patent system too frequently attracts speculators who prefer to acquire and enforce patents rather than engage in socially productive activity such as bringing new products and processes to the marketplace.[16]

Some experts argue that patents do not work as well in reality as in theory because they do not confer perfect appropriability. In other words, they allow the inventor to obtain a larger portion of the returns on his investment but do not permit him to capture all the benefits. Patents can be circumvented and infringement cannot always be proven. Thus, patents are not the only way, nor necessarily the most efficient means, for the inventor to protect the benefits generated by his efforts. A study by Yale University's Richard Levin and his colleagues concluded that lead time, learning curve advantages (e.g., familiarity with the science and technology under consideration), and sales/service activities were typically more important in exploiting appropriability than were patents. That was true for both products and processes. However, patents were found to be better at protecting products than processes. The novel ideas associated with a product often can be determined through reverse engineering—taking the item apart to assess how it was made. That information then could be used by competitors if not covered by a patent. Because it is more difficult to identify the procedures related to a process, other means of appropriation are seen as preferable to patents, with the attendant disclosure requirements.[17]

An analysis of the literature in this area performed for the World Intellectual Property Organization[18] highlights several conclusions concerning the use of patents that mirror much of the above discussion. The research surveyed indicates that "lead time and secrecy seem to be the most relevant appropriability devices for most sectors" and that while patents may not be the most effective means to protect inventions, they are still utilized by firms in all industries. There is a consensus that "disclosure and ease of inventing-around are the most important reasons for not patenting." At the same time, "patents are more relevant as an appropriability mechanism for product than for process innovations and for some sectors such as chemicals (especially pharmaceuticals), some machinery industries and biotechnology."

ROLE OF PATENTS IN BIOMEDICAL R&D

Research demonstrates that the value of patents is differs across industries and between firms of different maturation levels within a sector.[19] The pharmaceutical industry perceives patents as critical to protecting innovation. Several studies over the years have demonstrated the important role patents play in the pharmaceutical sector. Of the 18 major manufacturing industries analyzed by Richard Levin and his colleagues, only drug companies rated product patents the most effective means of insuring that firms can capture the profits associated with their innovations.[20]

Later research by Professor Wesley Cohen and his colleagues demonstrated that patents were considered the most effective method to protect inventions in the drug industry, particularly when biotechnology is included.[21] A recent paper by several professors at the Berkeley School of Law, University of California, found that there were "substantial differences between the health-related sectors (biotechnology and medical devices), in which patents are more commonly used and considered important, and the software and Internet fields, in which patents are reported to be less useful."[22] These studies reinforce earlier work by the late Professor Edwin Mansfield that indicated 65% of pharmaceutical inventions would not have been brought to market without patent protection in contrast to the 8% of innovations made in other industries.[23]

Patents may be particularly important in the pharmaceutical sector because of the relative ease of replicating the finished product. Imitation costs vary among industries. For example, while it is expensive, complicated, and time consuming to duplicate an airplane, it is relatively simple to chemically analyze a pill and reproduce it.[24] The degree to which industry perceives patents as effective has been characterized as "positively correlated with the increase in duplication costs and time associated with patents."[25] Early research in this area by Mansfield indicated that, in certain industries, patents significantly raise the costs incurred by nonpatent holders wishing to use the idea or invent around the patent—an estimated 40% in the pharmaceutical sector, 30% for major new chemical products, and 25% for typical chemical goods—and are thus viewed as significant. However, in other industries, patents have much smaller impact on the costs associated with imitation (e.g., in the 7%-15% range for electronics), and may be considered less successful in protecting resource investments.[26]

The costs associated with imitating pharmaceuticals "are extremely low relative to the innovator's costs for discovering and developing a new compound."[27] Studies by Dr. Joseph DiMasi of Tufts University and others indicate that the capitalized cost of bringing a new drug (defined as a "new molecular entity" rather than a new formulation of an existing pharmaceutical product) to the point of marketing approval was $802 million (2000 dollars).[28] Additional research done by analysts at the Federal Trade Commission found the costs to be even higher; between $839 million and $868 million (2000 dollars).[29] Later work argues that it now takes over $1 billion to bring a new drug to market.[30] At the same time, the total capitalized costs appear to be growing at an annual rate of 7.4% above general price inflation.[31]

A large portion of new drug costs (in terms of money and time) are associated with the size and breath of clinical trials necessary to obtain FDA marketing approval. According to a study supported by the Federal Reserve Bank of Boston, only 10% of potential drug candidates reach the human trial phase and only a small portion of these actually reach the market.[32] In research presented at a conference sponsored by the Federal Reserve Bank of Dallas, Duke University's Henry Grabowski found that only 1% of drug compounds reach the human trial stage and 22% of those entering clinical trials receive FDA approval.[33] Professor Iain Cockburn notes that "as drug discovery became more science-intensive, ... it became not just more expensive but also more difficult to manage."[34] Furthermore, returns to new drug introductions vary widely and the median new drug does not bring in sufficient profits to cover the costs of bringing the product to the marketplace.[35] According to research by Professors Grabowski, John Vernon, and DiMasi, only 34% of new drugs (new chemical entities) introduced generated profits that equaled the industry average R&D cost.[36]

The significant costs of pharmaceutical R&D, coupled with the uncertainty of the clinical trial process, lend consequence to patents in this area because "the disparity between the investments of innovators and those of imitators is particularly large in pharmaceuticals—almost as large as when software pirates simply copy the diskettes of an innovator."[37] While the capitalized cost of developing a new drug to the point of market approval is about $1 billion, it takes only between $1 million and $2 million to obtain approval for a generic version of the pharmaceutical.[38] This difference is a result of the costs associated with clinical trials needed to demonstrate the safety and efficacy of a new drug, data that could be utilized by generic companies if not protected by a patent.[39] A generic company does not have to fund these studies to get FDA marketing approval; under the provisions of the Hatch-Waxman Act generic firms only have to prove that their product is "bioequivalent" to the innovator drug.[40]

While patents are designed to spur innovation, some experts maintain that certain patents, particularly those on research tools[41] in biotechnology, hinder the innovation process. Professors Rebecca Eisenberg and Richard Nelson argue that ownership of research tools may "impose significant transaction costs" that result in delayed innovation and possible future litigation.[42] It also can stand in the way of research by others:

> Broad claims on early discoveries that are fundamental to emerging fields of knowledge are particularly worrisome in light of the great value, demonstrated time and again in history of science and technology, of having many independent minds at work trying to advance a field. Public science has flourished by permitting scientists to challenge and build upon the work of rivals.[43]

Eisenberg and her colleague at the University of Michigan Law School, Michael Heller, contend that in the future scientists might need to obtain numerous patent licenses in order to undertake basic research.[44] Similar concerns were expressed by Harold Varmus, President of Memorial Sloan-Kettering and formerly the Director of the National Institutes of Health. In July 2000 prepared testimony, he spoke to being "troubled by widespread tendencies to seek protection of intellectual property increasingly early in the process that ultimately leads to products of obvious commercial value, because such practices can have detrimental effects on science and its delivery of health benefits."[45]

However, other experts dispute this assertion. A study by Professors John Walsh, Ashish Arora, and Wesley Cohen found that although there are now more patents associated with biomedical research, and on more fundamental work, there is little evidence that work has been curtailed due to intellectual property issues associated with research tools.[46] Scientists are able to continue their research by "licensing, inventing around patents, going offshore, the development and use of public databases and research tools, court challenges, and simply using the technology without a license (i.e., infringement)." According to the authors of the report, private sector owners of patents permitted such infringement in academia (with the exception of those associated with diagnostic tests in clinical trials) "partly because it can increase the value of the patented technology."

Later research by Cohen, Walsh, and Charlene Cho found that "only 1% of academic researchers (i.e., those in universities, non-profits and government labs) report having to delay a project, and none abandoned a project due to others' patents, suggesting that neither anti-commons nor restrictions on access were seriously limiting academic research."[47] In addition to finding that patents did not interfere with ongoing R&D, the authors found that patents had "significantly less" impact on what projects were actually pursued than lack of funding, time constraints, or scientific competition. However, "respondents doing research on drugs and therapies were ... somewhat more likely to report that unreasonable terms demanded for research inputs were an important reason for them not to pursue a project."[48]

ROLE OF PATENTS IN THE SOFTWARE INDUSTRY

Over the past 25 years, there has been a demonstrable and sustained increase in the number of software patents granted in the United States. Research by James Bessen and Robert Hunt for the Federal Reserve Bank of Philadelphia noted that the 1,000 software patents issued annually in the early 1980s[49] had increased to an annual total of 5,000 by 1990. Today over 20,000 software patents are granted each year. While software patents comprised approximately 2% of all patents awarded in the early 1980s, they now account for approximately 15% of the total number of U.S. patent issued each year.[50]

Experts differ as to their assessment of the role of patents in promoting innovation in the computer software sector. This discussion centers around the issue of whether the increase in the number of patents is a result of inventive behavior generated by intellectual property protection or a result of changes in law during the 1980s and 1990s that made patents on software easier to obtain. Some experts argue that patent protection is not a significant factor in the development of computer software programs. Other analysts maintain that they play an important role in generating new technologies, particularly for small firms in the marketplace.

The nature of software development is such that inventions often are cumulative and new products generally embody numerous patentable inventions. This has led to what has been described by some observers as a

> poor match between patents and products in the [software] industry: it is difficult to patent an entire product in the software industry because any particular product is likely to include dozens if not hundreds of separate technological ideas.[51]

This situation may be augmented by the multiplicity of patents often associated with a finished computer product that utilizes the software. It is not uncommon for thousands of different patents (relating to hardware and software) to be embodied in one single computer. In addition, ownership of these patents may well be fractured among hundreds or thousands of different individuals and firms.

Studies by Bessen and Hunt explored the characteristics of software patents and determined that most are not owned by software companies but by large manufacturing companies. They found that

> Firms in just three manufacturing industries (machinery, electronics, and instruments) alone accounted for 66 percent of software patents [yet] ... Firms outside the manufacturing sector employed 90 percent of computer programmers, but together they accounted for only 25 percent of software patents.[52]

This data leads the authors to the conclusion that patents may not be closely tied to the development of new software technologies. Ownership of such patents is concentrated in sectors that have large patent portfolios and use them for strategic purposes.[53] Instead, they believe that companies are utilizing patents as a means to protect or leverage their investments rather than to generate more innovation through R&D spending.[54]

In industries where innovation is sequential and complementary, as with software and computers, some experts argue that strong patents interfere with the innovation process.[55] Inventions in these sectors typically are built upon earlier technologies and are integrated into existing systems. Commentators pose that patents inhibit or prevent enhancements to existing products because the patent owner may not have the interest or capability necessary to generate improvements at the same time that other firms cannot advance the technology without infringing on the original patent.

Not everyone agrees with this assessment. Professor Robert Merges maintains that patents have not hindered innovation in the software industry and that the significant ownership of title to inventions by large companies in this sector has not resulted in the demise of small firms developing new technologies.[56] Analysis of software companies by Professor Ronald Mann indicates the importance of software patents to small companies, particularly later-stage start-ups firms. He notes that the software industry is comprised primarily of small businesses and "the data suggests a different picture, one in which software R&D is impressively robust."[57] Mann's research indicates that small firms spend proportionally more on software R&D than large companies. Research and development spending by software firms "tends to be relatively stable over time as a percentage of sales. Indeed, company size seems to be more important in explaining variations in R&D spending within the industry."[58]

Studies by Mann also indicate that the importance of software patents is dependent on where the firm is in its development process. Patents play a more significant role in later-stage start-up companies when firms can generate revenues through licensing.[59] At that point, "patents are useful as "barter" in cross-licensing agreements that the firm enters if it reaches a sufficiently mature stage to be a significant player in the industry."[60] Patents may allow a firm to differentiate its areas of expertise and innovative activity.[61]

Patents enable a company to transform ideas into a tangible form of property that can provide value. This can be useful in negotiations for the acquisition of the firm. While intellectual property is important to some investors but not to others, it is considered a significant factor when a company is involved in acquisition negotiations or in an IPO.[62] It can prevent large companies from appropriating a small firm's technology. Bradford Smith and Susan Mann, writing in the University of Chicago Law Review, concur with the argument that patents are beneficial for small, software firms. They maintain that patents prevent larger companies from utilizing the technologies developed by small businesses while allowing these companies to attract venture capital.[63]

The multiplicity of patents involved in computer-related products has resulted in the extensive use of cross licensing in these industries such that one commentator argues: "licensing of software patents has become an industry unto itself."[64] Instead of promoting innovation, some experts maintain that the ownership of intellectual property has become an obstacle to the development and application of new ideas. The expansion in the number of patents associated with software is a consequence of the changes in patent law that make these patents easier to obtain, rather than an indication of increased innovative activity. There are indications, according to Bessen and Hunt, that patents are being substituted for increases in R&D.[65] The substitution occurs in industries that patent strategically but not in other sectors.[66] The propensity to patent software appears to be related to the utilization of the software by companies rather than to the R&D resources expended in developing the product.[67] This is of interest because a rationale behind the patent system is that it provides incentives for the additional investments necessary to bring a product to the marketplace.

Concerns have been expressed in the academic community that the propensity to patent and the extensive use of cross licensing has resulted in a "patent thicket" where ownership of patent title is used to block others from innovating. According to Bessen and Hunt, "This may have increased the attractiveness of a strategy that emphasizes patent rights over a strategy based on R&D."[68] However, other experts maintain that this might not be a true assessment of the situation. In an article for the Virginia Journal of Law and Technology, David Evans and Anne Layne-Farrar argue it is not clear that a patent thicket exists. "Other industries with longstanding histories of patenting could be categorized as having cumulative and sequential R&D, yet they do not display signs of innovation gridlock."[69] There are additional ways to prevent the use of patents to block innovation including the use of pro-competitive patent pools and antitrust enforcement.

Others agree that innovation in the software industry is not hindered by a patent thicket. In one study where actual software companies and investors were surveyed, the analyst found new companies were not concerned with existing patent portfolios as a barrier to their work as "none of the startup firms [interviewed] suggested a practice of doing prior art searches before beginning development of their products."[70] Because the software industry is so diverse, it is "difficult for any single patent or group of patents to control a major part of the whole industry."[71]

CONCLUDING OBSERVATIONS

Innovators in the biomedical and software industries tend to exhibit divergent views on the value of patents. Patent protection is critically important to the pharmaceutical and biotechnology sectors as a way to prohibit competitors from appropriating the results of a company's research and development efforts. However,

> patents are not among the key means used to protect innovations in either the computer or semiconductor industries. In those two industries, firms rely more heavily on secrecy, lead time and complementary capabilities to protect their inventions.[72]

A difference between the role of patents in the biomedical community and their role in the computer software sector lies with the dissimilar composition of the respective products. Typically only a few, often one or two, patents cover a particular drug. In contrast, the nature of software development is such that inventions often are cumulative and new products generally embody numerous patentable inventions. While few companies other than those that manufacture drugs need to deal with the relevant pharmaceutical patents,

> computers are ubiquitous—and as a result, so is software authorship ... Thus, a patent on a drug creates potential liability for those companies in the pharmaceutical business, while a software patent creates potential liability for any company with its own website or software customizations, regardless of its business.[73]

At the present time, the patent laws provide a system under which all inventions are subject to the same requirements of patentability regardless of the technical field in which they arose. The reforms proposed in recent legislative initiatives continue this approach. As a consequence, inventors and innovative companies in different industries, with varying patent experiences, may display diverse opinions on anticipated changes to the patent law. According to Professor Brian Kahin, these distinct views of the patent reform issue reflect

> the contrast between the discrete-product environment of pharmaceuticals and chemicals and the extreme complex-product environment associated with information technology.... In contract to the classic use of patents to exclude competitors in pharmaceuticals, ... the large volume of patents

86 Wendy H. Schacht

relative to [information technology]products imposes a cost burden and makes the IT sector prone to inadvertent infringement and vulnerable to patent trolls.[74]

Thus, it remains to be seen how these identified differences might affect any specific patent reform effort the U.S. Congress may chose to take under consideration.

End Notes

[1] U.S. Patent and Trademark Office, *U.S. Patent Statistics, Calendar Years 1963-2009*, available at http://www.uspto.gov/web/offices/ac/ido/oeip/taf/us_stat.pdf.

[2] National Research Council, National Academy of Sciences, *A Patent System for the 21st Century*, (Washington, National Academies Press, 2004) and Federal Trade Commission, *To Promote Innovation: The Proper Balance of Competition and Patent Law and Policy*, October 2003, available at http://www.ftc.gov.

[3] The specific legislative changes contained in several of the bills introduced in the 111th Congress are discussed in CRS Report R40481, *Patent Reform in the 111th Congress: Innovation Issues*, by Wendy H. Schacht and John R. Thomas. Patent reform efforts in the 110th Congress are analyzed in CRS Report RL33996, *Patent Reform in the 110th Congress: Innovation Issues*, by John R. Thomas and Wendy H. Schacht. Discussion of patent reform in the 109th Congress can be found in CRS Report RL32996, *Patent Reform: Innovation Issues*, by John R. Thomas and Wendy H. Schacht.

[4] 35 U.S.C.§101.

[5] For more information see CRS Report R41114, *The Hatch-Waxman Act: A Quarter Century Later*, by Wendy H. Schacht and John R. Thomas, and CRS Report RL30756, *Patent Law and Its Application to the Pharmaceutical Industry: An Examination of the Drug Price Competition and Patent Term Restoration Act of 1984 ("The Hatch-Waxman Act")*, by Wendy H. Schacht and John R. Thomas.

[6] For more information see CRS Report RL33288, *Proprietary Rights in Pharmaceutical Innovation: Issues at the Intersection of Patents and Marketing Exclusivities*, by John R. Thomas.

[7] For a list of relevant research in this area see Council of Economic Advisors. *Supporting Research and Development to Promote Economic Growth: The Federal Government's Role*, October 1995, 6-7.

[8] American Law Institute, Restatement of Unfair Competition Third §39, 1995.

[9] David D. Friedman, et al., "Some Economics of Trade Secret Law," 5 *Journal of Economic Perspectives*, 1991, 61.

[10] 35 U.S.C. §112 (2000).

[11] Robert P. Merges, "Commercial Success and Patent Standards: Economic Perspectives on Innovation," *California Law Review*, July 1988, 876.

[12] Kenneth W. Dam, "The Economic Underpinnings of Patent Law," *Journal of Legal Studies*, January, 1994, pp. 266-267. Scope is determined by the number of claims made in a patent. Claims are the technical descriptions associated with the invention. In order for an idea to receive a patent, the law requires that it be "new, useful [novel], and nonobvious to a person of ordinary skill in the art to which the invention pertains."

[13] Robert P. Merges and Richard R. Nelson, "On the Complex Economics of Patent Scope," *Columbia Law Review*, May 1990, 908.

[14] See John R. Thomas, "Collusion and Collective Action in the Patent System: A Proposal for Patent Bounties," *University of Illinois Law Review*, 2001, 305.

[15] *On the Complex Economics of Patent Scope*, 839.

[16] Elizabeth D. Ferrill, "Patent Investment Trusts: Let's Build a Pit to Catch the Patent Trolls," *6 North Carlina Journal of Law and Technology*, 2005, 367.

[17] Richard C. Levin, Alvin K. Klevorick, Richard R. Nelson, and Sidney G. Winter. "Appropriating the Returns for Industrial Research and Development," *Brookings Papers on Economic Activity*, 1987, in *The Economics of Technical Change*, eds. Edwin Mansfield and Elizabeth Mansfield (Vermont, Edward Elgar Publishing Co., 1993), 254.

[18] Andres Lopez, "Innovation and Appropriability, Empirical Evidence and Research Agenda," in *The Economics of Intellectual Property*, World Intellectual Property Organization, January 2009, 21, available at http://www.wipo/int/ export/sites/www/ip-development/en/ economics/pdf/wo_1012_e.pdf.

[19] Stuart J.H. Graham, Robert P. Merges, Pam Samuelson, and Ted Sichelman, "High Technology Entrepreneurs and the Patent System: Results of the 2008 Berkeley Patent Survey," *Berkeley Technology Law Journal*, April 16, 2010, 1255, available at http://www.btlj.org/data/articles/24_feature.pdf.

[20] *Appropriating the Returns for Industrial Research and Development*, 255 and 257.

[21] Wesley M. Cohen, Richard R. Nelson, and John P. Walsh, *Protecting Their Intellectual Assets: Appropriability Conditions and Why U.S. Manufacturing Firms Patent (or Not)*, NBER Working Paper 7552, Cambridge, National Bureau of Economic Research, February 2000, available at http://www.nber.org/papers/w7552.

[22] *High Technology Entrepreneurs and the Patent System: Results of the 2008 Berkeley Patent Survey*, 1255.

[23] Edwin Mansfield, "Patents and Innovation: An Empirical Study," *Management Science*, February 1986, 173-181.

[24] Federic M. Scherer, "The Economics of Human Gene Patents," 77 *Academic Medicine*, December 2002, 1350.

[25] *Appropriating the Returns for Industrial Research and Development*, 269.

[26] Edwin Mansfield, Mark Schwartz, and Samuel Wagner, "Imitation Costs and Patents: An Empirical Study," *The Economic Journal*, December 1981, in *The Economics of Technical Change*, 270.

[27] Henry Grabowski, "Patents and New Product Development in the Pharmaceutical and Biotechnology Industries," *Duke University Economics Working Paper*, July 2002, available at http://www.econ.duke.edu/Papers/Other/ Grabowski/Patents.pdf, 4.

[28] Joseph A. DiMasi, Ronald W. Hansen, and Henry G. Grabowski. "The Price of Innovation: New Estimates of Drug Development Costs," 22 *Journal of Health Economics*, 2003. Capitalized cost includes the "time cost" associated with an investment and the cost of testing drug products that fail.

[29] Christopher P. Adams and Van V. Brantner, *Estimating the Costs of New Drug Development: Is it Really $802m?*, Federal Trade Commission, December 2004, available at http://media.romanvenable.net/images/drugCost.pdf.

[30] Christopher Paul Adams and Van Vu Brantner, "Spending on New Drug Development," *Health Economics*, (published online 26 Feb.2009) Epub ahead of print.

[31] *The Price of Innovation: New Estimates of Drug Development Costs*, 180.

[32] Carrie Conway, "The Pros and Cons of Pharmaceutical Patents," *Regional Review*, Federal Reserve Bank of Boston, March 2003, available at http://www.findarticles.com.

[33] Henry G. Grabowski, "Patents, Innovation, and Access to New Pharmaceuticals," *Journal of International Economic Law*, 2002, 851.

[34] Iain Cockburn, "The Changing Structure of the Pharmaceutical Industry," *Health Affairs*, January/February 2004, 15.

[35] Henry G. Grabowski, "Patents and New Product Development in the Pharmaceutical and Biotechnology Industries," *Science and Cents: Exploring the Economics of Biotechnology*,

Proceedings of a 2002 Conference, Federal Reserve Bank of Dallas, pp. 95-96 available at http://www.dallasfed.org/research/pubs/science/grabowski.pdf and Henry Grabowski, John Vernon, and Joseph A. DiMasi, "Returns on Research and Development for 1990s New Drug Introductions," 20 *Pharmacoeconomics*, 2002.

[36] *Returns on Research and Development for 1990s New Drug Introductions*, 23.

[37] *The Economics of Human Gene Patents*, 1352.

[38] *Patents, Innovation, and Access to New Pharmaceuticals*, 852.

[39] *The Economics of Human Gene Patents*, 1352.

[40] For more information see CRS Report RL30756, *Patent Law and Its Application to the Pharmaceutical Industry: An Examination of the Drug Price Competition and Patent Term Restoration Act of 1984 ("The Hatch-Waxman Act")*, by Wendy H. Schacht and John R. Thomas.

[41] A biotechnology research tool is a cell line, reagent, or antibody used in research.

[42] Rebecca S. Eisenberg and Richard R. Nelson, "Public vs. Proprietary Science: A Fruitful Tension?," *Daedalus*, spring 2002.

[43] Ibid.

[44] Michael A. Heller and Rebecca S. Eisenberg, "Can Patents Deter Innovation? The Anticommons in Biomedical Research," 280 *Science*, 1998, 698-701.

[45] U.S. Congress, House Committee on the Judiciary, Subcommittee on Courts and Intellectual Property, *Hearings on Gene Patents and Other Genomic Inventions*, July 13, 2000, available at http://www.house.gov/judiciary/ seve0713.htm.

[46] John P. Walsh, Ashish Arora, Wesley M. Cohen, "Working Through the Patent Problem," *Science*, February 14, 2003, 1021.

[47] Wesley M. Cohen and John P. Walsh, *Real Impediments to Academic Biomedical Research*, NBER, May 15, 2007, 12 and forthcoming in *Innovation Policy and Economics*, Vol. 7, available at http://nber15.nber.org/books_in_progress/ innovation8/cohen-walsh6-19-07.pdf. See also John P. Walsh, Charlene Cho, and Welsely Cohen, "View from the Bench: Patents and Material Transfers," *Science*, 23 September 2005, 2002-2003.

[48] Ibid., 13.

[49] There is no official USPTO category for "software" patents; Bessen and Hunt use their own definition.

[50] James Bessen and Robert M. Hunt, *An Empirical Look at Software Patents*, Working Paper No. 03-17/R, Federal Reserve Bank of Philadelphia, March 2004, p. 3, available at http://www.phil.frb.org and Robert Hunt and James Bessen, "The Software Patent Experiment," *Q3 2004 Business Review*, 24, available at http://www.phil.frb.org.

[51] Ronald J. Mann, "Do Patents Facilitate Financing in the Software Industry?," *Texas Law Review*, March 2005, 979.

[52] *The Software Patent Experiment*, 26.

[53] *An Empirical Look at Software Patents*, 4.

[54] *The Software Patent Experiment*, 26.

[55] James Bessen and Eric Maskin, "Sequential Innovation, Patents, and Imitation," *Massachusetts Institute of Technology Working Paper, Department of Economics*, January 2000, p. 2 available at http://www.researchoninnovation.org/patent.pdf.

[56] Robert P. Merges, "The Uninvited Guest: Patents on Wall Street," *Federal Reserve Bank of Atlanta Economic Review*, 4th Quarter 2003, 9.

[57] *Do Patents Facilitate Financing in the Software Industry?*, 1002.

[58] Ibid., 1003.

[59] Ibid., 985.

[60] Ibid., 990.

[61] Ibid., 985.

[62] Ibid., 978.

[63] Bradford L. Smith and Susan O. Mann, "Innovation and Intellectual Property Protection in the Software Industry: An Emerging Role for Patents?," *University of Chicago Law Review*, winter 2004, 206.

[64] Mark H. Webbink, "A New Paradigm for Intellectual Property Rights in Software," *Duke Law and Technology Review*, 2005, 12 and 16.

[65] *The Software Patent Experiment*, 28-29.

[66] *An Empirical Look at Software Patents*, 34.

[67] *The Software Patent Experiment*, 27.

[68] Ibid., 30.

[69] David S. Evans and Anne Layne-Farrar, "Software Patents and Open Source: The Battle Over Intellectual Property Rights," *Virginia Journal of Law and Technology*, Summer 2004, 23.

[70] *Do Patents Facilitate Financing in the Software Industry?*, 1004.

[71] Ibid., 1007.

[72] *Protecting Their Intellectual Assets: Appropriability Conditions and Why U.S. Manufacturing Firms Patent (or Not)*, 8.

[73] Ben Klemens, *The Computer-Shaped Hole in the Patent Reform Act*, The Brookings Institution, July 28, 2005.

[74] Brian Kahin, "Patents and Diversity in Innovation," *Michigan Telecommunications and Technology Law Review*, April 27, 2007, 390, available at http://www.mttlr.org/volthirteen/kahin.pdf.

In: U.S. Patent System Reform ...
Editors: F. Parker and M. Lopez

ISBN: 978-1-61470-528-4
© 2011 Nova Science Publishers, Inc.

Chapter 4

DEFERRED EXAMINATION OF PATENT APPLICATIONS: IMPLICATIONS FOR INNOVATION POLICY

John R. Thomas

SUMMARY

Recent congressional interest in the patent system has in part focused upon the capabilities of the U.S. Patent and Trademark Office (USPTO). Many experts have expressed concern that the USPTO lacks the capacity to process the large number of patent applications that it receives. The USPTO's growing inventory of filed, but unexamined applications could potentially lead to longer delays in the USPTO patent-granting process.

Under current law, a USPTO examiner automatically reviews each patent application that is filed. Some observers have suggested that the USPTO instead adopt a system of "deferred examination" in order to alleviate its growing backlog. Under this system, the USPTO would not automatically review each application. Applicants would instead be required to submit a specific request for examination. Failure to file such a request within a specified time period—typically ranging from three to five years—would result in the abandonment of the application.

Deferred examination may hold potential benefits. For example, some inventors who file a patent application may subsequently decide ultimately not to expend further resources in obtaining a patent on that technology due to marketplace developments or other reasons. The USPTO then does not need to review those applications, allowing others to move through the agency more quickly. Deferred examination may be particularly suitable for enterprises that sell products, including pharmaceuticals and medical devices, that may have a long development cycle and be subject to regulatory approval. Proponents of deferred examination observe that numerous foreign patent offices have used this system for many years. They further explain that given increasingly lengthy delays, the USPTO effectively operates under a *de facto* deferral regime today.

On the other hand, some experts believe that deferred examination holds negative consequences. Deferred examination may cause many years to pass between the time an application was filed and the date a patent issues. Other firms may not know for some time whether their new products will infringe a patent that resulted from deferred examination. It is also possible that applicants could use the system strategically. They may choose to defer examination, monitor the industry, and then amend their applications in order to obtain patents that cover the successful products of their competitors. Opponents of deferred examination are also skeptical that a significant number of applications will "drop out" of the USPTO if this system were adopted. They also explain that the USPTO currently allows applicants to delay prosecution for up to three years, but that this procedure is rarely used.

Designers of a deferred examination system may potentially manipulate a number of parameters in an attempt to maximize potential benefits while minimizing perceived disadvantages. Among these parameters are the maximum length of the deferral period, the ability of third parties to request examination of a deferred application, the framing of the system as an "opt-in" or "opt-out" procedure for applicants, pre-grant publication of deferred applications, the fee structure, the impact of deferred examination upon patent term, and the availability of third party "intervening rights" for patents that issue from deferred applications. Options for implementing deferred examination include both legislation and USPTO rulemaking.

INTRODUCTION

Growing recognition of the crucial role that technological innovation plays in the U.S economy has led to increased congressional activity with

Deferred Examination of Patent Applications

respect to the intellectual property laws. As evidenced by provisions within several patent reform bills pending before the 111th Congress,[1] the operation of the U.S. Patent and Trademark Office (USPTO) is among the subjects of legislative interest. Many knowledgeable observers have expressed concern that the USPTO does not possess the capability to process the large number of patent applications that it receives.[2] The growing backlog of filed, but unexamined applications could potentially lead to long delays in the time the USPTO requires to grant patents.[3]

Some experts believe that the concept of "deferred examination" may assist in alleviating the growing USPTO inventory of applications that have yet to be reviewed.[4] Under current law, a USPTO examiner reviews each patent application that is filed.[5] In contrast, the patent offices of many foreign nations, including Canada, Germany, Japan, and the United Kingdom, do not automatically examine every application. In these offices, an examiner will not consider the application unless the applicant submits a request for examination, including an additional fee. Failure to file such a request within a specified time period—usually from three to five years—results in the abandonment of the application.[6]

Deferred examination may hold potential benefits. Some inventors who file patent applications may subsequently decide not to expend the additional resources needed to obtain patents. If, for example, an invention proves less promising than it initially appeared due to technical or marketplace developments, or government approval to market the technology cannot be obtained, a patent applicant may rationally decide not to pursue the matter further. The USPTO then does not need to review those applications, allowing others to move through the agency more quickly.[7] On the other hand, some experts believe that deferred examination holds negative consequences, such as marketplace uncertainty. Firms may not know for many years whether their new products will infringe a patent that resulted from deferred examination.[8]

This report provides an overview of deferred patent examination. It begins by offering a brief review of patent acquisition proceedings as well as challenges faced by the USPTO. The report then introduces the concept of deferred examination. The potential positive and negative consequences of deferred examination upon the environment for innovation within the United States are then explored. The report closes by identifying salient design parameters for deferred examination systems and reviewing congressional options.

FUNDAMENTALS OF PATENT ACQUISITION

The U.S. Constitution provides Congress with the power "To promote the Progress of Science and useful Arts, by securing for limited Times to ... Inventors the exclusive Right to their ... Discoveries."[9] In accordance with the Patent Act of 1952 (the "Patent Act"),[10] an inventor may seek the grant of a patent by preparing and submitting an application to the USPTO.[11] Under current law, each application is then placed into queue for eventual review by officials known as examiners.[12]

The USPTO publishes most, but not all, pending patent applications "promptly after the expiration of a period of 18 months" from the filing date.[13] Among the applications that are not published prior to grant are those that the applicant represents will not be the subject of patent protection abroad. In particular, if an applicant certifies that the invention disclosed in the U.S. application will not be the subject of a patent application in another country that requires publication of applications 18 months after filing, then the USPTO will not publish the application.

USPTO officials known as examiners then determine whether the invention disclosed in the application merits the award of a patent. The USPTO examiner will consider a number of legal requirements, including whether the submitted application fully explains and distinctly claims the invention.[14] In particular, the application must enable persons skilled in the art to make and use the invention without undue experimentation.[15] In addition, the application must provide the "best mode," or preferred way, that the applicant knows to practice the invention.[16]

The examiner will also determine whether the invention itself fulfills certain substantive standards set by the patent statute. To be patentable, an invention must meet four primary requirements. First, the invention must fall within at least one category of patentable subject matter.[17] According to the Patent Act, an invention which is a "process, machine, manufacture, or composition of matter" is eligible for patenting.[18] Second, the invention must be useful,[19] a requirement that is satisfied if the invention is operable and provides a tangible benefit.[20] Third, the invention must be novel, or different, from subject matter disclosed by an earlier patent, publication, or other state-of-the-art knowledge.[21] Finally, an invention is not patentable if "the subject matter as a whole would have been obvious at the time the invention was made to a person having ordinary skill in the art to which said subject matter pertains."[22] This requirement of "nonobviousness" prevents the issuance of patents claiming subject matter that a skilled artisan would have been able to implement in view of the knowledge of the state of the art.[23]

If the USPTO allows the patent to issue, its owner obtains the right to exclude others from making, using, selling, offering to sell, or importing into the United States the patented invention.[24] Those who engage in those acts without the permission of the patentee during the term of the patent can be held liable for infringement. Adjudicated infringers may be enjoined from further infringing acts.[25] The patent statute also provides for an award of damages "adequate to compensate for the infringement, but in no event less than a reasonable royalty for the use made of the invention by the infringer."[26]

The maximum term of patent protection is ordinarily set at 20 years from the date the application is filed.[27] At the end of that period, others may employ that invention without regard to the expired patent. Although patent term is based upon the filing date, the patentee gains no enforceable legal rights until the USPTO allows the application to issue as a granted patent. A number of Patent Act provisions may modify the basic 20-year term, including examination delays at the USPTO[28] and delays in obtaining marketing approval for the patented invention from other federal agencies.[29]

Like most rights, those provided by a patent are not self-enforcing. Patent owners who wish to compel others to respect their proprietary interests must commence enforcement proceedings, which most commonly consist of litigation in the federal courts.[30] Although issued patents enjoy a presumption of validity, accused infringers may assert that a patent is invalid or unenforceable on a number of grounds.[31] The Court of Appeals for the Federal Circuit (Federal Circuit) possesses nationwide jurisdiction over most patent appeals from the district courts.[32] The Supreme Court enjoys discretionary authority to review cases decided by the Federal Circuit.[33]

CONTEMPORARY CHALLENGES FOR THE USPTO

The growing popularity of the patent system has placed strains upon the resources of the USPTO. During 2009,[34] the USPTO received 485,500 applications—a decrease of 2.3% from the 496,886 applications it received during the 2008 fiscal year.[35] The number of applications filed in 2009 was still greater than the 468,330 filed in 2007,[36] however. In turn, this figure was substantially larger than the annual filings achieved just a few years ago. In 2000, for example, 293,244 applications were filed at the USPTO.[37]

The USPTO has candidly admitted that "the volume of patent applications continues to outpace our capacity to examine them."[38] As a consequence, the USPTO reportedly holds an inventory in excess of 1.2 million patent applications that have yet to be reviewed by an examiner.[39] In addition, a USPTO examiner in 2009 would not review a patent application until, on average, 25.8 months after it was filed.[40] The "first action pendency" during 2000 was 13.6 months.[41] Many observers believe that if current conditions continue, the backlog and delay are likely to grow at the USPTO in coming years.[42]

Long delays for patent approvals may negatively impact high technology industries by increasing uncertainty about the availability and scope of patent rights. For market segments that feature a rapid pace of innovation and short product cycles, such as consumer electronics, lengthy USPTO delays may also significantly devalue the patent right. Put simply, by the time a patent issues, the entire industry might have moved on to more advanced technologies.[43] Commerce Secretary Gary Locke reportedly described the length of time the USPTO requires to issue patents as "unacceptable," explaining that "[t]his delay causes uncertainty for inventors and entrepreneurs and impedes our economic recovery." USPTO Director David Kappos recently opined that "[e]very quality patent application that sits on the shelf represents jobs not created."[44]

In addition, under current law, USPTO delays may qualify certain patents for an extension of term.[45] For example, if the USPTO does not respond to an application within 14 months of the day it is filed, the term of a patent that results from that application is extended by one day for each day of delay. Given that the average first action pendency is now almost 26 months, this rule of "Patent Term Adjustment" may cause many U.S. patents to have a term that exceeds 20 years.[46] A patent with a longer term may be of greater value to its proprietor, but also may impact the ability of others to develop competing products.[47]

The USPTO has developed a number of initiatives in order to address its backlog of unexamined patent applications. The agency has hired many new examiners, including 1,193 in 2006; 1,215 in 2007; and 1,211 in 2008.[48] The significance of this hiring rate should be assessed in view of the fact that in 2009, the total size of the patent examining corps was 6,242.[49] The recent economic downturn has caused the USPTO to limit new hiring, however.[50] As the title of recent congressional testimony by the Government Accountability Office—"Hiring Efforts Are Not Sufficient to Reduce the Patent Application Backlog"[51]—indicates, many observers are of the view that "[d]ue to both

Deferred Examination of Patent Applications

monetary and infrastructure constraints, the USPTO cannot simply hire examiners to stem the tide of applications."[52]

In 2007, the USPTO also proposed rules with respect to claims and so-called continued applications that were designed to reduce its examination burdens. These rules would have limited the number of claims that could be filed in a particular patent application, unless the applicant supplied the USPTO with an "Examination Support Document" in furtherance of that application.[53] They would have also limited the number of continued applications that could be filed, absent a petition and showing by the patent applicant of the need for such applications.[54] These rules never came into effect due to a temporary court ruling enjoining their implementation.[55] In the face of considerable opposition to these rules by many members of the patent bar and innovative firms, the USPTO announced on October 8, 2009, that it was rescinding the rules package entirely.[56]

More recently, the USPTO announced a "Patent Application Backlog Reduction Stimulus Plan."[57] Under that program, an individual, small firm, or other enterprise that qualifies as a "small entity" may choose to abandon a previously filed application. If the applicant does so, he may select another application to be examined on an expedited basis. According to the USPTO, "[t]his procedure allows a small entity applicant who has multiple applications currently pending before the USPTO to have one of the applications accorded special status for examination if the applicant is willing to expressly abandon an application that has not been examined."[58] The Patent Application Backlog Reduction Stimulus Plan has reportedly been the subject of only limited participation.[59]

As record-setting patent filing rates continue to strain agency resources, the USPTO has actively considered new concepts for administering the patent examination system. Explaining that it "frequently receives suggestions that the USPTO adopt a deferral of examination procedure,"[60] the USPTO held a roundtable on February 12, 2009, in order to obtain input on the possibility of adopting this system. The remainder of this report reviews the concept of deferred examination.

THE CONCEPT OF DEFERRED EXAMINATION

The Patent Act currently requires the USPTO to review each patent application to determine whether it should issue into a patent or not.[61]

Inventors pay for this service upon filing their applications. The USPTO has established an optional deferral procedure through regulation.[62] In order to defer, the applicant must pay an additional $130 processing fee and, at the outset, choose the number of months of deferral.[63] The maximum period of deferral is 36 months. However, applicants have reportedly used this procedure infrequently.[64]

An alternative regime employed by certain other patent-granting nations is termed "deferred examination," or, more rarely, "examination on request."[65] Under this procedure, patent applications are not automatically placed into queue to be examined. Rather, the applicant must make an additional, affirmative request for examination, and pay an additional fee. This request must be made within a stipulated period of time—for example, three, five, or seven years—or the application is deemed to have been abandoned.[66]

Deferred examination is reportedly employed by many patent-granting nations, including each of the top 10 U.S. trading partners with the exception of Mexico.[67] Jurisdictions that have adopted deferred examination report that many applicants never request a substantive examination. Further, the number of applications that are never examined appears to increase as the period of deferral is lengthened. For example, the European Patent Office (EPO) requires that a request for examination be made within six months of the EPO's publication of the so-called European Search Report. Because the EPO typically takes about one year to publish its search report, examination must be requested within approximately 18 months. In 2008, the EPO reported that requests for examination were received with respect to 93.5% of all applications.[68]

In contrast, the Japan Patent Office (JPO) currently operates under a longer, three-year period of deferral. In 2008, the JPO reported that only 65.6% of all applications proceeded to examination.[69] Prior to 2001, when the JPO allowed an even lengthier seven-year period of deferral, the dropout rate was correspondingly greater. According to one estimate, as many as 65% of JPO applications were never examined.[70] The experience of the Canadian Intellectual Property Office (CIPO) is similar. Canadian law allows for a five-year period of deferral that reportedly results in a "dropout rate" of about 35% of filed applications.[71] Other patent offices have also reported substantial dropout rates as well.[72]

Applicants may choose not to pursue their filed applications further for a number of reasons. They may determine that marketplace, regulatory, or technical developments have made further prosecution of that application not worthwhile. Some inventors may also determine that the inventions disclosed in their filed applications do not meet the legal standards of patentability. In particular, the EPO and certain other patent offices provide all applicants with a "Search Report" that lists other patents, journal articles, and other references that document the state of the art.[73] Upon reviewing this information, some applicants may determine that it is unlikely their inventions would be considered patentable, and therefore decline to request examination. Other applicants may no longer be in business or lack funding to continue to advance their applications.[74]

The possibility of U.S. adoption of deferred examination has proven to be a controversial topic. While some patent professionals believe that the possibility of "examination upon request" would advantage both patent applicants and the USPTO, others believe that this system has too many negative aspects to be worthy of adoption. This report next considers some of the possible benefits and drawbacks of deferred examination.

INNOVATION ISSUES

Potential Benefits of Deferred Examination

Supporters of deferred examination assert that U.S. adoption would result in a reduction of workload for the USPTO.[75] Under this view, many inventors who file applications at the USPTO might subsequently choose not to pursue them further. This set of applications need not receive any review whatsoever by agency examiners. This application dropout would in turn provide more resources for the USPTO to examine undeferred applications. Although the potential application dropout rate in the United States may be difficult to predict, some observers believe that the experience of foreign patent offices suggests that the reduction of USPTO workload could potentially be significant.[76] Others note that even a small decrease in applications that require examination would nonetheless assist the USPTO.[77]

Proponents of a deferred examination system also contend that with increasing application pendency rates at the USPTO, the United States effectively operates under a *de facto* deferral regime today.[78] As a result, any potential negative consequences of deferred examination have to some extent already been realized, while the advantages of a formal "examination upon request" system have yet to be obtained.

Some firms within the life sciences industry also explain that deferred examination provides a good match for products that are subject to lengthy regulatory approval delays. For example, drugs and certain medical devices require the approval of the Food and Drug Administration (FDA) prior to being sold to the public. Innovators of those products may need to file a patent application earlier in their development cycle in order to attract venture capital. However, the final design of the product is not certain until later in the development cycle. A delay during examination may allow the applicant to more closely tailor the claims of the patent to the final design of the product.[79]

In addition, some products submitted for regulatory review do not obtain FDA approval. The FDA may determine that some drugs and medical devices are not safe and effective within the meaning of the Federal Food Drug & Cosmetic Act.[80] In such cases, as journalist Steve Seidenberg describes the matter, sponsors of rejected products "wind up with patents they can't use."[81] Deferred patent examination may also make better use of government resources with respect to products that may never receive regulatory approval.

Other advocates of deferred examination observe that this system has been used by leading patent offices for many years. As explained by Robert J. Yarbrough, chairman of the Pennsylvania Intellectual Property Forum, the "benefits and pitfalls of deferred examination should be well known."[82] Mr. Yarbrough asserts that the United States could potentially draw upon this experience in designing its own system.

Potential Drawbacks of Deferred Examination

Although some experts believe that adoption of a deferred examination would work to the advantage of the patent community, others believe that this approach might fail to realize its purported benefits and also involves additional detriments. Many observers have suggested the possibility that deferred examination might increase uncertainty in the marketplace.[83] As explained by David M. Simon, chief patent counsel of Intel Corporation

> [D]eferred examination that results in patents not issuing until perhaps ten years after filing could result in substantial claw back from the public domain when those deferred applications issue. Businesses will be surprised with patents suddenly issuing to preclude successful products.[84]

Other observers go further, suggesting that some patent applicants may attempt to manipulate the deferral system strategically. Some applicants may elect not to pursue allowance of their patents while monitoring the activities of their competitors. They might then attempt to amend their patent applications in an effort to obtain patent coverage of a competitor's product.[85] Although this possibility exists under current law,[86] deferred examination may provide another mechanism for creating so-called "submarine patents"—patents that remain submerged within the USPTO for many years, only to surface and surprise the marketplace.[87]

Skeptics of deferred examination recognize that the USPTO currently houses a significant inventory of unexamined applications and experiences long examination pendencies, trends that may lead both to marketplace uncertainty and strategic behavior by applicants. But they are concerned that adoption of deferred examination may exaggerate these unwelcome trends. Writing for the American Intellectual Property Law Association (AIPLA), Executive Director Q. Todd Dickinson asserts that "although inventories tend to rise and fall over time, the creation of a deferred examination system would institutionalize a delay option in examination and may create further uncertainty in the system."[88]

Others believe that the relatively high dropout rates associated with foreign deferred examination systems will not be realized in the United States. According to these accounts, elements that contribute to the abandonment of applications abroad may not exist to the same extent domestically. In particular, the United States is a large market that has a long tradition of enforcing patents. Under this view, a U.S. patent might be more valuable to firms than patents granted by other nations. In turn, applicants may be less willing to abandon a U.S. application than an application filed elsewhere.[89]

Seemingly supporting this argument is the fact that the current USPTO rule allowing for deferred examination is little used.[90] The USPTO reported on January 28, 2009, that since the deferral alternative commenced on November 29, 2000, fewer than 200 applications have been deferred.[91] The reason for this low usage rate may be due to a variety of factors, potentially including lack of widespread knowledge of the provision and long application pendency rates even absent an express deferral. Given the potential complexity of each individual decision to abandon an application, a precise estimate of dropout rates within a proposed U.S. deferred examination system is likely unachievable.

Other commentators have expressed concern that a deferred examination system may have a negative impact upon the revenue that the USPTO receives through the fees it charges. AIPLA Executive Director Q. Todd Dickinson observes that the potential risk to USPTO income "will largely depend on the fees established for participating in deferred examination, on the assumed drop-out rate and loss of income from other fees."[92]

On the other hand, to the extent deferred examination leads to a decrease in initial filing fees, this system could potentially increase patent filing rates. This step could cause inventors to decrease the care with which they prepare applications, however, out of the recognition that they may not request examination for all of them. As Tom DiLenge, general counsel and vice president of the Biotechnology Industry Organization (BIO) writes, "some BIO members are concerned that a deferred examination system with a low threshold for initial application filings would lead to an increase in poor-quality filings, thereby triggering more public criticism of the patent system."[93]

DEFERRED EXAMINATION DESIGN PARAMETERS

This brief discussion suggests that a deferred patent examination system potentially holds both positive and negative aspects. It also indicates a number of system parameters that the designers of a deferred examination system for the United States could potentially manipulate in an attempt to maximize its perceived advantages while minimizing its perceived disadvantages. Perhaps the most obvious of these parameters is the period of possible deferral. Leading foreign patent offices offer maximum periods of deferral ranging from approximately two years (at the European Patent Office)[94] to seven years (at the German Patent and Trademark Office),[95] with other patent offices providing intermediate periods of deferral. Experience suggests that the longer the period of maximum deferral, the greater the number of applications for which examination will never be requested. However, longer periods of deferral may also increase marketplace uncertainty about the availability and scope of patent rights.[96]

In deferral systems, the party who requests examination is usually the applicant. However, some deferral systems allow third parties to request examination as well. Upon receiving notice that a third party has exercised its "activation right," the applicant must either enter examination or abandon the application.[97] The activation right is intended to allow competitors of the patent applicant and other interested members of the public to obtain earlier

Deferred Examination of Patent Applications 103

certainty regarding the existence and extent of patent rights. Some commentators have expressed concern that liberal use of activation rights may burden patent applicants, however, and propose that the USPTO impose a fee in order to prevent abuses.[98]

Designers of a deferred examination system must also decide whether it applies to all patent applications, or instead to a more limited number based upon a particular field of technology or other factor.[99] In addition, the system could require deferral to be affirmatively elected, or alternatively apply deferral as a default. The current USPTO regulation allowing for deferral of application operates on an "opt-in" basis. As typically framed abroad, however, deferral is an "opt-out" system that obliges applicants to request examination.[100]

Whether deferred applications should be subject to different rules with respect to the pre-grant publication of applications has also been discussed. Under current law, not all applications are published "promptly after the expiration of a period of 18 months" from the filing date. Notably, if an applicant certifies that the invention disclosed in the U.S. application will not be the subject of a patent application in another country that requires publication of applications 18 months after filing, then the USPTO will not publish the application.[101]

Many commentators have suggested that all deferred applications should be published, regardless of whether the applicant will pursue foreign patents or not. Under this position, the policy goal of alerting the public about pending patent applications is of particular significance when a deferred application may not issue for many years after it is filed. As a result, the exception for domestic-only applications would be eliminated if the application is deferred.[102]

The fee structure with respect to deferred applications may also be adjusted in view of the policy goals and fiscal needs of the USPTO. As one possibility, patent attorney Robert J. Yarbrough, who generally supports a deferred examination system, writes that the deferred "applicant should pay no higher fees than any other applicant and, preferably, should be given a discount."[103] For example, the USPTO currently assesses a $220 examination fee that could be waived until the applicant requests that the USPTO perform this service.[104]

Another issue for consideration is the impact of deferred examination upon the term of a patent. Under current law, the maximum term of a patent is 20 years from the date the application was filed.[105] Because the applicant obtains no enforceable rights until the USPTO allows the patent to issue, each day the application spends at the USPTO effectively reduces the period during which the patent owner enjoys propriety rights.[106] Deferred examination implies that the effective term of patent would be reduced by the period measured from the filing date until the date the patent owner requests examination.[107]

At least one commentator has proposed that deferred examination be "term neutral."[108] Under this proposal, each day that an application is deferred would result in one day of term extension for any patent that results from that application. As an example, if a period of three years elapses between the date of filing and the date that examination is requested, then the maximum term of the patent would be 23 years from the date of filing. No current system of deferred examination is believed to provide for patent term extension in this manner.

Some observers have also proposed that patents that result from deferred applications be subject to "intervening rights."[109] Intervening rights allows a specific enterprise to engage in activities that would otherwise infringe an issued patent. The Patent Act currently allows third parties to enjoy intervening rights when a patent is amended by either reissue or reexamination,[110] or where a patent is revived after failure to pay a maintenance fee.[111] Some commentators have suggested that intervening rights should also apply to patents that issued from deferred applications, provided that an enterprise commercialized a product during the deferral period that subsequently became subject to a patent.[112]

CONCLUDING OBSERVATIONS

A variety of options are available for Congress with respect to deferred examination. If the current situation is deemed appropriate, then no action need be taken. Alternatively, Congress could introduce a statutory deferred examination regime into the U.S. patent system via legislation. A third congressional option is to allow or encourage the USPTO to enact regulations that would encourage, or perhaps mandate, deferred examination of patent applications.

Whether deferred examination may be achieved by the USPTO through rulemaking, or whether congressional intervention would be required, is not entirely certain. The Patent Act currently requires the USPTO to examine each filed application.[113] However, Congress has also granted to the USPTO the power to "establish regulations, not inconsistent with law, which ... shall govern the conduct of proceedings in the Office."[114] The USPTO apparently relied upon this procedural rulemaking authority in order to enact its current regulation regarding deferred examination.[115] Assuming that the USPTO reasoned correctly, this regulation could potentially be expanded in order to develop a more full-fledged deferred examination system. As explained by Arti Rai, administrator for external affairs at the USPTO, "an improved system of deferred examination could in all likelihood be implemented through PTO regulation, so long as the PTO's procedural-rulemaking authority is not interpreted in an unduly cramped fashion."[116]

On the other hand, uncertainty over the precise extent of USPTO procedural rulemaking authority may prevent or limit further adaption of a deferred examination system absent congressional intervention.[117] Because this proposal potentially requires many changes to existing law with respect to such matters as fees, pre-grant publication of applications, intervening rights, and patent term, a court could potentially consider expanded deferred examination regulations to be substantive in nature and therefore beyond the ability of the USPTO to promulgate.[118] A legislative rather than regulatory response may therefore provide the most appropriate mechanism for adopting a deferred examination system.

The growing value of intellectual property within the world economy has placed increased demands upon the USPTO to process accurately a quantity of patent applications that was nearly unimaginable a generation ago. The USPTO has in part responded by encouraging policy discussion regarding new procedures for managing its increasingly strained resources. The possibility of U.S. adoption of deferred examination—a patent office practice that is accepted globally but controversial domestically—has once more become part of the discussion regarding patent reform. Ultimately, whether or not a deferred patent examination system would benefit the environment for innovation in the United States remains an open question.

ACKNOWLEDGMENTS

This report was funded in part by a grant from the John D. and Catherine T. MacArthur Foundation.

End Notes

[1] *See* CRS Report R40481, *Patent Reform in the 111th Congress: Innovation Issues*, by Wendy H. Schacht and John R. Thomas.

[2] *See, e.g.,* Michael J. Meurer, "Patent Examination Priorities," 51 *William and Mary Law Review* (Nov. 2009), 675.

[3] *See* Patrick A. Doody, "How to Eliminate the Backlog at the Patent Office," 37 *American Intellectual Property Law Association Quarterly Journal* (2009), 395.

[4] *See, e.g.,* Jason D. Grier, "Chasing Its Own Tail? An Analysis of the USPTO's Efforts to Reduce the Patent Backlog," 31 *Houston Journal of International Law* (Summer 2009), 617.

[5] 35 U.S.C. § 131.

[6] *See generally* Nancy J. Linck, *et al.*, "A New Patent Examination System for the New Millennium," 35 *Houston Law Review* (1998), 305.

[7] *See* Michael Abramowicz & John F. Duffy, "Ending the Patenting Monopoly," 157 *University of Pennsylvania Law Review* (2009), 1541.

[8] *See* "Franklin Pierce Law Center's Eighth Intellectual Property System Major Issues Conference," 47 *IDEA: The Intellectual Property Law Review* (2006), 1 (comments of Herb Wamsley, Executive Director, Intellectual Property Owners Association).

[9] Article I, Section 8, Clause 8.

[10] P.L. 82-593, 66 Stat. 792 (codified at Title 35 United States Code).

[11] 35 U.S.C. § 111.

[12] 35 U.S.C. § 131.

[13] 35 U.S.C. § 122(b).

[14] 35 U.S.C. § 112.

[15] *See Martek Biosciences Corp. v. Nutrinova, Inc.*, 579 F.3d 1363 (Fed. Cir. 2009).

[16] 35 U.S.C. § 112.

[17] *See Bilski v. Kappos*, ___ U.S. ___ (2010).

[18] 35 U.S.C. § 101.

[19] *Id.*

[20] *See In re '318 Patent Infringement Litigation*, 583 F.3d 1317 (Fed. Cir. 2009).

[21] 35 U.S.C. § 102.

[22] 35 U.S.C. § 103.

[23] *See KSR Int'l Co. v. Teleflex Inc.*, 550 U.S. 398 (2007).

[24] 35 U.S.C. § 271.

[25] 35 U.S.C. § 283.

[26] 35 U.S.C. § 284.

[27] 35 U.S.C. § 154(a)(2).

[28] 35 U.S.C. § 154(b).

[29] 35 U.S.C. § 156.

[30] 35 U.S.C. § 281.

[31] 35 U.S.C. § 282.

[32] 28 U.S.C. § 1295(a)(1).

[33] 28 U.S.C. § 1254(1).

[34] References to particular years in this discussion refer to the USPTO fiscal year, which extends from October 1st to September 30th of each calendar year.

[35] *See* David Goldman, "Recession's Latest Victim: U.S. Innovation," (Dec. 11, 2009) (available at http://money.cnn.com).

[36] *See* "Patent Applications" (available at http://uspatentstatistics.com/).

[37] USPTO, A New Organization for a New Millennium: Performance and Accountability Report Fiscal Year 2000 (available at http://www.uspto.gov/about/stratplan/ar).

Deferred Examination of Patent Applications   107

[38]   USPTO, *2007–2012 Strategic Plan*, at 6 (available at http://patents.uspto.gov/web/offices/com/strat2007/ stratplan2007-2012.pdf)

[39] See John Schmid & Ben Poston, "Patent Delays Harmful to U.S. Economy, Commerce Secretary Says," *Milwaukee Journal Sentinel* (Aug. 23, 2009) (available at http://www.jsonline.com/business/54199852.html).

[40] USPTO, *Performance and Accountability Report Fiscal Year 2009* (available at http://www.uspto.gov/web/ offices/com/ annual/2009/mda_02_02.html).

[41] USPTO, *2003 Performance and Accountability Report* (available at http://www.uspto.gov/about/ stratplan/ar/2003/040201_patentperform.jsp).

[42] *See, e.g.,* Jon Dudas *et al.*, "Let the PTO Pay Its Own Way," 198 *New Jersey Law Journal* no. 12 (Dec. 21, 2009), 975; Steven Andersen, "Out of Balance," *Inside Counsel* (Nov. 1, 2009).

[43] *See* Goldman, *supra.*

[44] Intellectual Property Office (UK), *UK and US Announce Action Plan to Reduce Global Patent Backlogs* (March 10, 2010) (available at http://www.ipo.gov.uk/about/press/press-release/press-release-2010/press-release-20100310.htm).

[45] 35 U.S.C. § 154(b).

[46] *See* PatentlyO, *Patent Term Adjustment Statistics* (Jan. 13, 2010) (available at http://www.patentlyo.com/ patent/2010/01/patent-term-adjustment-statistics.html).

[47] *See generally* Scott E. Kamholz, "Patent Term Adjustment for Fun and Profit," *Intellectual Property Today* (Aug. 2006), 24.

[48] USPTO, A New Organization for a New Millennium: Performance and Accountability Report Fiscal Year 2008 (available at http://www.uspto.gov/web/offices/com/annual/2008/mda_02_02.html).

[49] USPTO, A New Organization for a New Millennium: Performance and Accountability Report Fiscal Year 2009 (available at http://www.uspto.gov/about/stratplan/ar/2009/2009annualreport.pdf).

[50] *Id.*

[51] Government Accountability Office, *U.S. Patent and Trademark Office: Hiring Efforts Are Not Sufficient to Reduce the Patent Application Backlog* (Feb. 27, 2008) (available at http://www.gao.gov/new.items/d08527t.pdf).

[52] *See* Kevin Myhre, "*Tafas v. Dudas* and *Tafas v. Doll*: The Problem of Efficient Innovation," 16 *Boston University Journal of Science and Technology Law* (2010), 157.

[53] *See* Dept. of Commerce, USPTO, Final Rule, "Change to Practice for Continued Examination Filings, Patent Applications Containing Patentably Indistinct Claims, and Examination of Claims in Patent Applications," 72 *Federal Register* (August 21, 2007), 46716.

[54] *Id.*

[55] *See* Tafas v. Doll, 559 F.3d 1345 (Fed. Cir.), *vacated*, 328 Fed. Appx. 658 (Fed. Cir. 2009).

[56] USPTO, Press Release, *USPTO Rescinds Controversial Patent Regulations Package Proposed by Previous Administration* (Oct. 8, 2009) (available at http://www.uspto.gov/news/09_21.jsp).

[57] Dept. of Commerce, USTPO, "Patent Application Backlog Reduction Stimulus Plan," 74 *Federal Register* 62285 (Nov. 27, 2009).

[58] *Id.* at 62286.

[59] See Perry E. Van Over, "A New Pilot Program: Patent Application Backlog Reduction Stimulus Plan," *Orthopreneur* (March/April 2010), 36.

[60] Dept. of Commerce, USPTO, "Request for Comments and Notice of Roundtable on Deferred Examination for Patent Applications," 74 *Federal Register* (Jan. 28, 2009), 4946 ("USPTO Roundtable Notice").

[61] 35 U.S.C. § 131.

[62] *See* Changes to Implement Eighteen-Month Publication of Patent Applications, 65 *Federal Register* (Sept. 20, 2000), 57023.

[63] *See* 37 CFR 1.103(d).

[64] USPTO Roundtable Notice, *supra.*

[65] *See, e.g.,* Letter from Tom DiLenge, General Counsel, Biotechnology Industry Organization, to the Honorable John J. Doll, Acting Director of the USPTO (May 29, 2009) (available at http://www.uspto.gov/web/offices/ pac/dapp/opla/comments/deferredcomments/bio.pdf) ("BIO Letter").

[66] *See* Sean A. Pager, "Patents on a Shoestring: Making Patent Protection Work for Developing Countries," 23 *Georgia State University Law Review* (2007), 755.

[67] *See* Letter from Alan Hammond, Chief Intellectual Property Officer, Life Technologies, to to the Honorable John J. Doll, Acting Director of the USPTO (Feb. 26, 2009) (available at http://www.uspto.gov/web/offices/pac/ dapp/opla/comments/deferredcomments/lifetechcorp.pdf).

[68] The Trilateral Offices, *Four Offices Statistical Report* (2008) (available at http://www.trilateral.net).

[69] *Id.*

[70] *See* Robert A. Clarke, "U.S. Continuity Law and its Impact on the Comparative Patenting Rates of the U.S., Japan and the European Patent Office," 85 *Journal of the Patent and Trademark Office Society* (2003), 335.

[71] *See* James Rogan, Director, USPTO, *Keynote Remarks at the ABA/Intellectual Property Law Section IPL Summer Conference* (June 27, 2002).

[72] *See* Paul F. Prestia and Brian A. Cocca, *Deferred Patent Examination: De Facto or De Jure?* (Nov. 8, 2008) (available at http://www.ratnerprestia.com/143?article=213).

[73] *See* Marco T. Connor & Lin Yasong, "How to Get Patent Protection in Europe?," 90 *Journal of the Patent and Trademark Office Society* (2008), 169.

[74] *See generally* Steve Seidenberg, "Novel Ideas: PTO Proposes a New Suite of Patent Products to Streamline Applications," *Inside Counsel* (Jan. 1, 2007), at 22.

[75] *See* Grier, *supra.*

[76] *See* David P. Irimies, "Why the USPTO Should Adopt a Deferred Patent Examination System," 20 *DePaul Journal of Art, Technology, and Intellectual Property* (March 2010).

[77] *See* Letter from Jimmy Jackson, Vice President of Public Policy & Communications, BIOCOM to Commissioner for Patents (May 29, 2009) (available at http://www.uspto.gov/web/offices/pac/dapp/opla/comments/deferredcomments/ biocom.pdf) ("BIOCOM Letter").

[78] *See* Prestia & Cocca, *supra.*

[79] Letter from Christopher L. White, Executive Vice President, AdvaMed, to the Hon. David Kappos, Director of the USPTO (Aug. 31, 2009) (available at http://www.uspto.gov/web/ offices/pac/dapp/opla/comments/deferredcomments/ advamed.pdf).

[80] Pub. L. No. 75-717, 52, Stat 1040 (1938).

[81] Seidenberg, *supra.*

[82] Letter from Robert J. Yarbrough, Chairman, Pennsylvania Intellectual Property Law Forum, to Commissioner of Patents (Feb. 25, 2009) (available at http://www.uspto.gov/web/ offices/pac/dapp/opla/comments/ deferredcomments/paipforum.pdf) ("PIPLF Letter").

[83] *See* Seidenberg, *supra.*

[84] Letter from David M. Simon, Chief Patent Counsel, Intel Corporation, to Commissioner for Patents (Feb. 24, 2009) (available at http://www.uspto.gov/web/offices/pac/dapp/opla/ comments/deferredcomments/intel.pdf).

[85] *See* BIO Letter, *supra.*

[86] *See* Michael Meehan, "Increasing Certainty and Harnessing Private Information in the U.S. Patent System: A Proposal for Reform," 2010 *Stanford Technology Law Review* (Feb. 18, 2010), 1.

[87] *See* Brian J. Love, "The Misuse of Reasonable Royalty Damages as a Patent Infringement Deterrent," 74 *Missouri Law Review* (2009), 909.

Deferred Examination of Patent Applications   109

[88] Letter from Q. Todd Dickinson, Executive Director, AIPLA, to the Honorable John Doll, Acting Director, USPTO (Feb. 26, 2009) (available at http://www.uspto.gov/web/offices/pac/dapp/opla/comments/deferredcomments/aipla.pdf) ("AIPLA Letter").

[89] AIPLA Letter, *supra*.

[90] *See* 37 C.F.R. § 1.103.

[91] USPTO Roundtable Notice, *supra*.

[92] AIPLA Letter, *supra*.

[93] BIO Letter, *supra*.

[94] *See* IP Federation, *Deferred Examination of European Patent Applications* (July 2009) (available at http://www.ipfederation.com/document_download.php?id=92).

[95] *See* Joachim Henkel & Florian Jell, *Alternative Motives to File for Patents: Profiting from Pendency and Publication* (April 2009) (available at http://www.ssrn.com).

[96] *See* AIPLA Letter, *supra*.

[97] *See* Irimies, *supra*.

[98] *See* Letter from Kathleen A. Asher, Intellectual Property Counsel, Philips Intellectual Property & Standards, to Commissioner for Patents (Feb. 25, 2009) (available at http://www.uspto.gov/web/offices/pac/dapp/opla/comments/   deferredcomments/philips.pdf).

[99] *See* AIPLA Letter, *supra*.

[100] *See* BIOCOM Letter, *supra*.

[101] 35 U.S.C. § 122(b).

[102] *See* Steven Bennett & David Kappos, "Inside Views: Deferred Examination: A Solution Whose Time Has Come," *Intellectual Property Watch* (Mar. 12, 2009) (available at http://www.ip-watch.org/weblog//2009/03/12/inside-views-deferred-examination-a-solution-whose-time-has-come/).

[103] PIPLF Letter, *supra*.

[104] 37 C.F.R. § 1.

[105] 35 U.S.C. § 154(a)(2).

[106] *See* Patricia Montalvo, "How Will the New Twenty-Year Patent Term Affect You? A Look at the TRIPS Agreement and the Adoption of a Twenty-Year Patent Term," 12 *Santa Clara Computer & High Technology Law Journal* (Feb. 1996), 139.

[107] *See* Irimies, *supra*.

[108] Letter from Duane J. Roth, CEO, CONNECT, to the Honorable John J. Doll, Acting Director of the USPTO (Feb. 26, 2009) (available at http://www.uspto.gov/web/offices/pac/dapp/opla/comments/deferredcomments/connect.pdf).

[109] Irimes, *supra*.

[110] 35 U.S.C. §§ 251, 307.

[111] 35 U.S.C. §41(c)(2).

[112] Irimes, *supra*.

[113] 35 U.S.C. § 131.

[114] 35 U.S.C. § 2(b)(2).

[115] 35 C.F.R. § 1.103(d).

[116] Arti Rai, "Growing Pains in the Administrative State: The Patent Office's Troubled Quest for Managerial Control," 157 *University of Pennsylvania Law Review* (2009), 2051, 2061 n.45

[117] *See* Tafas v. Doll, 559 F.3d 1345, 1356 (Fed. Cir.), *vacated*, 328 Fed. Appx. 658 (Fed. Cir. 2009) (acknowledging difficulties in distinguishing between substantive and procedural rulemaking by the USPTO and concluding that "we do not purport to set forth a definitive rule for distinguishing between substance and procedure in this case.... ").

[118] *See* Irimies, *supra*.

In: U.S. Patent System Reform …
Editors: F. Parker and M. Lopez

ISBN: 978-1-61470-528-4
© 2011 Nova Science Publishers, Inc.

Chapter 5

FALSE PATENT MARKING:
LITIGATION AND LEGISLATION

Brian T. Yeh

SUMMARY

A patent holder that manufactures or sells a patented product will usually mark it with the patent number or other words that provide notice to the public that the article is patented. Such marking also permits the patent holder to recover an increased amount of damages in patent infringement lawsuits. However, marking a product with an expired patent number or inapplicable patent number is a violation of the false marking statute, Section 292 of the Patent Act. Section 292 provides that anyone who *falsely* marks an *unpatented* product with either a patent number, the words "patent," "patent pending," or any other words or numbers implying that the product is protected by a current or pending patent when, in fact, it is not, *and* does so with the intent of deceiving the public, shall "be fined not more than $500 for every such offense."

Until late 2009, false marking lawsuits were relatively rare, and federal courts often assessed one $500 fine for the decision to falsely mark, without regard to the number of articles that had been mismarked by the defendant. Yet in December 2009, the U.S. Court of Appeals for the Federal Circuit issued *Forest Group, Inc. v. Bon Tool Company*, which interpreted § 292 to require a penalty of up to $500 for *every* article that is falsely marked. The

Federal Circuit explained that this calculation is mandated by the plain language of the statute. Furthermore, the Federal Circuit identified policy considerations that support its interpretation of § 292, noting that false marking deters innovation and stifles competition in the marketplace because a falsely marked article may dissuade potential competitors from entering the same market.

The Patent Act's false marking provision expressly allows qui tam civil actions—any member of the public may sue a false marking offender on behalf of the federal government, in which event the fine is shared evenly between the person bringing the suit and the United States. The *Forest Group* decision helped fuel a surge of false patent marking lawsuits nationwide, filed by so-called "whistleblower" plaintiffs who targeted defendants that sold thousands of products marked with expired patent numbers, such as plastic cups, dental floss, and mouse traps. Such product manufacturers could face considerable financial liability for false patent marking.

Two decisions by the Federal Circuit in 2010 have addressed several questions that have arisen during the false patent marking litigation. *Pequignot v. Solo Cup Co.* held that a product covered with an expired patent is "unpatented" for purposes of the false marking statute. *Solo Cup* also explained that a defendant can escape liability if, despite knowing that a marking is false, it can prove that it did not consciously desire to deceive the public. *Stauffer v. Brooks Brothers, Inc.* determined that although a qui tam plaintiff in a false marking complaint may not have suffered an injury to himself, the United States has suffered an injury from the false marking violation—and because the false marking statute operates as a statutory assignment of the United States' interests, a private plaintiff (acting as the government's assignee) has standing to enforce § 292.

The 112th Congress may consider legislation similar to that introduced (but not passed) in the 111th Congress to amend the false marking statute in an effort to curb the proliferation of false patent marking suits. H.R. 4954 would have required that the person bringing a false marking suit must have suffered a competitive injury as a result of the violation, thus eliminating § 292's qui tam provision. The bipartisan manager's amendment to the Senate version of the Patent Reform Act of 2009, S. 515, contained a similar amendment to § 292. H.R. 6352, the Patent Lawsuit Reform Act of 2010, would have made the same changes to § 292 and, in addition, would have specifically limited the damages available for the false marking offense to a single fine of not more than $500.

INTRODUCTION

Under Section 287(a) of the Patent Act, a patent holder that manufactures or sells a patented product may give notice to the public that the product is patented either by marking it with the word "patent" or the abbreviation "pat.," together with the number of the patent.[1] If the patent holder does not mark the product with such information, the patent holder cannot receive damages for any infringement that occurred before the patent holder has filed a lawsuit against an infringer; the only damages that may be recovered are for infringement occurring after the infringer has been given notice of the infringement and continued to infringe thereafter. Therefore, the Patent Act provides the patent holder with an incentive to mark its products in order to obtain a greater amount of damages in infringement actions. In addition, the public benefits from a patent holder marking its products, as marking provides "a ready means of discerning the status of intellectual property embodied in an article of manufacture or design."[2]

However, Section 292 of the Patent Act imposes civil penalties upon anyone who *falsely* marks products for the purpose of deceiving the public. The following kinds of false marking are prohibited by Section 292, including (1) unauthorized marking without the consent of the patent holder, (2) marking a product that is not covered by a patent, and (3) marking a product with the words "patent-pending" when in fact no patent application has been made.[3] The U.S. Supreme Court has recognized that federal patent policy furthers an "important public interest in permitting full and free competition in the use of ideas which are in reality a part of the public domain."[4] Yet false marking "clearly injure[s]" that public interest "because the act of false marking misleads the public into believing that a patentee controls the article in question."[5] The public is thus defrauded by false marking, and the patent system is injured as well because of the erosion of the public notice function that the act of marking provides.[6]

False patent marking is subject to a fine of "not more than $500 for every such offense." To enforce the false patent marking statute, Congress permitted a qui tam[7] action: "Any person may sue for the penalty, in which event one-half shall go to the person suing and the other to the use of the United States."[8]

Until late 2009, lawsuits claiming a violation of § 292 were fairly rare,[9] and federal courts often assessed a single $500 fine for the defendant's decision to falsely mark, without regard to the number of products that had been mismarked by the defendant.[10] However, in December 2009, the U.S.

Court of Appeals for the Federal Circuit ("Federal Circuit") ruled that § 292 requires a fine of up to $500 *per article* that has been falsely marked by the defendant. Because the appellate court's interpretation of the false marking statute has "exponentially raised the potential recoveries in false patent marking actions," the year 2010 has seen a "meteoric rise in false patent marking suits."[11] As one observer has described, "false marking plaintiffs [are] scouring store shelves for *any* mass-manufactured product with inaccurate patent markings, with hopes for a massive payday."[12]

This report will describe and analyze the Federal Circuit's 2009 decision that requires a per-article penalty for false marking, as well as two subsequent Federal Circuit decisions in 2010 that answer several questions that have arisen during the recent false patent marking litigation. It also discusses legislation that was introduced, but not passed, in the 111th Congress that would have amended § 292 in order to retroactively end qui tam false marking suits and with the intent of reducing the number of false marking suits filed in the future. The 112th Congress may consider similar legislation.

CASE LAW

In order to prevail under the most commonly used prongs of the false marking statute, the plaintiff must establish by a preponderance of the evidence two elements of the false marking claim: (1) marking an unpatented article with (2) intent to deceive the public.[13] Courts have explored the contours of both of these elements, as well as the amount of the penalty imposed for the offense.

In an opinion from a century ago, *London v. Everett H. Dunbar Corp.*, the U.S. Court of Appeals for the First Circuit held that the false marking language from the Patent Act of 1870 (that required a penalty of not less than $100 for every such offense) should be interpreted as imposing a single fine for continuous false marking of multiple articles.[14] Many district courts followed the *London* interpretation even after Congress in 1952 changed the false marking penalty from a $100 minimum fine to a $500 maximum fine.[15]

Forest Group, Inc. v. Bon Tool Company

On December 28, 2009, the Federal Circuit in *Forest Group, Inc. v. Bon Tool Company* distinguished the *London* precedent, explaining that the 1952 amendment to the false marking statute eliminated the policy considerations that had justified the *London* court's interpretation.[16] The *London* court had expressed a concern that a $100 minimum penalty applied on a per article basis would "result in the accumulation of an enormous sum of penalties, entirely out of proportion to the value of the articles."[17] However, with Congress amending the penalty in 1952 to a "not more than $500" maximum fine, district courts were given the discretion to assess a *per article* fine of any amount up to $500 for the false marking offense, the Federal Circuit asserted.[18]

The patent at issue in the *Forest Group* decision pertains to a spring-loaded parallelogram stilt commonly used in the construction industry. The patent holder, Forest Group, had sued Bon Tool for infringement of its patent; Bon Tool counterclaimed alleging false marking by Forest Group of its own stilts. However, the district court found that there was no patent infringement, and then turned to Bon Tool's counterclaims. The court held that the stilts produced by Forest Group were not covered by its own patent because they did not include a "resiliently lined yoke," as the patent claim required. However, the court found that Forest Group had knowledge that its stilts were not covered by the patent (after a district court in a related case granted summary judgment of noninfringement), yet Forest Group continued to mark its stilts with the patent number after that other case.[19] The district court in *Forest Group* fined Forest Group $500 for a single offense of false marking.

Bon Tool appealed to the Federal Circuit, arguing among other things that the district court had erred in its interpretation of the false marking statute, when it determined that the statute provided for a penalty based on each *decision* to mark rather than on a per article basis. The Federal Circuit agreed with Bon Tool:

> The plain language of the statute does not support the district court's penalty of $ 500 for a decision to mark multiple articles. Instead, the statute's plain language requires the penalty to be imposed on a per article basis. The statute prohibits false marking of "*any* unpatented *article*," and it imposes a fine for "*every* such offense." ... The statute requires a fine to be imposed for every offense of marking any unpatented article. The act of false marking is the offense punished by the statute. The phrase "for the purpose of deceiving the public" creates an additional

requirement of intent but does not change the relationship between the act of marking an article and the penalty. We conclude that the statute clearly requires that each article that is falsely marked with intent to deceive constitutes an offense under 35 U.S.C. § 292.[20]

In addition to relying on the literal words of the statute, the Federal Circuit cited policy considerations to support its interpretation of § 292. The appellate court explained that false marking deters innovation and stifles competition in the marketplace: potential competitors are dissuaded from entering the same market as the falsely marked product because they do not want to be sued for infringement, among other things. Others might invest unnecessarily in "designing around" the falsely marked product to avoid infringement, or they may incur costs to determine whether the patent numbers marked on the products are valid and enforceable. But a single $500 fine for each decision to falsely mark (or $500 per continuous act of marking that "could span years and countless articles") would, in the Federal Circuit's opinion, "render the statute completely ineffective" and fail to provide sufficient deterrence against false marking.[21]

Furthermore, the Federal Circuit observed that the fact that Congress provided qui tam actions to enforce the false marking statute lends further support to its "per article" penalty construction:

Penalizing false marking on a per decision basis would not provide sufficient financial motivation for plaintiffs—who would share in the penalty—to bring suit. It seems unlikely that any qui tam plaintiffs would incur the enormous expense of patent litigation in order to split a $500 fine with the government.[22]

However, the Federal Circuit cautioned that its ruling does not mean that a district court must fine defendants $500 per article marked; rather, the $500 fine is a maximum limit:

[T]he statute provides district courts the discretion to strike a balance between encouraging enforcement of an important public policy and imposing disproportionately large penalties for small, inexpensive items produced in large quantities. In the case of inexpensive mass-produced articles, a court has the discretion to determine that a fraction of a penny per article is a proper penalty.[23]

On remand from the Federal Circuit, the district court in *Forest Group* imposed a per article fine of $180 for each of the 38 stilts that had evidence of false marking (a total fine of $6,840).[24] The lower court observed that Forest Group had sold the falsely marked stilts at prices between $103 and $180; it determined that the highest point of the price range to be most appropriate in order to "deprive Forest of more than it received for the falsely-marked stilts, fulfilling the deterrent goal of § 292's fine provision."[25]

Pequignot v. Solo Cup Co.

With its June 10, 2010, decision in *Pequignot v. Solo Cup Co.,*[26] the Federal Circuit provided answers to several outstanding questions regarding false patenting marking. Solo is a company that manufactures disposable cups, bowls, plates, and utensils, and it holds patents regarding plastic drink cup lids. Solo marked its lids with the patent numbers using a stamping machine that contains "mold cavities" that produce the lids.[27] The molds can last 15 to 20 years. One of Solo's patents expired in 1988 and the other expired in 2003, yet Solo continued to mark the lids with these patent numbers after they had expired. When Solo became aware that it was marking its products with expired patent numbers, it requested the advice of outside intellectual property counsel. Based on the counsel's advice:

> Solo developed a policy under which, when mold cavities needed to be replaced due to wear or damage, the new molds would not include the expired patent marking. According to deposition testimony, Solo indicated to its attorneys that a wholesale replacement of the mold cavities would be costly and burdensome, and Solo's attorneys concluded that Solo's policy was permissible under § 292.[28]

In September 2007, a patent attorney, Pequignot, filed a qui tam action under § 292, alleging that Solo had falsely marked at least 21,757,893,672 of its products with the patent numbers for the purpose of deceiving the public, despite knowing that those patents had expired. He sought an award of $500 per article, which the Federal Circuit observed would amount to an award to the United States of approximately $ 5.4 trillion, or 42% of the country's total national debt.[29] The Federal Circuit affirmed the district court's decision to grant summary judgment to Solo Cup, finding that there was a lack of evidence that Solo Cup intended to deceive the public with its expired patent number markings.[30]

Solo Cup answered several questions concerning a false patent marking claim. The first is the meaning of the statutory term "unpatented article." Solo had argued that products that were previously protected by patents which have since expired are not "unpatented articles." The appellate court disagreed, holding that "an article covered by a now-expired patent is 'unpatented'" because it is just as much in the public domain as an article that had never been patented.[31] The Federal Circuit noted that "many of the same public policies apply to falsely marked products with inapplicable patent numbers and expired patent numbers."[32]

The second question concerned whether an expired patent marking and a defendant's knowledge of that marking provides conclusive proof of § 292's second element, the defendant's intent to deceive the public by falsely marking. The Federal Circuit first announced that "the combination of a false statement and knowledge that the statement was false creates a rebuttable presumption of intent to deceive the public, rather than irrebuttably proving such intent."[33] The appellate court, however, opined that "the bar for proving deceptive intent here is particularly high" and held that "mere knowledge that a marking is false is insufficient to prove intent if Solo can prove that it did not consciously desire the result that the public be deceived."[34] The appellate court explained that "a purpose of deceit, rather than simply knowledge that a statement is false, is required" by § 292.[35]

The third question concerned what kind of evidence the defendant may provide to rebut the presumption of intent to deceive the public. The appellate court approved Solo's reliance in good faith on the specific advice of counsel and that it had followed that advice. The court noted that Solo had continued to falsely mark "out of a desire to reduce costs and business disruption" that would have occurred by removing the markings immediately upon the patents' expiration dates.[36] Such actions demonstrated to the appellate court's satisfaction that Solo "acted not for the purpose of deceiving the public" in falsely marking its products.[37]

Stauffer v. Brooks Brothers, Inc.

In the second significant opinion issued by the Federal Circuit in 2010 regarding the false patent marking statute, the appellate court examined questions about standing and injury in fact under a § 292 qui tam suit. *Stauffer v. Brooks Brothers, Inc.* involved a claim brought by a patent attorney, Stauffer, against the clothing company Brooks Brothers for falsely marking men's bow ties with patents that had expired over 50 years ago (Stauffer had purchased some of these falsely marked ties). The district court judge had granted Brooks Brothers' motion to dismiss the suit because he found that Stauffer lacked standing to sue because he had not suffered an injury in fact.[38]

On August 31, 2010, the Federal Circuit reversed the district court's decision on standing.[39] The appellate court observed that although a qui tam plaintiff in a false marking complaint may not have suffered an injury to himself, the United States has suffered an injury. The court remarked that "Congress has, by enacting section 292, defined an injury in fact to the United States. In other words, a violation of that statute inherently constitutes an injury to the United States."[40] Because the false marking statute operates as a statutory assignment of the United States' interests and rights, a private plaintiff (acting as the government's assignee) has standing to enforce § 292, the Federal Circuit held.[41]

However, the Federal Circuit instructed the district court on remand "to address the merits of the case, including Brooks Brothers' motion to dismiss ... on the grounds that the complaint fails to state a plausible claim to relief because it fails to allege an 'intent to deceive' the public—a critical element of a section 292 claim—with sufficient specificity to meet the heightened pleading requirements for claims of fraud imposed by Rule 9(b)" of the Federal Rules of Civil Procedure.[42] Note that the Federal Circuit did not definitively hold that false patent marking cases must be subject to the elevated pleading standard; the appellate court only directed the district court to examine the question. If a false marking claim must meet the heightened pleading standard of fraud cases, this requirement may pose a barrier for some plaintiffs in bringing a successful false marking claim, according to some observers.[43] Several federal district courts have disagreed about whether the heightened pleading requirement of Rule 9(b) applies to false marking claims.[44]

The Federal Circuit is currently considering a petition for writ of mandamus regarding the proper pleading standard for false marking cases.[45] In an amicus curiae brief submitted to the Federal Circuit in *In re BP Lubricants USA Inc.*,[46] the U.S. Department of Justice advised the appellate court to rule that the enhanced pleading standard applies to false marking actions: "The position of the United States is that, consistent with other cases 'sounding in fraud,' False Marking cases should be subject to the pleading requirements of Rule 9(b)."[47] The Federal Circuit's decision on this mandamus petition has not been issued as of the date of this report.

LEGISLATION IN THE 111TH CONGRESS

Legislation was introduced but not passed in the 111th Congress to amend § 292 of the Patent Act in an effort to curb the proliferation of false patent marking suits. Introduced by Representative Issa on March 25, 2010, H.R. 4954 would have required that the person bringing a false marking suit suffer a "competitive injury" as a result of the violation—which would eliminate § 292's qui tam provision. The new standing requirement would have applied to future false marking suits as well as retroactively, thereby barring any qui tam lawsuit that had been filed prior to the bill's enactment. The bill would have limited entitlement to bring suit to those who have suffered direct harm (no longer "any person" as the current law allows). In addition, the bill would have changed the calculation of damages, requiring a recovery "adequate to compensate for the injury."

The bipartisan manager's amendment to the Senate version of the Patent Reform Act of 2009, S. 515, released on March 4, 2010, contained a similar amendment to § 292.[48]

H.R. 6352, the Patent Lawsuit Reform Act of 2010, would have made the same changes to § 292 as H.R. 4954, but in addition, it would have specifically limited the damages available for false marking to a single fine of not more than "$500, in the aggregate, for all offenses in connection with" falsely marked articles.[49]

End Notes

[1] 35 U.S.C. § 287(a).

[2] Bonito Boats, Inc. v. Thunder Craft Boats, Inc., 489 U.S. 141, 162 (1989).

[3] 35 U.S.C. § 292(a) ("Whoever, without the consent of the patentee, marks upon, or affixes to, or uses in advertising in connection with anything made, used, offered for sale, or sold by such person within the United States, or imported by the person into the United States, the name or any imitation of the name of the patentee, the patent number, or the words "patent," "patentee," or the like, with the intent of counterfeiting or imitating the mark of the patentee, or of deceiving the public and inducing them to believe that the thing was made, offered for sale, sold, or imported into the United States by or with the consent of the patentee; or Whoever marks upon, or affixes to, or uses in advertising in connection with any unpatented article, the word "patent" or any word or number importing that the same is patented, for the purpose of deceiving the public; or Whoever marks upon, or affixes to, or uses in advertising in connection with any article, the words "patent applied for," "patent pending," or any word importing that an application for patent has been made, when no application for patent has been made, or if made, is not pending, for the purpose of deceiving the public— Shall be fined not more than $ 500 for every such offense.")

[4] Lear, Inc. v. Adkins, 395 U.S. 653, 670 (1969).

False Patent Marking: Litigation and Legislation

[5] Clontech Labs., Inc. v. Invitrogen Corp., 406 F.3d 1347, 1356 (Fed. Cir. 2005).

[6] Elizabeth I. Winston, *The Flawed Nature of the False Marking Statute,* 77 TENN. L. REV. 111, 115 (Fall 2009).

[7] Qui tam is short for the Latin phrase *qui tam pro domino rege quam pro se ipso in hac parte sequitur,* which means "who pursues this action on our Lord the King's behalf as well as his own." Qui tam is the process whereby an individual sues or prosecutes in the name of the government and shares in the proceeds of any successful litigation or settlement. The qui tam plaintiff need not have been a victim of the misconduct giving rise to the litigation. The U.S. Supreme Court has recognized § 292 of the Patent Act as a qui tam statute. Vermont Agency of Natural Resources v. United States ex rel. Stevens, 529 U.S. 765, 769 n.1 (2000). For a comprehensive overview of qui tam, *see* CRS Report R40785, *Qui Tam: The False Claims Act and Related Federal Statutes*, by Charles Doyle.

[8] 35 U.S.C. § 287(b).

[9] *See* Winston, *supra* note 6, at 135 ("[I]n the one hundred sixty-seven years of existence of the false marking qui tam action, only eleven circuit court decisions have addressed the statute.").

[10] S. Christian Platt and Jeffrey D. Comeau, *The Rise of False Patent Marking Suits,* BNA PATENT, TRADEMARK & COPYRIGHT JOURNAL, April 30, 2010.

[11] *Id. See also* Sheri Qualters, *A Surge of Patent Whistleblower Suits,* NATIONAL LAW JOURNAL, April 5, 2010. For a listing of cases that allege false patent marking that have been filed since January 1, 2010, *see* http://www.grayonclaims.com/storage/False%20Marking%20Cases.pdf.

[12] Scott E. Scioli, *Patently Unproved: False Patent Marking Defendants Breathe Sigh of Relief,* Corporate Counsel, July 13, 2010, *at* http://www.law.com/jsp/cc/PubArticleCC.jsp?id=120246344 7109 (emphasis in original).

[13] *See Clontech Labs,* 406 F.3d at 1352.

[14] 179 F. 506 (1st Cir. 1910).

[15] *See, e.g.,* A.G. Design & Assocs., LLC v. Trainman Lantern Co., 2009 U.S. Dist. LEXIS 8320, at *9-10 (W.D. Wash. Jan. 23, 2009); Undersea Breathing Sys., Inc. v. Nitrox Techs., Inc., 985 F. Supp. 752, 782 (N.D. Ill. 1997); Sadler-Cisar, Inc. v. Commercial Sales Network, Inc., 786 F. Supp. 1287, 1296 (N.D. Ohio 1991); Joy Mfg. Co. v. CGM Valve & Gauge Co., 730 F. Supp. 1387, 1399 (S.D. Tex. 1989); Precision Dynamics Corp. v. Am. Hosp. Supply Co., 241 F. Supp. 436, 447 (S.D. Cal. 1965).

[16] 590 F.3d 1295 (Fed. Cir. 2009).

[17] *London,* 179 F. at 508.

[18] *Forest Group,* 590 F.3d at 1302.

[19] *Id.* at 1299.

[20] *Id.* at 1301 (emphasis in original).

[21] *Id.* at 1303.

[22] *Id.* at 1304.

[23] *Id.*

[24] Forest Group, Inc. v. Bon Tool Co., 2010 U.S. Dist. LEXIS 41291 (S.D. Tex. Apr. 27, 2010), at *2.

[25] *Id.* at *6-7.

[26] 608 F.3d 1356 (Fed. Cir. 2010).

[27] *Id.* at 1358.

[28] *Id.* at 1359.

[29] *Id.* at n.1.

[30] *Id.* at 1357.

[31] *Id.* at 1361.

[32] *Id.* at 1362.

[33] *Id.* at 1362-63.

[34] *Id.* at 1363.

[35] *Id.*

[36] *Id.* at 1364.

[37] *Id.*

[38] Stauffer v. Brooks Bros., 615 F. Supp. 2d 248, 255 (S.D.N.Y. 2009).

[39] Stauffer v. Brooks Bros., 2010 U.S. App. LEXIS 18144 (Fed. Cir. 2010).

[40] *Id.* at *11.

[41] *Id.* at *11-12 (citing Vermont Agency of Natural Resources v. United States ex rel. Stevens, 529 U.S. 765, 773 (2000)).

[42] *Id.* at *19 (citation and internal quotations omitted). Rule 9(b) requires that a party alleging fraud "must state with particularity the circumstances constituting fraud..." FED. R. CIV. P. 9(b).

[43] Sheri Qualters, *Despite Broad Holding On Whistleblower Standing in False Marking Cases, Pleading Hurdle is High*, NATIONAL LAW JOURNAL, Sept. 1, 2010.

[44] Jim Lennon, Texas Split on Applicability of Rule 9(b) to False Marking Pleadings, Dec. 17, 2010, *at* http://falsepatentmarking.blogspot.com/2010/12/texas-split-on-applicability-of-rule-9b.html.

[45] *See* Justin E. Gray, *United States Files Amicus Curiae Brief Arguing that Rule 9(b) Should Apply in False Marking Cases*, *at* http://www.grayonclaims.com/home/2010/12/7/united-states-files-amicus-curiae-brief-arguing-that-rule-9b.html.

[46] In re: BP Lubricants USA Inc., Misc. Docket No. 2010-960 (Fed. Cir. 2010).

[47] Response of the United States as Amicus Curiae in Support of the Petitioner, at 2, *available at* http://www.grayonclaims.com/storage/BPLubricantsDOJ.pdf.

[48] Manager's Amendment to S. 515, In the Nature of a Substitute, page 16, *available at* http://www.aipla.org/Content/ContentGroups/Legislative_Action/111th_Congress1/Senate5/S515PatentReformAmendment-March-2010.pdf.

[49] H.R. 6352, § 2(a)(1)(C).

In: U.S. Patent System Reform ...
Editors: F. Parker and M. Lopez

ISBN: 978-1-61470-528-4
© 2011 Nova Science Publishers, Inc.

Chapter 6

THE DESIGN AND IMPLEMENTATION OF PATENT REVOCATION PROCEEDINGS: INNOVATION ISSUES

John R. Thomas

SUMMARY

Congressional recognition of the role patents play in promoting innovation and economic growth has resulted in the introduction of legislation proposing changes to the patent system. Among other goals, these changes would potentially decrease the cost of resolving disputes concerning patents, increase commercial certainty regarding the validity of particular patents, address potential abuses committed by speculators, and account for the particular needs of individual inventors, universities, and small firms with respect to the patent system.

In pursuit of these goals, several bills introduced in the 111th Congress would alter the current system of "patent revocation proceedings" administered by the U.S. Patent and Trademark Office (USPTO). The term "patent revocation proceeding" commonly refers to a legal procedure through which members of the public may challenge the validity of an issued patent.

Current law provides for two types of patent revocation proceedings: an *ex parte* reexamination and *inter partes* reexamination. Any individual may cite a patent or printed publication to the USPTO and request that an *ex parte* reexamination occur. If the USPTO determines that the request raises "a substantial new question of patentability," then it will commence the *ex parte* reexamination. The USPTO will then review the patent with special dispatch. The proceeding results in either a certificate upholding the claims in original or amended form, or a certificate of cancellation rejecting all of the claims of the patent. *Inter partes* reexamination operates similarly to an *ex parte* reexamination, but allows more significant participation by the individual requesting the proceeding.

Some observers believe that both types of reexamination have not been widely used and could be improved. As a result, previous legislative proposals have called for their elimination or modification. These bills would have also created a new, more expansive "post-grant review proceeding." This proposed procedure was intended to provide a predictable, cost-effective, and timely mechanism for resolving patent validity disputes and limit repetitive claims against the patent owner.

Patent revocation proceedings involve a number of design parameters that may be adjusted in order to meet certain policy goals. Among these parameters are the time at which the proceeding may begin, the patentability issues that may be addressed, the availability of discovery, and the extent to which participants may reassert unsuccessful arguments in subsequent administrative or judicial proceedings. These parameters may be modified in order to encourage certain policy goals, including timely use and resolution of the proceedings, limiting the possibility of harassment of the patent owner, and providing predictable, effective, and transparent decisions.

Increased congressional interest in the patent system has reflected growing recognition of the role patents play in promoting innovation and economic growth. In recent years, a number of Ibills have proposed changes to the patent system designed to address perceived deficiencies. Several of these bills would have altered the current system of "patent revocation proceedings" administered by the U.S. Patent and Trademark Office (USPTO). These proposals built upon several earlier laws, including the American Inventors Protection Act of 1999,[1] that provided interested parties with a mechanism for challenging a patent outside of the federal court system.

The term "patent revocation proceeding" commonly refers to a legal procedure through which members of the public may challenge the validity of an issued patent. Patent revocation proceedings are administrative in nature and are conducted before the USPTO. Current law provides for two types of patent revocation proceedings: an *ex parte* reexamination[2] and *inter partes* reexamination.[3] The chief distinction between these two sorts of proceedings is the level of participation by the individual who requested the reexamination. Once the USPTO decides to pursue an *ex parte* reexamination, the requestor no longer participates in the proceedings.[4] In contrast, the requestor participates in an *inter partes* reexamination throughout the duration of the proceedings.

Reexamination proceedings were intended to serve several goals, including allowing firms to resolve patent disputes in a more timely and less costly manner than litigation in the federal courts,[5] harnessing the technological and legal expertise of the USPTO,[6] and improving public confidence in the patent system.[7] Some observers believe that these proceedings are underutilized due to shortcomings in their design. Among the expressed concerns over reexamination proceedings is that they are too slow, too susceptible to abuse by patent opponents, and not truly an effective substitute for litigation in the federal courts.[8]

Legislative proposals in the 111th Congress would address existing patent revocation proceedings and also establish a new, more expansive "post-grant review proceeding."[9] Proponents of reform assert that these changes would better fulfill the original purposes of reexamination, ultimately allowing more efficient resolution of patent disputes and improving patent quality. On the other hand, concerned observers note that patent revocation proceedings may hold disdavantages. In their view, these procedures may increase uncertainty about patent rights in the marketplace, be used strategically to harass patent proprietors, and strain USPTO administrative capabilities.[10] Proponents maintain that the design features of the different patent revocation proceedings endeavor to realize their potential advantages while minimizing their possible drawbacks.

This report introduces issues with respect to the design and implementation of patent revocation proceedings. It begins by providing an overview of the basic workings and policy aspirations of the patent system. The report then provides a more detailed review of *ex parte* and *inter partes* reexamination proceedings currently administered by the USPTO. Next, the report reviews changes to patent revocation proceedings that were proposed in pending legislation. The report closes by identifying a number of congressional issues and options with respect to patent revocation proceedings.

Patents and Innovation Policy

The Mechanics of the Patent System

The U.S. Constitution grants Congress the power "To promote the Progress of Science and useful Arts, by securing for limited Times to ... Inventors the exclusive Right to their ... Discoveries...."[11] The Patent Act of 1952 allows inventors to request the grant of a patent by preparing and submitting an application to the USPTO.[12] USPTO officials known as examiners then determine whether the invention disclosed in the application merits the award of a patent.[13]

In deciding whether to approve a patent application, a USPTO examiner will consider whether the submitted application fully discloses and distinctly claims the invention.[14] In particular, the application must enable persons skilled in the art to make and use the invention without undue experimentation.[15] In addition, the application must disclose the "best mode," or preferred way, that the applicant knows to practice the invention.[16]

The examiner will also determine whether the invention itself fulfills certain substantive standards set by the patent statute. To be patentable, an invention must meet four primary requirements. First, the invention must fall within at least one category of patentable subject matter. An invention that qualifies as a "process, machine, manufacture, or composition of matter" is eligible for patenting.[17] Second, the invention must be useful, a requirement that is satisfied if the invention is operable and provides a tangible benefit.[18]

Third, the invention must be new, or different, from subject matter disclosed by an earlier patent, publication, or other state-of-the-art knowledge.[19] Finally, an invention is not patentable if "the subject matter as a whole would have been obvious at the time the invention was made to a person having ordinary skill in the art to which said subject matter pertains."[20] This requirement of "nonobviousness" prevents the issuance of patents claiming subject matter that a skilled artisan would have been able to implement in view of the knowledge of the state of the art.[21]

If the USPTO allows the patent to issue, its owner obtains the right to exclude others from making, using, selling, offering to sell, or importing into the United States the patented invention.[22] Those who engage in those acts without the permission of the patentee during the term of the patent can be held liable for infringement. The maximum term of patent protection is ordinarily set at 20 years from the date the application is filed.[23] At the end of that period, others may employ that invention without regard to the expired patent.

Patent proprietors who wish to compel others to respect their rights must commence enforcement proceedings, which most commonly consist of litigation in the federal courts. Adjudicated infringers may be enjoined from further infringing acts.[24] The patent statute also provides for an award of damages "adequate to compensate for the infringement, but in no event less than a reasonable royalty for the use made of the invention by the infringer."[25]

Although issued patents are presumed to be valid, accused infringers may assert that a patent is invalid or unenforceable on a number of grounds.[26] If the court agrees that the patented invention would have been obvious in view of the state of the art, for example, then it will declare the patent invalid. Several empirical studies have attempted to track the percentage of litigated patents that the courts conclude the USPTO improvidently granted. One study conducted by John R. Allison, a member of the University of Texas business school faculty, and Mark A. Lemley, a member of the Stanford Law School faculty, concluded that courts hold 46% of patents litigated to a final judgment to be invalid.[27] Other studies have reported results broadly consistent with the Allison & Lemley research.[28]

The Court of Appeals for the Federal Circuit (Federal Circuit) possesses nationwide jurisdiction over most patent appeals from the district courts.[29] The Supreme Court enjoys discretionary authority to review cases decided by the Federal Circuit.[30]

Policy Goals

The patent system is intended to promote innovation, which in turn leads to industry advancement and economic growth. The patent system in particular attempts to address "public goods problems" that may discourage individuals from innovating. Innovation commonly results in information that may be deemed a "public good," in that it is both non-rivalrous and non-excludable. Stated differently, consumption of a public good by one individual does not limit the amount of the good available for use by others, and no one can be prevented from using that good.[31]

The lack of excludability in particular is believed to result in an environment where too little innovation would occur. Absent a patent system, "free riders" could easily duplicate and exploit the inventions of others. Further, because they incurred no cost to develop and perfect the technology involved, copyists could undersell the original inventor. Aware that they would be unable to capitalize upon their inventions, individuals might be discouraged from innovating in the first instance. The patent system corrects this market failure problem by providing innovators with an exclusive interest in their inventions for a period of time, thereby allowing them to capture their marketplace value.[32]

The patent system potentially serves other goals as well. The patent law may promote the disclosure of new products and processes, as each issued patent must include a description sufficient to enable skilled artisans to practice the patented invention.[33] At the close of the patent's 20-year term,[34] others may employ the claimed invention without regard to the expired patent. In this manner the patent system ultimately contributes to the growth of information in the public domain.

Issued patents may encourage others to "invent around" the patentee's proprietary interest. A patent proprietor may point the way to new products, markets, economies of production, and even entire industries. Others can build upon the disclosure of a patent instrument to produce their own technologies that fall outside the exclusive rights associated with the patent.[35]

The patent system also has been identified as a facilitator of markets. If inventors lack patent rights, they may have scant assets to sell or license. In addition, an inventor might otherwise be unable to police the conduct of a contracting party. Any technology or know-how that has been disclosed to a prospective licensee might be appropriated without compensation to the inventor. The availability of patent protection decreases the ability of contracting parties to engage in opportunistic behavior. By lowering such transaction costs, the patent system may make transactions concerning information goods more feasible.[36]

Through these mechanisms, the patent system may act in a more socially desirable way than its chief legal alternative, trade secret protection. Trade secrecy guards against the improper appropriation of valuable, commercially useful, and secret information. In contrast to patenting, trade secret protection does not result in the disclosure of publicly available information. That is because an enterprise must take reasonable measures to keep secret the information for which trade secret protection is sought. Taking the steps necessary to maintain secrecy, such as implementing physical security measures, also imposes costs that may ultimately be unproductive for society.[37]

The patent system has long been subject to criticism, however. Some observers have asserted that the patent system is unnecessary due to market forces that already suffice to create an optimal level of innovation. The desire to obtain a lead time advantage over competitors may itself provide sufficient inducement to invent without the need for further incentives.[38] Other commentators believe that the patent system encourages industry concentration and presents a barrier to entry in some markets.[39]

Each of these arguments for and against the patent system has some measure of intuitive appeal. However, they remain difficult to analyze on an empirical level. We lack rigorous analytical methods for studying the impact of the patent system upon the economy as a whole. As a result, current economic and policy tools do not allow us to calibrate the patent system precisely in order to produce an optimal level of investment in innovation.

An Introduction to Patent Revocation Proceedings

Once the USPTO formally issues a patent, the agency's involvement with that legal instrument ordinarily comes to a close.[40] However, the USPTO may be called upon to reconsider its initial decision to approve a patent application through several "post-grant proceedings" that apply to issued patents. Two of these proceedings, *ex parte* reexamination and *inter partes* reexamination, are revocation proceedings—that is to say, they are primarily used by individuals who wish to challenge the validity of an issued patent.

Both types of reexamination proceedings address a perceived shortcoming in the patent system. Absent such proceedings, interested individuals would be unable to challenge the validity of a patent unless they became involved in a "substantial controversy" with the patent's proprietor.[41]

This requirement that an immediate, concrete dispute between the patent owner and another individual arises because the Constitution vests the federal courts with jurisdiction only where a "case or controversy" exists.[42] A charge of patent infringement typically satisfies the "case or controversy" requirement.[43]

The "case or controversy" requirement significantly limits the ability of members of the public to challenge the USPTO's decision to grant a patent. Unless the patent proprietor becomes involved in an actual, continuing controversy with another person, that person cannot successfully request that a court determine whether the patent is valid or not. Reticent patent proprietors may therefore potentially create uncertainty in the marketplace. Manufacturers, researchers, investors, and others who question the validity of

130   John R. Thomas

a patent, but possess no forum to address their concerns, may be unable to make informed decisions regarding the subject matter of that patent.[44]

Patent revocation proceedings address this perceived gap by allowing any interested person to challenge any U.S. patent at the USPTO. Because these proceedings are administrative in nature, the constitutional "case or controversy" requirement does not apply to them.[45] As a result, the USPTO may be called upon to review the validity of an issued patent at any time during its term.

Ex Parte Reexamination

Congress introduced reexamination proceedings into the patent law in 1980.[46] The American Inventors Protection Act of 1999 renamed the traditional sort of reexamination as an "*ex parte* reexamination" and also provided for the possibility of an "*inter partes* reexamination."[47]

Under the *ex parte* reexamination regime, any individual, including the patentee, a licensee, and even the USPTO Director himself, may cite a patent or printed publication to the USPTO and request that a reexamination occur.[48] The reexamination request must be in writing and explain the relevance of the cited reference to every claim for which reexamination is requested. The request must also be accompanied by the appropriate fee, which as of January 1, 2010, was $2,520. Although the USPTO does not maintain the identity of the requester in confidence, individuals desiring anonymity may authorize a patent agent or attorney to file the request in the agent's own name.

A USPTO examiner then must determine whether the patents or printed publications cited in the request raise "a substantial new question of patentability."[49] This standard is met when there is a significant likelihood that a reasonable examiner would consider the reference important in deciding whether the claim is patentable. If the USPTO determines that the cited reference does not raise "a substantial new question of patentability," then it will refund a large portion of the requestor's fee. The USPTO's denial of a reexamination request may not be appealed.[50]

On the other hand, if the USPTO determines that the cited reference does present a substantial new patentability question, then it will issue an order for reexamination.[51] The patentee is then afforded the opportunity to file a preliminary statement for consideration in the reexamination. If the patentee does so, then the requestor may then file a reply to the patentee's statements.[52]

As a practical matter, because most patentees do not wish to encourage further participation by the requestor, few preliminary statements are filed.[53]

Following this preliminary period, the USPTO will essentially reinitiate examination of the patent. Prosecution then continues following the usual rules for examination of applications.[54] However, several special rules apply to reexaminations. First, the USPTO conducts reexaminations with special dispatch.[55] Examiners must give priority to patents under reexamination, and will set aside their work on other patent applications in favor of the reexamination proceeding. To further ensure their timely resolution, patentees may not file a continuation application in connection with a reexamination.[56] Second, the patent owner may not update the patent with additional information not originally found within the patent during reexamination.[57]

If the reexamined claims are upheld in original or amended form, the USPTO will issue a reexamination certificate. Once this certificate has issued, the reexamined patent once more enjoys the statutory presumption of validity.[58] If the USPTO finds the claims to be unpatentable over the cited reference, then it will issue a certificate of cancellation.[59] Patentees adversely affected by a reexamination may appeal the USPTO's decisions to the Federal Circuit.[60]

Frequently, a defendant accused of infringement before a court files a reexamination request at the USPTO. If the USPTO accepts the request, the USPTO and a court will find themselves in the awkward situation of simultaneously considering the validity of the same patent. In *Ethicon, Inc. v. Quigg*,[61] the Federal Circuit concluded that because the Patent Act required reexaminations to be conducted with "special dispatch," the USPTO may not stay reexamination proceedings due to ongoing litigation. Whether a court will stay litigation in favor of the reexamination lies within the discretion of the judge. Such factors as the technical complexity of the invention, the overall workload of the court, and whether the reexamination request was filed early or late in the litigation typically influence this determination.[62]

Congress recognized that third parties may have made commercial decisions based upon the precise wording of the claims of an issued patent. If that patent is reexamined and survives with different claims, this reliance interest could be frustrated. In order to protect individuals who may have relied upon the scope of the claims of the original patent, the Patent Act allows for so-called intervening rights.[63] Intervening rights allow third parties to sell off existing inventory free of the patent right. In addition, courts may allow continued practice of an invention claimed in a reexamined patent to the extent

132 John R. Thomas

they deem equitable "for the protection of investments made or business commenced" before the grant of the reexamination certificate.[64]

Inter Partes Reexamination

As the title "*ex parte* reexamination" suggests, the role of the reexamination requestor is very limited in these proceedings. Only the patentee may participate in the dialogue with the examiner, and only the patentee may appeal the matter to the courts if the USPTO reaches an unsatisfactory conclusion. Some potential patent challengers did not believe the limited role provided for them offered a viable alternative to validity challenges in court.[65] As a result, some observers believed that the ability of *ex parte* reexamination to provide an expert forum as a faster, less expensive alternative to litigation of patent validity was compromised. In particular, far fewer *ex parte* reexaminations were requested than some observers had originally anticipated.[66]

The Optional Inter Partes Reexamination Procedure Act of 1999 responded to these concerns by providing patent challengers with an additional option.[67] They may employ the traditional reexamination system, which was renamed an *ex parte* reexamination. Or, they may opt for a considerable degree of participation in a new procedure known as *inter partes* reexamination.[68] Under this legislation, third party requesters may choose to submit written comments to accompany patentee responses to the USPTO.[69] The requester also may appeal USPTO determinations that a reexamined patent is not invalid to the courts.[70] The filing fee for *inter partes* reexaminations is $8,800 as of January 1, 2010.

Congress was concerned that competitors of the patent proprietor might attempt to litigate a patent validity issue in the courts following an unsuccessful *inter partes* reexamination at the USPTO, or the reverse, requesting *inter partes* reexamination based upon the same validity issue they had unsuccessfully raised in court.[71] The potential need for repetitive defensive efforts was deemed to be abusive to patent proprietors. As a result, the *inter partes* reexamination statute provides that third party participants may not raise issues that they raised or could have raised during the *inter partes* reexamination during subsequent litigation.[72] Similarly, an individual who loses a validity challenge in federal court may not later initiate an *inter partes* reexamination proceeding on any grounds it raised or could have raised in federal court.[73] These provisions are termed "estoppel" provisions because

The Current State of Post-Grant Review

The USPTO regularly releases to the public current data concerning both sorts of reexamination proceedings. This data supplies considerable information concerning the practical workings of these proceedings. With respect to *ex parte* reexamination, a total of 10,066 requests had been filed from the July 1, 1981, conception date of these proceedings through June 30, 2009. Approximately 36% of these requests were filed by the patent owner,[74] 2% by the USPTO Director, with the remaining 62% filed by third parties. The USPTO granted 9,675, or approximately 92%, of these requests. *Ex parte* reexamination proceedings had an average pendency of 25.1 months and a median pendency of 19.5 months. *Ex parte* reexamination proceedings resulted in a certificate cancelling all the claims 11% of the time, a certificate confirming all the claims 25% of the time, and a certificate amending at least one claim 64% of the time.[75]

A total of 671 *inter partes* reexamination requests had been filed from the November 29, 1999, conception date of the proceedings through June 30, 2009.[76] The USPTO granted 583, or approximately 95%, of these requests. *Inter partes* reexamination proceedings had an average pendency of 36.1 months and a median pendency of 33.0 months. *Inter partes* reexamination proceedings resulted in a certificate cancelling all the claims 60% of the time, a certificate confirming all the claims 5% of the time, and a certificate amending at least one claim 35% of the time.[77]

In combination with commentary from members of the patent community, this data supports a number of observations. First, the number of both types of reexamination requests is fewer than some observers had anticipated.[78] Although some commentators expected that thousands of reexamination requests would be filed each year, the actual number has been considerably less.[79] Both forms of reexamination appear to be growing in popularity in recent years, however.[80] In 2007, for example, 643 *ex parte* reexamination requests were filed, as compared to 375 in 1997 and 240 in 1987. The small but growing number of *inter partes* reexamination requests may in part be explained because this proceeding is only available to challenge patents that issued from applications filed after November 29, 1999.[81] As a result, no *inter partes* reexamination requests were filed at all in 1999, and only one such request was made in 2001. In 2007, 126 *inter partes* requests were filed, and 128 requests were filed between January 1, 2008, and June 30, 2008.[82]

Second, *ex parte* reexamination requests result in the cancellation of all of a patent's claims only 11% of the time. This data supports the view of some observers that *ex parte* reexamination requests favor the patent proprietor in practice.[83] One explanation for this perceived tendency is that *ex parte* reexamination proceedings are seen as restrictive in nature, with limited grounds for challenging a patent and minimal participation by the patent challenger.[84] On the other hand, 64% of reexamination certificates result in amendments to the claims of the challenged patents. These amendments may narrow the scope of patent protection in such a way to allow competitors more readily to design around the patent, thereby providing a satisfactory result to the reexamination requestor. Indeed, another way to perceive these statistics is that 75% of the time, the USPTO finds the patent subject to *ex parte* reexamination at least partially invalid.[85] These critiques also do not apply to *inter partes* reexamination proceedings, where all the claims of the patent are cancelled 60% of the time.

Third, both sorts of reexamination requests take over two years on average to complete. The length of this proceeding is explained in part by the demands of the workload of the USPTO and complexity of some of the technologies involved. Some commentators believe that these proceedings take too much time to complete. During the pendency of the reexamination, litigation or licensing of the patent may prove difficult due to the pending USPTO decision.[86]

Other concerns have arisen with respect to reexamination. The estoppel provisions associated with *inter partes* reexaminations are among those that have attracted criticism.[87] The *inter partes* reexamination statute provides that third party participants may not raise during subsequent litigation issues that they raised or could have raised during the *inter partes* reexamination.[88] Similarly, an individual who loses a validity challenge in federal court may not later provoke an *inter partes* reexamination proceeding on any grounds it raised or could have raised in federal court.[89] Some experts believe that these provisions weigh too heavily against patent challengers and therefore discourage use of *inter partes* reexaminations.[90] However, other commentators observe that an infringer who fails to convince a court that the asserted patent is invalid stands in the same position as the party that loses in an *inter partes* reexamination—in either setting, the law provides a single opportunity to argue that the patent was invalid.[91] Further, Congress intended that these provisions would limit possibilities for harassing patent owners through repetitive litigation and reexaminations proceedings.[92]

Other observers have criticized a tactic sometimes employed once a court concludes that an individual infringes a patent. The adjudicated infringer may employ reexamination proceedings in an effort to convince the USPTO to invalidate a patent that a court had previously upheld. Some observers believe that it is inappropriate for the USPTO to strike down a patent that a court had recently confirmed.[93] These tactics may also raise concerns over separation of powers between the executive and judicial branches.[94] On the other hand, differences between judicial and USPTO proceedings may contribute to divergent outcomes between these fora. For example, although patents enjoy a presumption of validity in the courts,[95] they are not entitled to this presumption during reexamination proceedings.[96]

In sum, divergent views exist with respect to *ex parte* and *inter partes* reexamination proceedings. Although individual commentators vary in their assessments of the effectiveness and fairness of these patent revocation proceedings, persistent discussion has occurred within the patent community concerning their potential modification. In addition, many observers have proposed the creation of additional mechanisms for allowing members of the public to challenge the USPTO's patentability determination without subjecting patent proprietors to harassment.[97] As this report next discusses, some features of these proposals have become the subject of congressional legislative proposals.

PROPOSALS FOR REFORM IN THE 111TH CONGRESS

Legislative interest in improving upon current patent revocation proceedings in part motivated the introduction of three bills in the 111th Congress. These bills were H.R. 1260 (introduced by Congressman Conyers on March 3, 2009), S. 515 (introduced by Senator Leahy on March 3, 2009, and reported by Senator Leahy with amendments on April 2, 2009), and S. 610 (introduced by Senator Kyl on March 17, 2009). Each of these bills was styled as the "Patent Reform Act of 2009."

With respect to existing patent revocation proceedings, S. 610 would entirely eliminate *inter partes* reeexamination. In contrast, H.R. 1260 and S. 515 would retain these proceedings. Each of the three bills would retain *ex parte* reexamination proceedings.

136 — John R. Thomas

Each of the bills would also introduce a new administrative procedure termed a "post-grant review proceeding" or "post-grant review procedures." The post-grant proceeding proposed by the three bills shares certain common features. First, the maximum length of the proceeding was set to one year, with an extension by six months possible for good cause shown. Second, each post-grant proceeding would be administered by a newly established "Patent Trial and Appeal Board." Third, any participant dissatisfied with the outcome would be able to bring an appeal to the Federal Circuit. Finally, with the exception of confidential material that has been sealed by the USPTO, the file of this procedure would be made available to the public. The following table identifies selected features with respect to each of these bills.

As this table demonstrates, patent revocation proceedings involve a number of parameters. The particular choices made in selecting these parameters may reflect the following policy goals:

Timely Challenges

Many observers believe that interested members of the public should be encouraged to bring patent challenges as soon as possible after the patent issues.[98] Balanced against this goal was the desire to provide members of the public access to USPTO review throughout the term of the patent.[99] The three bills endeavor to balance these goals by setting varying time limits for commencing a post-grant proceeding. S. 610 also appears to encourage timely challenges by augmenting the presumption of validity and limiting the scope of the challenge for proceedings not brought within nine months of the date the patent issues.

Timely USPTO Decision-Making

The three bills each would require the USPTO to complete the post-grant proceeding within one year, with the possibility of a single extension of up to six months. In addition, the bills would provide the USPTO with the ability to merge different proceedings that involve the same or similar issues. These features may increase the possibility that the USPTO will expeditiously administer post-grant proceedings.[100] However, these time limits may be difficult for the USPTO to meet and may require the USPTO to devote considerable resources to post-grant proceedings.

Table 1. Selected Features of Proposed Patent Revocation Proceedings.

Selected Issues	H.R. 1260	S. 515	S. 610
Individuals who may request the USPTO to conduct the post-grant proceeding.	A "person who is not the patent owner."	A "person who is not the patent owner."	A "person who has a substantial economic interest adverse to the patent."
The time period during which an individual may request that the USPTO conduct the post-grant proceeding.	12 months after the patent issues; or any time if the patent owner consents in writing.	12 months after the patent issues; or any time if the patent owner consents in writing.	9 months after the patent issues (termed a "first-period proceeding") or any time, so long as a first-period proceeding is not pending (termed a "second-period proceeding").
The range of patent validity issues that the USPTO may consider during the post-grant proceeding.	Any relevant validity issue except for best mode.	Any relevant validity issue except for best mode.	In a first-period proceeding, any relevant validity issue. In a second-period proceeding, validity issues are limited to novelty and nonobviousness based upon patents and printed publications.
The required showing in order for the USPTO to grant a request to conduct a post-grant proceeding.	The petition must establish a substantial question of patentability for at least one claim in the patent.	The petition must establish a substantial question of patentability for at least one claim in the patent.	The petition must present information that, if not rebutted, would provide a sufficient basis to conclude that at least one claim is invalid.
The ability of the patent owner to amend the patent's claims during the post-grant proceeding.	One amendment may be filed as a matter of right, with additional amendments permitted only for good cause shown. The scope of the claims may not be enlarged.	One amendment may be filed as a matter of right, with additional amendments permitted only for good cause shown. The scope of the claims may not be enlarged.	One amendment may be filed as a matter of right, with additional amendments per-mitted only for good cause shown or upon the joint request of the parties in order materially to advance settlement. The scope of the claims may not be enlarged.

Table 1. (Continued)

Selected Issues	H.R. 1260	S. 515	S. 610
The presumption of validity enjoyed by the patent subject to the post-grant proceeding.	The patent is not presumed to be valid. The petitioner shall have the burden of proving invalidity by a preponderance of the evidence.	The patent is not presumed to be valid. The petitioner shall have the burden of proving invalidity by a preponderance of the evidence.	The patent is presumed to be valid. The petitioner shall have the burden of proving invalidity by a preponderance of the evidence in a first-period proceeding and by clear and convincing evidence in a second-period proceeding.
The ability of the individual requesting the post-grant proceeding to raise validity issues with respect to that patent in later proceedings.	The requestor is prevented from raising validity issues in later proceedings based on an issue raised in the post-grant proceeding.	The requestor is prevented from raising validity issues in later proceedings based on an issue raised in the post-grant proceeding.	The requestor is prevented from raising validity issues in later proceedings based on an issue raised or that could have been raised in the post-grant proceeding.
The availability of discovery in the post-grant proceeding.	Discovery is available to the participants in the post-grant proceeding.	Discovery is available to the participants in the post-grant proceeding.	Discovery is available to the participants in the post-grant proceeding. In a second-period proceeding, such discovery is limited to depositions of witnesses who submit affidavits or otherwise necessary in the interest of justice.
The relationship of the post-grant proceeding to other proceedings before the USPTO.	An individual may not file more than one petition with respect to the same patent. The Director may determine the manner in which other proceedings are stayed, transferred, consolidated, or terminated.	An individual may not file more than one petition with respect to the same patent. The Director may determine the manner in which other proce-edings are stayed, transferred, consolidated, or terminated.	Multiple first-period proceedings will be consolidated. In a second-period proceeding ordered by the Director, the Director may join other petitioners to that proceeding in his discretion. The Director may determine the manner in which other proceedings are stayed, transferred, consolidated, or terminated.

Selected Issues	H.R. 1260	S. 515	S. 610
The relationship of the post-grant proceeding to litigation in the courts.	The Director may stay a post-grant review proceeding if a pending civil action for infringement addresses the same or substantially the same questions of patentability.	The Director may stay a post-grant review proceeding if a pending civil action for infringement addresses the same or substantially the same questions of patentability.	The Director may stay a first-period proceeding until after infringement litigation is complete if the infringement action were filed within 3 months after grant of a patent, the patent owner requests a stay, the litigation and post-grant proceeding concern the same or substantially the same issues of patentability, and such a stay would not be contrary to the interests of justice. A post-grant review proceeding may not be maintained if the petitioner has filed a civil action challenging the patent's validity. A second-period proceeding may not be instituted if the petition is filed more than 3 months after the petitioner must respond to a charge of patent infringement in the courts.

Predictable Decisions

Each of the three bills would create a Patent Trial and Appeal Board with exclusive responsibility for administering the post-grant proceeding. Such concentrated authority may potentially increase the uniformity of decisions reached by the USPTO in post-grant proceedings.[101]

Effective Decisions

In comparison with existing reexamination proceedings, the proposed post-grant proceedings would provide for a broader range of patentability issues that the USPTO must consider.[102] Unlike reexaminations, the post-grant proceedings also would allow the participants to engage in discovery. Discovery potentially allows one party to the proceeding to obtain information about the case from the other party in order to assist in trial preparation. These substantive and procedural rules potentially allow the USPTO to resolve a broad range of patentability issues in a lower-cost, more expedient procedure than federal litigation. The breadth of potential patentability issues may make post-grant proceedings more difficult for the USPTO to resolve, however.

Transparent Decisions

Each of the bills calls for the record of the proceedings to be made available to the public.

Minimizing Repetitive Charges against the Patent Owner

The bills also incorporate features that may decrease the possibility that post-grant proceedings may be used against a patent owner in an arguably abusive manner.[103] Among them is the requirement that the USPTO must assess whether the petitioner has raised legitimate patentability arguments prior to commencing the post-grant proceeding. The patent owner is also afforded at least one opportunity to amend the claims in view of prior art references that are cited by the petitioner. Finally, each of the bills would bar an unsuccessful petitioner in a post-grant proceeding from raising the same issues in other proceedings. Although these provisions were intended to shield the patent owner from repetitive arguments, they may also make the proceedings less attractive to potential challengers.

PATENT REVOCATION PROCEEDINGS AND INNOVATION POLICY

Patents derive their value from the rights they confer to exploit proprietary technologies. The increased focus on intellectual property in our information-based, knowledge-driven economy has arguably caused industry to raise its expectations with respect to the quality, timeliness, and efficiency of the granting of patents.[104] As the USPTO currently employs approximately 6,000 patent examiners with varying degrees of experience, legal training, and technical education,[105] maintaining consistency in patent grant determinations presents a challenging task for USPTO management.[106]

By recruiting members of the public to act as "private patent examiners,"[107] post-grant proceedings allow the USPTO to confirm its earlier determinations regarding that subset of patents that prove to be of marketplace significance.[108] In this respect, it should be appreciated that the validity of only a small subset of issued patents is ever called into question.[109] For example, one commentator estimated that only about five percent of issued patents are litigated or licensed.[110] Post-grant proceedings may therefore direct the attention of the USPTO to those patents that industry believes to be of particular significance and arguable validity.

In addition, an administrative process for reassessing patentability determinations in a reliable, cost-effective, and timely manner could potentially allow members of the public to make commercial decisions with more certainty over the impact of patent rights.[111] By reducing costs to patent owners, it could also channel resources that innovative firms currently spend on defending their patent rights in the courts into further research and development.[112]

The designers of a patent revocation proceeding may need to take into account a number of potentially conflicting policy goals. A sufficiently robust, efficient, and predictable proceeding may attract individuals with a valid adverse interest to a patent. In this respect, it should be recognized that patent validity adjudications potentially benefit the public even though they take place between the patent owner and the petitioner. Because such determinations may either confirm that the award of a patent was appropriate, or dedicate the previously patented subject matter to the public domain, members of the public may benefit when the validity of a patent is upheld or denied.[113]

On the other hand, baseless or repetitive challenges potentially reduce the value of intellectual property ownership. They may ultimately reduce the value of the innovation that results from the grant of the patent as well.[114] Unmeritorious challenges may also strain USPTO capabilities and divert administrative resources from more worthwhile tasks.[115]

In view of these and other innovation policy concerns, Congress possesses a range of options with respect to patent revocation proceedings. If the current *ex parte* and *inter partes* reexamination proceedings are deemed satisfactory, then no action need be taken. If reform is believed to be desirable, making limited changes to the existing reexamination proceedings presents another option. Legislation might, for example, alter the estoppel provisions associated with *inter partes* reexamination, expand the range of substantive patent law issues that could form the basis for the patent challenge, or provide for some form of discovery in these proceedings.

A third option, taken in part by H.R. 1260, S. 515, and S. 610, is to establish a new revocation proceeding more robust than the two types of reexamination available under current law. Such a proceeding is adversarial in nature and may include discovery, estoppel effects, a broad range of patentability issues subject to review, and other features found in litigation in the federal courts. This sort of proceeding may potentially form a more desired substitute for litigation in the federal courts. However, as more litigation features are incorporated into patent revocation proceedings, they potentially grow more costly for the participants and more difficult for the USPTO to administer.[116]

As discussed earlier in this report, patent revocation proceedings are defined through a number of parameters. In the event that reform is considered desirable, these features may be adjusted in view of particular policy goals. For example, to avoid prolonged uncertainty over a patent's validity, H.R. 1260, S. 515, and S. 610 each establish a one-year time period, potentially extendable to 18 months, for the USPTO to complete the proceeding. Other legislative strategies for achieving this goal exist. Legislation might set no fixed time limit upon the proceeding, for example, but rather provide for extension of the term of any patent involved in a revocation proceeding that exceed a certain time limit on a day-per-day basis.

The Design and Implementation of Patent ... 143

Arguably one of the more controversial features of the various patent revocation proceeding proposals is the determination of when such a proceeding could be brought. Some observers believe that revocation proceedings should be conducted as soon as possible during a patent's term. They observe that patent owners commonly expend greater resources in developing and marketing an invention as the term of a patent progresses. Earlier resolution of validity challenges may decrease uncertainty and allow for better investment decisions.

Prompt determinations may also benefit the public by increasing clarity over the precise scope of the patent right. Uncertainty over patent title may adversely affect the ability of start-up firms, as well as other enterprises that rely significantly upon their intellectual property rights, to obtain funding from investors.[117] These observers support a brief time limit on bringing a revocation proceeding.[118]

On the other hand, some commentators believe that the value of many patents is not realized until later in their terms. In particular, the developers of new pharmaceuticals, medical devices, and other regulated products often do not receive government permission to market these products until several years after they have procured a patent.[119] Because many products fail to achieve government marketing approval,[120] discerning which patents will be of marketplace significance in the future may be a difficult inquiry. Significant temporal restrictions may in effect remove certain patents on regulated products from post-grant proceedings altogether.

These observers further note that post-grant proceedings at the USPTO have traditionally been available at any time during the term of the patent. In addition, the validity of a patent may be challenged any time the patent is asserted during litigation. These commentators do not favor any sort of time limit on bringing a patent revocation proceeding.[121] By establishing different time frames for initiating a patent revocation proceeding, the three bills in the 111th Congress balance these competing views in distinct ways.

Patent revocation proceedings were among the notable intellectual property issues discussed in recent hearings before Congress. Much of this discussion focused upon the experience of innovative industry with existing reexamination proceedings. Legislation proposing more expansive patent revocation proceedings may be viewed as attempting to achieve the goals of the earlier reexamination statutes: The creation of a predictable, cost-effective, and timely mechanism for resolving patent validity disputes while limiting harassment of the patent owner.

144 John R. Thomas

ACKNOWLEDGMENTS

This report was funded in part by a grant from the John D. and Catherine T. MacArthur Foundation..

End Notes

[1] Intellectual Property and Communications Omnibus Reform Act of 1999, Title IV (American Inventors Protection Act of 1999), P.L. 106-113, 113 Stat. 1501 (1999).

[2] The term "ex parte" means "done or made at the instance and for the benefit of one party only." *Black's Law Dictionary* (8th ed. 2004). The provisions governing *ex parte* reexamination proceedings are codified at 35 U.S.C. §§ 302-307 (2006).

[3] The term "inter partes" means "between two or more parties." *Black's Law Dictionary* (8th ed. 2004). The provisions governing *inter partes* reexamination proceedings are codified at 35 U.S.C. §§ 311-318 (2006).

[4] One exception exists to this general rule. In an *ex parte* reexamination, the requestor may possess one opportunity to participate in the proceeding once the USPTO has granted the request. Once a reexamination is declared, the patent owner may optionally file a preliminary statement. If the patent owner does so, then the requestor may then file a reply to the patentee's statements. 35 U.S.C. § 304 (2006).

[5] *See* Amy J. Tindell, "Final Adjudication of Patent Validity in USPTO Reexamination and Article III Courts: Whose Job Is It Anyway?", 89 *Journal of the Patent and Trademark Office Society* (2007), 787.

[6] *See* William Barrow, "Creating a Viable Alternative: Reforming Patent Reexamination Procedure for the Small Business and Small Inventor," 59 *Administrative Law Review* (2007), 629.

[7] *See* Mark D. Janis, "*Inter Partes* Patent Reexamination," 10 *Fordham Intellectual Property, Media & Entertainment Law Journal* (2000), 481.

[8] *Id.*

[9] *See* H.R. 1260; S. 515; S. 610 (each styled the "Patent Reform Act of 2009").

[10] *See* Mark D. Janis, "Rethinking Reexamination: Toward a Viable Administrative Revocation System for U.S. Patent Law," 11 *Harvard Journal of Law and Technology* (1997), 1.

[11] U.S. Constitution, Article I, Section 8, Clause 8.

[12] P.L. 82-593, 66 Stat. 792 (codified at Title 35 of the United States Code).

[13] 35 U.S.C. § 131 (2006).

[14] 35 U.S.C. § 112 (2006).

[15] *See* Invitrogen Corp. v. Clontech Labs., Inc., 429 F.3d 1052, 1070-71 (Fed. Cir. 2005).

[16] *See* High Concrete Structures, Inc. v. New Enterprise Stone and Lime Co., 377 F.3d 1379, 1382 (Fed. Cir. 2004).

[17] 35 U.S.C. § 101 (2006).

[18] *Id. See* In re Fischer, 421 F.3d 1365, 1371 (Fed. Cir. 2005).

[19] 35 U.S.C. § 102 (2006).

[20] 35 U.S.C. § 103(a) (2006).

[21] *See* KSR International Co. v. Teleflex Inc., 550 U.S. 398 (2007).

[22] 35 U.S.C. § 271(a) (2006).

[23] 35 U.S.C. § 154(a)(2) (2006). Although the patent term is based upon the filing date, the patentee obtains no enforceable legal rights until the USPTO allows the application to issue as a granted patent. A number of Patent Act provisions may modify the basic 20-year term

The Design and Implementation of Patent ... 145

for certain reasons, including examination delays at the USPTO and delays in obtaining marketing approval for the patented invention from other federal agencies.

[24] 35 U.S.C. § 283 (2006). *See* eBay Inc. v. MercExchange L.L.C., 547 U.S. 388 (2006).

[25] 35 U.S.C. § 284 (2006).

[26] 35 U.S.C. § 282 (2006).

[27] John R. Allison & Mark A. Lemley, "Empirical Evidence on the Validity of Litigated Patents," 26 *American Intellectual Property Law Association Quarterly Journal* (1998), 185.

[28] *See* Rebecca S. Eisenberg, "Pharma's Nonobvious Problem," 12 *Lewis & Clark Law Review* (2008), 375 (discussing several empirical studies pertaining to patent invalidity rates).

[29] 28 U.S.C. § 1295(a)(1) (2006).

[30] 28 U.S.C. § 1254(1) (2006).

[31] *See* Dotan Oliar, "Making Sense of the Intellectual Property Clause: Promotion of Progress as a Limitation on Congress's Intellectual Property Power," 94 *Georgetown Law Journal* (2006), 1771.

[32] *See* Dan L. Burk & Mark A. Lemley, "Is Patent Law Technology-Specific?," 17 *Berkeley Technology Law Journal* (2002), 1155.

[33] 35 U.S.C. § 112 (2006).

[34] 35 U.S.C. § 154 (2006).

[35] *See* Rebecca Eisenberg, "Patents and the Progress of Science: Exclusive Rights and Experimental Use," 56 *University of Chicago Law Review* (1989), 1017.

[36] Robert P . Merges, "Intellectual Property and the Costs of Commercial Exchange: A Review Essay," 93 *Michigan Law Review* (1995), 1570.

[37] David D. Friedman *et al.*, "Some Economics of Trade Secret Law," 5 *Journal of Economic Perspectives* (1991), 61.

[38] *See* Frederic M. Sherer, *Industrial Market Structure and Economic Performance* (1970), 384-87.

[39] *See* John R. Thomas, "Collusion and Collective Action in the Patent System: A Proposal for Patent Bounties," *University of Illinois Law Review* (2001), 305.

[40] The USPTO does accept maintenance fees, which are due 3½, 7½, and 11½ years after the grant of the patent. The patent will expire if the maintenance fee is not paid. *See* 35 U.S.C. § 41(b) (2006).

[41] *See* MedImmune, Inc. v. Genentech, Inc., 549 U.S. 118 (2007).

[42] U.S. Const., Art. III, sec. 2, cl. 1.

[43] *See* Prasco, LLC v. Medicis Pharm. Corp., 537 F.3d 1329 (Fed. Cir. 2008).

[44] *See* Cat Tech LLC v. TubeMaster, Inc., 528 F.3d 871 (Fed. Cir. 2008).

[45] *See* Amy J. Tindell, "Final Adjudication of Patent Validity in PTO Reexamination and Article III Courts: Whose Job Is It Anyway?," 89 *Journal of the Patent and Trademark Office Society* (2007), 787.

[46] 35 U.S.C. §§ 301, 302 (2006).

[47] P.L. 106-113.

[48] *See* 35 U.S.C. § 302 (2006).

[49] 35 U.S.C. § 303(a) (2006).

[50] 35 U.S.C. § 303(c) (2006).

[51] 35 U.S.C. § 304 (2006).

[52] *Id.*

[53] *See* Paul Morgan, "Reexamination vs. Litigation—Making Intelligent Decisions in Challenging Patent Validity," 86 *Journal of the Patent and Trademark Office Society* (2004), 441.

[54] 35 U.S.C. § 305 (2006).

[55] *Id.*

[56] *Id.*

[57] *Id.*

[58] 35 U.S.C. § 307(a) (2006).

[59] *Id.*

[60] *See* 35 U.S.C. § 306 (2006).

[61] 849 F.2d 1422 (Fed. Cir. 1988).

[62] *See* Soverain Software LLC v. Amazon.com, Inc., 356 F.Supp.2d 660 (E.D. Tex. 2005).

[63] 35 U.S.C. § 252 (2006).

[64] *Id.*

[65] *See* J. Steven Baughman, "Reexamining Reexaminations: A Fresh Look at the *Ex Parte* and *Inter Partes* Mechanisms for Reviewing Issued Patents," 89 *Journal of the Patent and Trademark Office Society* (2007), 349.

[66] Katherine M. Zandy, "Too Much, Too Little, or Just Right? A Goldilocks Approach to Patent Reexamination Reform," 61 *New York University Annual Survey of American Law* (2006), 865.

[67] Enacted in the 106th Congress, this legislation formed Subtitle F of the American Inventors Protection Act of 1999, which in turn was Title IV of the Intellectual Property and Communications Omnibus Reform Act of 1999, P.L. 106-113, 113 Stat. 1501 (1999).

[68] *See generally* Tun-Jen Chiang, "The Advantages of *Inter Partes* Reexamination," 90 *Journal of the Patent and Trademark Office Society* (2008), 579.

[69] 35 U.S.C. § 314 (2006).

[70] 35 U.S.C. § 315 (2006).

[71] Janis, *supra* note 8, at 481.

[72] 35 U.S.C. § 315(c) (2006).

[73] *Id.*

[74] The notion that a rights holder would wish to oppose its own patent may at first seem anomalous. However, a patent proprietor may request a reexamination against its own patent so that it may amend the patent's claims. Amended claims may be more likely to withstand validity challenges by third parties, present a stronger case for infringement against a competitor's products or processes, or provide other advantages. *See* Jeffrey G. Sheldon, "Strengthening and Weakening the Patent Through Reexamination and Reissue," 492 *Practising Law Institute/PAT* (Sept. 25, 2007), 119.

[75] USPTO, *Ex Parte* Reexamination Filing Data—June 30, 2009 (available at http://www.fr.com/news/ articledetail.cfm?articleid=771).

[76] USPTO, *Inter Partes* Reexamination Filing Data—June 30, 2009 (available at http://www.fr.com/news/ articledetail.cfm?articleid=772).

[77] *Id.*

[78] *See* William Barrow, "Creating a Viable Alternative: Reforming Patent Reexamination Procedure for the Small Business and Small Inventor," 59 *Administrative Law Review* (2007), 629.

[79] *See* Shannon M. Casey, "The Patent Reexamination Reform Act of 1994: A New Era of Third Party Participation," 2 *Journal of Intellectual Property Law* (1995), 559.

[80] *See* James W. Hill & M. Todd Hales, "Patent Reexamination After *KSR*," 50 *Orange County Lawyer* (Aug. 2008), 30.

[81] *See* Betsy Johnson, "Plugging the Holes in the *Ex parte* Reexamination Statute: Preventing a Second Bite at the Apple for a Patent Infringer," 55 *Catholic University Law Review* (2005), 305.

[82] USPTO, "*Inter Partes* Reexamination Filing Data—June 30, 2007" (available at http://www.fr.com/news/ articledetail.cfm?articleid=772).

[83] *See* Roger Shang & Yar Chaikovsky, "*Inter Partes* Reexamination of Patents: An Empirical Evaluation," 15 *Texas Intellectual Property Law Journal* (2006), 1.

[84] *See* Kristen Jakobsen Osenga, "Rethinking Reexamination Reform: Is It Time for Corrective Surgery, or Is It Time to Amputate?," 14 *Fordham Intellectual Property, Media & Entertainment Law Journal* (2003), 217.

[85] Johnson, *supra*, at 305.

[86] *Id.* at 330.

[87] *See* David L. Steward, *"Inter Partes* Reexam—On Steroids," 85 *Journal of the Patent and Trademark Office Society* (2003), 656.

[88] 35 U.S.C. § 315(c) (2006).

[89] *Id.*

[90] *See* Joseph D. Cohen, "What's Really Happening in *Inter Partes* Reexamination," 87 *Journal of the Patent and Trademark Office Society* (2005), 207; Susan Perng Pan, "Considerations for Modifying *Inter-Partes* Reexam and Implementing Other Post-Grant Review," 45 *IDEA: The Journal of Law and Technology* (2004), 1.

[91] Chiang, *supra*, at 580.

[92] Qin Shi, "Reexamination, Opposition, or Litigation? Legislative Efforts to Create a Post-Grant Patent Quality Control System," 31 *American Intellectual Property Law Association Quarterly Journal* (2003), 433.

[93] *See* Tremesha S. Willis, "Patent Reexamination Post Litigation: It's Time to Set the Rules Straight," 12 *Journal of Intellectual Property Law* (Spring 2005), 597.

[94] Tindell, *supra*.

[95] 35 U.S.C. § 282 (2006).

[96] *See In re* Swanson, 540 F.3d 1368, 1377 (Fed. Cir. 2008).

[97] *See, e.g.,* Eric Williams, "Remembering the Public's Interest in the Patent System—A Post-Grant Opposition Designed to Benefit the Public," 2006 *Boston College Intellectual Property and Technology Forum* (Nov. 7, 2006), 110702.

[98] *See* Eric E. Williams, "Patent Reform: The Pharmaceutical Industry Prescription for Post-Grant Opposition and Remedies," 90 *Journal of the Patent and Trademark Office Society* (2008), 354.

[99] *See* D. Ward Hobson Jr., "Reforming the Patent System: A Closer Look at Proposed Legislation," 3 *Oklahoma Journal of Law and Technology* (2006), 29.

[100] Kunin & Fetting, *supra*.

[101] *Id.*

[102] *See* Kevin R. Davidson, "Retooling Patents: Current Problems, Proposed Solutions, and Economic Implications for Patent Reform," 8 *Houston Business and Tax Law Journal* (2008), 425.

[103] *See* Matthew Sag & Kurt Rohde, Patent Reform and Differential Impact," 8 *Minnesota Journal of Law, Science & Technology* (2007), 1.

[104] *See* Chris J. Katopis, "Perfect Happiness?: Game Theory as a Tool for Enhancing Patent Quality," 10 *Yale Journal of Law and Technology* (2007-08), 360.

[105] *See* Government Accountability Office, *U.S. Patent and Trademark Office: Hiring Efforts Are Not Sufficient to Reduce the Patent Application Backlog* (Sept. 2007).

[106] Stephen G. Kunin & Anton W. Fetting, "The Metamorphosis of *Inter Partes* Reexamination," 19 *Berkeley Technology Law Journal* (2004), 971.

[107] *See* John R. Thomas, "Collusion and Collective Action in the Patent System: A Proposal for Patent Bounties," 2001 *University of Illinois Law Review* (2001), 305.

[108] *See* Mark A. Lemley, "Rational Ignorance at the Patent Office," 95 *Northwestern University Law Review* (2001), 1495.

[109] In 2007, the USPTO granted 183,901 patents and received 484,955 applications. *See* USPTO, *U.S. Patent Statistics Chart Calendar Years 1963-2007* (available at http://www.uspto.gov/web/offices/ac/ido/oeip/taf/us_stat.htm).

[110] *See* Lemley, *supra*, at 1507.

[111] *See* Osenga, *supra*, at 254.

[112] Kunin & Fetting, *supra*, at 973.

[113] Thomas, *supra*.

[114] *See* Zandy, *supra*, at 890-91.

[115] Doug Harvey, "Reinventing the U.S. Patent System: A Discussion of Patent Reform Through An Analysis of the Proposed Patent Reform Act of 2005," 38 *Texas Tech Law Review* (2006), 1133.

[116] *See* Zandy, *supra*, at 880.

[117] *See generally* CRS Report RL33367, *Patent Reform: Issues in the Biomedical and Software Industries*, by Wendy H. Schacht (discussing role of patents in process of procuring venture capital).

[118] *See* Williams, *supra*, at 360-61 (discussing these views).

[119] *See* Rebecca S. Eisenberg, "The Role of the FDA in Innovation Policy," 13 *Michigan Telecommunications and Technology Law Review* (2007), 345.

[120] *See generally* Carl Tobias, "FDA Regulatory Compliance Reconsidered," 93 *Cornell Law Review* (2008), 1003.

[121] *Id.*

In: U.S. Patent System Reform ...
Editors: F. Parker and M. Lopez

ISBN: 978-1-61470-528-4
© 2011 Nova Science Publishers, Inc.

Chapter 7

CURRENT ISSUES IN PATENTABLE SUBJECT MATTER: BUSINESS METHODS, TAX PLANNING METHODS, AND GENETIC MATERIALS

John R. Thomas

SUMMARY

Congressional interest in the patent system has grown in recent years, tracking increasing recognition of the importance of intellectual property to innovative U.S. industries. One of the areas of interest is the topic of patentable subject matter—that is, the sorts of inventions for which patents may be obtained. In particular, patents on business methods, tax planning methods, and genetic materials have proven controversial. Legislation introduced in recent sessions of Congress would restrict the availability of patents in these fields. None of these bills has been enacted.

The patent statute currently provides that patents may be obtained on any invention that is a process, machine, manufacture, or composition of matter. The range of patentable subject matter under this provision has been characterized as extremely broad. The courts have nonetheless concluded that certain subject matter, including abstract ideas, mathematical algorithms, laws of nature, and mental processes may not be patented no matter how innovative they might be. They have reasoned that these inventions comprise the fundamental tools of scientific research, and that allowing them to be privately appropriated might interfere with future advancement.

Business method patents relate to a method of administering, managing, or conducting a business or organization. Tax planning method patents concern a method of reducing or deferring taxes. The 2010 decision of the U.S. Supreme Court in *Bilski v. Kappos* addressed whether particular methods are patentable, although opinions vary as to the conclusiveness of the Courts' ruling.

Patents claiming the products of biotechnology, and in particular genetic materials, have also led to considerable debate. Genetic material patents cover such technologies as DNA sequences, amino acid sequences, individual mutations known to cause disease, and testing kits for detecting genetic mutations. Since the 1980 decision of the Supreme Court in *Diamond v. Chakrabarty*, the U.S. Patent and Trademark Office (USPTO) has viewed genetic materials and related technologies as patentable. However, the March 29, 2010, district court opinion in *Association for Molecular Pathology v. USPTO* cast doubt upon the patentability of isolated DNA. Proceedings in the so-called "Myriad" litigation were pending as of the date this report issued.

Numerous arguments have been advanced in opposition to patents on business methods, tax planning methods, and genetic materials. Some commentators believe that business method patents ultimately discourage competition, that tax strategy patents provide undesirable innovation incentives, and that patents on genetic materials lead to deleterious effects on healthcare and medical research. Other experts assert that these concerns are overstated, and further contend that the patent system provides a powerful incentive for innovation, investment, and public disclosure of technology across many fields of endeavor.

Several legislative options present themselves. If Congress decides the current rules with respect to patent eligibility are appropriate, then no action need be taken. Other possibilities include amendments to the Patent Act either to bar the issuance of patents in particular disciplines, or to limit the ability to enforce certain kinds of patents. The desire to comply with certain international agreements, in particular the WTO Agreement on Trade-Related Aspects of Intellectual Property (TRIPS), may restrict certain legislative alternatives.

INTRODUCTION

Recent congressional discussion of patent system reform has included consideration of provisions that would restrict the sorts of inventions for which patents may be obtained. Legislation introduced in the 111th Congress would have prevented the patenting of tax planning methods,[1] while one hearing regarding patent reform focused in part upon the propriety of patenting business methods.[2] Legislation introduced in previous sessions of Congress would have banned patents relating to genetic materials as well.[3] None of this legislation has been enacted.

Under current law, one of the requirements to obtain a patent is that the invention must consist of a "process, machine, manufacture, or composition of matter."[4] The courts and the U.S. Patent and Trademark Office (USPTO) have understood this language to allow an expansive range of patentable subject matter.[5] Patents have therefore been obtained upon diverse inventions, including living organisms, genetic materials, tax avoidance strategies, insurance methods, and marketing techniques.[6] Some observers believe that recent judicial opinions have narrowed the extent of patentable subject matter, however.[7]

The proper scope of patentable subject matter has been the subject of an often impassioned debate. Among other concerns, critics believe that business method patents are unnecessary to promote innovation,[8] that tax strategy patents conflict with public policy,[9] and that patents on generic materials raise ethical concerns.[10] However, other observers believe that the patent system has served as a fair and effective mechanism for promoting advances in a broad range of disciplines.[11] In their view, arbitrary restrictions upon the patent incentive are inappropriate.[12]

This report introduces the current debate concerning the appropriate range of patentable subject matter. It begins by providing an introduction to the patent system. It then reviews the ongoing discussion concerning the merits of business method and tax planning method patents. The current controversy concerning patents on genetic materials is then reviewed. The report then provides a broader discussion of innovation policy concerns that arise as policy makers consider the appropriate range of patentable subject matter. A summary of congressional issues and options concludes the report.

FUNDAMENTALS OF THE PATENT SYSTEM

The U.S. Constitution confers upon Congress the power "To promote the Progress of ... useful Arts, by securing for limited Times to ... Inventors the exclusive Right to their ... Discoveries."[13] In accordance with the Patent Act of 1952,[14] an inventor may seek the grant of a patent by preparing and submitting an application to the USPTO. USPTO officials known as examiners then determine whether the invention disclosed in the application merits the award of a patent.[15]

USPTO procedures require examiners to determine whether the invention fulfills certain substantive standards set by the patent statute. To be patentable, the invention must be novel, or different, from subject matter disclosed by an earlier patent, publication, or other state-of-the-art knowledge.[16] In addition, an invention is not patentable if "the subject matter as a whole would have been obvious at the time the invention was made to a person having ordinary skill in the art to which said subject matter pertains."[17] This requirement of "nonobviousness" prevents the issuance of patents claiming subject matter that a skilled artisan would have been able to implement in view of the knowledge of the state of the art.[18] The invention must also be useful, a requirement that is satisfied if the invention is operable and provides a tangible benefit.[19]

Even if these requirements of novelty, nonobviousness, and utility are met, an invention is not patentable unless it falls within at least one category of patentable subject matter. According to section 101 of the Patent Act of 1952, an invention which is a "process, machine, manufacture, or composition of matter" may be patented.[20] The range of patentable subject matter under this statute has been characterized as "extremely broad."[21] The courts and USPTO have nonetheless concluded that certain subject matter, including abstract ideas and laws of nature, is not patentable under section 101.[22] This report further discusses this legal standard below.

In addition to these substantive requirements, the USPTO examiner will consider whether the submitted application fully discloses and distinctly claims the invention.[23] In particular, the application must enable persons skilled in the art to make and use the invention without undue experimentation.[24] In addition, the application must disclose the "best mode," or preferred way, that the applicant knows to practice the invention.[25]

If the USPTO allows the patent to issue, its owner obtains the right to exclude others from making, using, selling, offering to sell, or importing into the United States the patented invention.[26] Those who engage in those acts without the permission of the patentee during the term of the patent can be held liable for infringement. Adjudicated infringers may be enjoined from further infringing acts.[27] The patent statute also provides for an award of damages "adequate to compensate for the infringement, but in no event less than a reasonable royalty for the use made of the invention by the infringer."[28]

The maximum term of patent protection is ordinarily set at 20 years from the date the application is filed.[29] At the end of that period, others may employ that invention without regard to the expired patent.

Patent rights do not enforce themselves. Patent owners who wish to compel others to respect their rights must commence enforcement proceedings, which most commonly consist of litigation in the federal courts. Although issued patents enjoy a presumption of validity, accused infringers may assert that a patent is invalid or unenforceable on a number of grounds. The Court of Appeals for the Federal Circuit (Federal Circuit) possesses nationwide jurisdiction over most patent appeals from the district courts.[30] The Supreme Court enjoys discretionary authority to review cases decided by the Federal Circuit.[31]

PATENTS ON BUSINESS AND TAX PLANNING METHODS

The Patent Act of 1952 allows a patent to issue upon a "process," which the statute defines to mean a "process, art, or method."[32] Process patents claim a series of steps that may be performed to achieve a specific result. Process patents typically relate to methods of manufacture or use.[33] A process patent may claim a method of making a product, for example, or a method of using a chemical compound to treat a disease.

Although the statutory term "process" is broad, courts and the USPTO have nonetheless established certain limits upon the sorts of processes that may be patented. In particular, abstract ideas, mathematical algorithms, mental processes, and scientific principles have been judged not to be patentable.[34] The Supreme Court has described these sorts of inventions as the "basic tools of scientific and technological work"[35] that should be "free to all men and reserved exclusively to none."[36] As explained by Supreme Court Justice Stephen Breyer, this rule "reflects a basic judgment that protection in such cases, despite its potentially positive incentive effects, would too severely interfere with, or discourage, development and the further spread of future knowledge itself."[37]

154 John R. Thomas

In recent years, two controversial categories of process patents have been identified. The first of these, business method patents, have been defined to include "a method of administering, managing, or otherwise operating a business or organization, including a technique used in doing or conducting business."[38] The second, tax strategy patents, have been defined as "a plan, strategy, technique, or scheme that is designed to reduce, minimize, or defer, or has, when implemented, the effect of reducing, minimizing, or deferring, a taxpayer's tax liability."[39] This report discusses these two sorts of process patents in turn.

Business Method Patents

Prior to 1998, some courts had held that methods of doing business were not patentable subject matter under § 101 of the Patent Act. For example, the Court of Appeals for the First Circuit held that:

> [A] system for the transaction of business, such, for example, as the cafeteria system for transacting the restaurant business, or similarly the open-air drive-in system for conducting the motion picture theatre business, however, novel, useful, or commercially successful is not patentable apart from the means for making the system practically useful, or carrying it out.[40]

The Federal Circuit revisited the issue in 1998, however, and in its well-known decision in *State Street Bank & Trust Co. v. Signature Financial Group* held that no business method exclusion from patentability existed.[41] The patent at issue in that case concerned a data-processing system for implementing an investment structure known as a "Hub and Spoke" system.[42] This system allowed individual mutual funds ("Spokes") to pool their assets in an investment portfolio ("Hub") organized as a partnership. According to the patent, this investment regime provided the advantageous combination of economies of scale in administering investments coupled with the tax advantages of a partnership.[43] The patented system purported to allow administrators to monitor financial information and complete the accounting necessary to maintain this particular investment structure. In addition, it tracked "all the relevant data determined on a daily basis for the Hub and each Spoke, so that aggregate year end income, expenses, and capital gain or loss can be determined for accounting and tax purposes for the Hub and, as a result, for each publicly traded Spoke."[44]

Litigation arose between Signature, the patent owner, and State Street Bank over the latter firm's alleged use of the patented invention. Among the defenses offered by State Street Bank was that the asserted patent claimed subject matter that was not within one of the four categories of statutory subject matter,[45] and hence was invalid. The district court sided with State Street Bank.[46] The trial judge explained:

> At bottom, the invention is an accounting system for a certain type of financial investment vehicle claimed as [a] means for performing a series of mathematical functions. Quite simply, it involves no further physical transformation or reduction than inputting numbers, calculating numbers, outputting numbers, and storing numbers. The same functions could be performed, albeit less efficiently, by an accountant armed with pencil, paper, calculator, and a filing system.[47]

The trial court further relied upon "the long-established principle that business 'plans' and 'systems' are not patentable."[48] The court judged that "patenting an accounting system necessary to carry on a certain type of business is tantamount to a patent on the business itself."[49] Because the court found that "abstract ideas are not patentable, either as methods of doing business or as mathematical algorithms,"[50] the patent was held to be invalid.

Following an appeal, the Federal Circuit reversed. The court of appeals concluded that the patent claimed not merely an abstract idea, but rather a programmed machine that produced a "useful, concrete, and tangible result."[51] Because the invention achieved a useful result, it constituted patentable subject matter even though its result was expressed numerically.[52] The Federal Circuit further explained that:

> Today, we hold that the transformation of data, representing discrete dollar amounts, by a machine through a series of mathematical calculations into a final share price, constitutes a practical application of a mathematical algorithm, formula, or calculation, because it produces "a useful, concrete and tangible result"—a final share price momentarily fixed for recording and reporting purposes and even accepted and relied upon by regulatory authorities and in subsequent trades.[53]

The court of appeals then turned to the district court's business methods rejection, opting to "take [the] opportunity to lay this ill-conceived exception to rest."[54] The court explained restrictions upon patents for methods of doing

156   John R. Thomas

business had not been the law since at least the enactment of the 1952 Patent Act. The Federal Circuit then concluded that methods of doing business should be subject to the same patentability analysis as any other sort of process.[55]

Following *State Street Bank,* numerous patents that arguably claim business methods have issued from the USPTO.[56] Katherine Strandburg, a member of the faculty of the New York University School of Law, has characterized business method patents as involving four categories: "(1) 'back office' or administrative operational methods; (2) customer service operational methods; (3) methods of providing personal or professional service; and (4) intangible 'products.'"[57] Several of these patents have been the subject of litigation in the federal courts.[58]

Patents on methods of doing business have attracted controversy. Some observers believe that such patents are appropriate supporters of the costly research and development efforts that occur in our service-oriented, information-based economy.[59] Others believe that business method patents are unnecessary to promote innovation and may raise unique concerns over competition.[60] A subsequent portion of this report will review this debate.

Congressional reaction to the patenting of business methods has to this point been limited. In 1999, Congress enacted the First Inventor Defense Act as part of the American Inventors Protection Act.[61] That statute provides an earlier inventor of a "method of doing or conducting business" that was later patented by another to assert a defense to patent infringement in certain circumstances.

In enacting the First Inventor Defense Act, Congress recognized that some firms may have operated under the impression that business methods could not be patented prior to the *State Street Bank* decision. As a result, they may have maintained their innovative business methods as trade secrets. Having used these trade secrets in furtherance of their marketplace activities for a period of time, however, these firms may be unable to obtain a patent upon their business method. Further, should a competitor later independently invent and patent the same business method, the trade secret holder would potentially be liable for patent infringement. Following the confirmation of the patenting of business methods by the *State Street Bank* court, the creation of the first inventor defense was intended to provide a defense to patent infringement in favor of the first inventor/trade secret holder.[62]

By stipulating that the first inventor defense applied only to a "method of doing or conducting business," Congress arguably recognized the validity of these sorts of patents.[63] The First Inventor Defense Act did not define the term

Tax Planning Method Patents

Although the *State Street Bank* opinion rejected a *per se* rule denying patents on business methods, the invention claimed by the Signature patent was arguably motivated by a desire to reduce tax liability.[65] In some sense, then, *State Street Bank* may be seen as the first tax patent case. Some commentators believe that the "increase in the number of tax strategy patents requested and approved by the [USPTO] came on the heels" of *State Street Bank*.[66]

Generally stated, tax planning method patents may be defined as those that disclose and claim a system or method for reducing or deferring taxes.[67] As of January 6, 2011, the USPTO identified 130 issued patents and 155 published applications under classification number 705/36T.[68] As the USPTO received 482,871 patent applications in 2009, and granted 191,927 patents during that year, it should be appreciated that tax strategy patents represent a very small share of that agency's workload.[69] Among the titles of the issued patents are:

- System and method for forecasting tax effects of financial transactions (U.S. Patent No. 7,305,353)
- Method and apparatus for tax efficient investment management (U.S. Patent No. 7,031,937)
- Method and apparatus for tax-efficient investment using both long and short positions (U.S. Patent No. 6,832,209)
- Computerized system and method for optimizing after-tax proceeds (U.S. Patent No. 6,115,697)

Tax planning method patents have resulted in a lively discussion among interested parties. Some observers, and in particular tax professionals, have found tax planning method patents to be "ridiculous,"[70] "bizarre,"[71] and "deeply unsettling."[72] On the other hand, other commentators, including many patent professionals, believe both that concerns over tax patents are overstated, and that the patenting of tax strategies may lead to numerous positive consequences. This report will review this debate below.

In the 111th Congress, three bills have been introduced that would stipulate that patents may not be obtained on methods of tax planning.[73] H.R. 1265 and

S. 506 define the excluded category of "tax planning invention[s]" to mean "a plan, strategy, technique, scheme, process, or system that is designed to reduce, minimize, determine, avoid, or defer, or has, when implemented, the effect of reducing, minimizing, determining, avoiding, or deferring, a taxpayer's tax liability or is designed to facilitate compliance with tax laws, but does not include tax preparation software and other tools or systems used solely to prepare tax or information returns."[74] H.R. 2584 would prevent any patent claiming a "tax planning method," which is defined similarly.[75] The legislation would apply to any application filed at the USPTO on or after the date of enactment.[76]

Bilski v. Kappos

Increasing public scrutiny of business and tax strategy patents in recent years has corresponded with heightened attention to patent eligibility issues by the USPTO and the courts. On June 28, 2010, the Supreme Court issued its decision in *Bilski v. Kappos* concerning patentable subject matter.[77] Bilski's application concerned a method of hedging risk in the field of commodities trading. In particular, his application claimed the following method:

> A method for managing the consumption risk costs of a commodity sold by a commodity provider at a fixed price comprising the steps of:
> initiating a series of transactions between said commodity provider and consumers of said commodity wherein said consumers purchase said commodity at fixed rate based upon historical averages, said fixed rate corresponding to a risk position of said consumer;
> identifying market participants for said commodity having a counter-risk position to said consumers; and
> initiating a series of transactions between said commodity provider and said market participants at a second fixed rate such that said series of market participant transactions balances the risk position of said series of consumer transactions.[78]

The USPTO rejected the application as claiming subject matter that was ineligible for patenting under section 101.

On appeal, the Federal Circuit characterized the "true issue before us then is whether Applicants are seeking to claim a fundamental principle (such as an abstract idea) or a mental process." The Federal Circuit explained:

> A claimed process is surely patent-eligible under § 101 if: (1) it is tied to a particular machine or apparatus, or (2) it transforms a particular article into a different state or thing.[79]

Current Issues in Patentable Subject Matter 159

Applying this standard, the Federal Circuit concluded that Bilski's application did not claim patentable subject matter. The Court of Appeals acknowledged Bilski's admission that his claimed invention was not limited to any specific machine or apparatus, and therefore did not satisfy the first prong of the section 101 inquiry.[80] The Federal Circuit also reasoned that the claimed process did not achieve a physical transformation. According to Chief Judge Michel, "[p]urported transformations or manipulations simply of public or private legal obligations or relationships, business risks, or other such abstractions cannot meet the test because they are not physical objects or substances, and they are not representative of physical objects or substances."[81] As a result, the USPTO decision to deny Bilski's application was affirmed.

After agreeing to hear the case, the Supreme Court issued a total of three opinions, consisting of a plurality opinion for the Court and two concurring opinions. No single opinion was joined by a majority of Justices for all of its parts. The opinion for the Court, authored by Justice Kennedy, agreed that Bilski's invention could not be patented. But the plurality rejected the Federal Circuit's conclusion that the machine or transformation test was the sole standard for identifying patentable processes. Rather, that standard was deemed "an important and useful clue."[82] The Court also confirmed that laws of nature, physical phenomenon, and abstract ideas were not patentable subject matter.

The majority also rejected the assertion that business methods should not be considered patentable subject matter *per se*. In reaching this conclusion, Justice Kennedy pointed to the First Inventor Defense Act, which explicitly speaks to patents claiming a "method of doing or conducting business."[83] As he explained, the "argument that business methods are categorically outside of § 101's scope is further undermined by the fact that federal law explicitly contemplates the existence of at least some business method patents."[84]

Justice Stevens, joined by Justices Breyer, Ginsburg, and Sotomayor, issued a lengthy concurring opinion on the day of his retirement from the Supreme Court. He agreed that the machine-or-transformation test was "reliable in most cases" but "not the exclusive test."[85] In his view, the Court should "restore patent law to its historical and constitutional moorings" by declaring that "methods of doing business are not, in themselves, covered by the statute."[86]

Justice Breyer also issued a concurring opinion that Justice Scalia joined in part. Justice Breyer identified four points on which all nine justices agreed: (1) the range of patentable subject matter is broad but not without limit; (2) the machine-or-transformation test has proven to be of use in determining whether a process is patentable or not; (3) the machine-or-transformation test is not the sole standard for assessing the patentability of processes; and (4) not everything that merely achieves a "useful, concrete, and tangible result" qualifies as patentable subject matter.[87]

Opinions vary upon the impact of *Bilski v. Kappos*, particularly with respect to tax strategy patents. Attorney Marvin Petry explains that "*Bilski* seems, once and for all, to have ended the tax practitioners' concern with tax strategy patents because it conclusively rejects tax strategy patents which were of significant concern, those that involve pure method steps...."[88] On the other hand, Ellen P. Aprill, a member of the faculty of Loyola Law School of Los Angeles, writes that *Bilski v. Kappos* "leaves us in a greater state of uncertainty than that which existed before it was decided." In her view, the Supreme Court ruling "demonstrates that for those who believe that tax strategies should not be patented, legislation is needed." Future developments will provide better perspectives upon the effect of the *Bilski* opinion upon business method and tax strategy patents.[89]

PATENTS ON GENETIC MATERIALS

Controversy concerning patentable subject matter has not been confined to methods of doing business and tax planning methods. Patents claiming the products of biotechnology, and in particular genetic materials, have also led to considerable debate. In recent years, advances in biotechnology have resulted in a growing body of knowledge concerning the genetic material of living organisms. In turn, thousands of patents have been granted that assert rights in specific sequences of deoxyribonucleic acid (DNA)—the nucleic acid that contains the genetic instructions that all known living organisms use in order to develop and function.[90] Other patents claim related technologies, including individual mutations known to cause disease, testing kits for detecting genetic mutations, amino acid sequences (proteins), and the use of these proteins as medicines.[91]

The availability of patents pertaining to genetic technologies may be traced to the well-known decision of the U.S. Supreme Court in *Diamond v. Chakrabarty*.[92] That 1980 opinion held that a genetically engineered microorganism constituted patentable subject matter, qualifying as both a "composition of matter" or "manufacture" within the meaning of §101 of the

Patent Act.[93] In so doing, the Supreme Court confirmed the traditional rule that "laws of nature, physical phenomenon, and abstract ideas have been held not patentable. Thus, a new mineral discovered in the earth or a new plant found in the wild is not patentable subject matter." The Court reasoned that the traditional rule denying patents to "products of nature" was inapplicable to the invention before it, however. Chief Justice Burger explained:

> [T]he patentee has produced a new bacterium with markedly different characteristics from any found in nature and one having the potential for significant utility. His discovery is not nature's handiwork, but his own; accordingly it is patentable subject matter under § 101.[94]

As applied to genetic materials, the reasoning of *Diamond v. Chakrabarty* may be read to allow patents to issue where scientists have isolated these materials from their natural environment or produced through artificial techniques. As a result, patent claims directed towards DNA typically employ such terms as "isolated" or "recombinant" in order to reflect these conditions. Notably, this claim language restricts the scope of patent to isolated or artificially produced substances. As a result, the genes naturally possessed by humans and other living organisms are not included within the scope of proprietary rights.[95]

The March 29, 2010, decision of the District Court for the Southern District of New York in *Association for Molecular Pathology v. USPTO* cast serious doubt upon this reasoning, however.[96] Judge Sweet's lengthy opinion struck down several patents owned by Myriad Genetics claiming isolated DNA and various analytical methods:

> The claims-in-suit directed to "isolated DNA" containing human BRCA1/2 gene sequences reflect the USPTO's practice of granting patents on DNA sequences so long as those sequences are claimed in the form of "isolated DNA." This practice is premised on the view that DNA should be treated no differently from any other chemical compound, and that its purification from the body, using well-known techniques, renders it patentable by transforming it into something distinctly different in character. Many, however, including scientists in the field of molecular biology and genomics, have considered this practice a "lawyer's trick" that circumvents the prohibitions on the direct patenting of DNA in our bodies but which, in practice, reaches the same result. The resolution of these motions is based upon long recognized principles of molecular biology and genetics: DNA represents the physical embodiment of biological information, distinct in its essential characteristics from any

other chemical found in nature. It is concluded that DNA's existence in an "isolated" form alters neither this fundamental quality of DNA as it exists in the body nor the information it encodes. Therefore, the patents at issue directed to "isolated DNA" containing sequences found in nature are unsustainable as a matter of law and are deemed unpatentable subject matter under 35 USC 101.

Similarly, because the claimed comparisons of DNA sequences are abstract mental processes, they also constitute unpatentable subjct matter under Section 101.

Some observers believe that the broad language employed by Judge Sweet implies that virtually all gene patents are invalid under §101 as claiming unpatentable subject matter.[97] At the time this report goes to press, this litigation is the subject of an appeal to the Federal Circuit.

As with patents claiming business methods and tax strategies, patents pertaining to genetic materials are controversial.[98] Critics have asserted that genetic materials should remain accessible to all, rather than subject to intellectual property rights, and that such patents may depress research efforts and have a deleterious impact upon public health.[99] Other experts believe these critiques are overstated or misplaced, however.[100] In their view, patent rights in DNA are no more expansive or worthy of concern than for other sorts of inventions. This report reviews this debate below.

Congress has previously considered restricting patents relating to genetic materials. In the 110th Congress, Representative Becerra introduced the Genetic Research and Accessibility Act, H.R. 977. That bill would have provided:

> Notwithstanding any other provision of law, no patent may be obtained for a nucleotide sequence, or its functions or correlations, or the naturally occurring products it specifies.[101]

The proposed amendment would not have applied to a patent issued prior to the date of enactment of the Genetic Research and Accessibility Act.[102] This legislation was not enacted. As well, the Genomic Research and Diagnostic Disability Act of 2002 was introduced, but not enacted, in the 107th Congress.[103] That legislation would have created a research exemption from infringement for research on genetic sequence information and an infringement exemption for genetic diagnostic testing.

Innovation Policy Issues

The patenting of business methods, tax strategies, genetic materials, and other sorts of post-industrial technologies has raised controversy. Some observers have expressed concerns that these sorts of inventions should not be patented, no matter how innovative they might be. They believe that section 101 of the Patent Act, the provision governing patentable subject matter, should be interpreted, and if necessary amended, to exclude these sorts of inventions from patenting.[104] Others believe that these concerns are overstated. They further assert that the patenting of inventions of the Information Age, as well as biotechnologies, will be beneficial for innovation and competition.[105] This report reviews some of the primary arguments that have been raised in this debate.

Proponents of a broad notion of patentable subject matter assert that the patent system has traditionally offered a powerful incentive for innovation across many industries. For example, the chemical, electronics, manufacturing, telecommunications, and pharmaceutical industries are among those that have long sought and enforced patents. In the view of these commentators, the patent system will readily adapt to new fields of endeavor as well. Further, many inventions of the 21st century—including business methods and genetic inventions—are as subject to costly research and development efforts as more traditional technologies. Observers question why the patent incentive exists in one field of costly research and development and not in another.[106]

The patent system also provides the benefit of public disclosure. In order to obtain patent rights, inventors must fully disclose their inventions such that a skilled artisan could practice them without undue experimentation.[107] A patent system that denies protection to entire categories of inventions may cause inventors to conceal them as trade secrets. In contrast to patenting, trade secret protection does not result in the disclosure of publicly available information. Taking the steps necessary to maintain secrecy, such as implementing physical security measures, also imposes costs that may ultimately be unproductive for society.[108]

Another argument in favor of a broad notion of patentable subject matter is that distinguishing patentable and unpatentable inventions may at times prove difficult. For example, assessing whether a particular invention is sufficiently technologically embedded to constitute patentable subject matter may not constitute a straightforward, routine inquiry. Aware of the legal requirements to obtain a patent, lawyers may draft patent instruments in such as a way as to make software inventions appear to be hard-wired machines. Such artful claims drafting may ultimately make patents more difficult to read and interpret.[109]

Supporters of an expansive patent system also observe that patents have been identified as facilitators of markets. If inventors lack patent rights, they may have scant tangible assets to sell or license. In addition, an inventor might otherwise be unable to police the conduct of a contracting party. Any technology or know-how that has been disclosed to a prospective licensee might be appropriated without compensation to the inventor. The availability of patent protection decreases the ability of contracting parties to engage in opportunistic behavior. By lowering such transaction costs, the patent system may make transactions concerning information goods more feasible.[110] Categorical exclusion of certain sorts of inventions from the patent system may deny entire industries this potential benefit.

Studies have also indicated that entrepreneurs and small, innovative firms rely more heavily upon the patent system than larger enterprises. Large firms often possess a number of alternative means for achieving a proprietary interest in a particular technology. For example, trade secrecy, ready access to markets, trademark rights, speed of development, and consumer goodwill may to some degree act as substitutes for the patent system. However, individual inventors and small firms often do not have these mechanisms at their disposal. As a result, the patent system may enjoy heightened importance with respect to these enterprises.[111]

Legal experts also assert that patents do not provide the affirmative right to use the patented invention, but rather the right to exclude others from doing so. This perspective implies that the grant of patent neither implies government approval of an invention, nor allows meaningful control of a technology. As a result, the grant of a patent on, for example, a particular tax strategy, should not be deemed as an indication that the strategy is legally sound.[112] Similarly, disallowing patents on genetic materials would not necessarily suppress the technology as a general matter.[113]

Although these and other assertions weigh in favor of an ambitious scope of patentable subject matter, other observers are less optimistic. Some commentators believe that innovation in areas such as business methods, tax planning methods, and genetic materials has flourished even though the availability of patent rights has been uncertain. For example, the American Institute of Certified Public Accountants [AICPA] asserts that "[p]eople already have substantial incentives to comply with tax law and lower their taxes."[114] Under this line of reasoning, the patent incentive is unnecessary to promote a socially optimal level of innovation within these disciplines.

Other observers go further, believing that patents in these areas may not merely be unnecessary, but also socially detrimental. With respect to business methods, some commentators believe that these patents are commonly of such broad scope as to "effectively appropriate all possible solutions to a particular problem."[115] This extent of proprietary rights may limit the ability of others to design around the patented invention and ultimately discourage competition.[116]

With respect to tax strategy patents, some believe that an incentive to develop methods of lowering one's taxes is not socially desirable. William A. Drennan, a member of the law faculty at Southern Illinois University, contrasts the grant of tax strategy patents with recent Treasury Department Regulations that, in his view, "reduce the economic incentive to create tax loopholes."[117] Mr. Drennan thus explains:

> [O]ne government agency—the Treasury Department—is taking action to discourage loopholes. In contrast, the Patent Office (at the direction of the Federal Circuit) is providing a new incentive to create loopholes. Since the Treasury Department is in charge of the sound administration of the U.S. tax system, the Treasury Department's views on sound tax policy should be given greater weight than the view of the Patent Office on this subject.[118]

Other experts believe that tax strategy patents are inappropriate because they are said to inject private control over a system of public laws.[119] Under this view, a patent may potentially grant one individual the ability to prevent others from using a new tax provision. In turn, private actors may affect the ability of federal, state, and local governments to raise revenue, influence taxpayer behavior, and otherwise achieve the intended purposes of the tax laws.[120] These concerns were voiced by the AICPA in the following way:

> Tax strategy patents also preempt Congress's prerogative to have full legislative control over tax policy. Congress enacts tax law provisions applicable to various taxpayers and intends that taxpayers will be able to use them. Tax strategy patents thwart this Congressional intent by giving tax strategy patent holders the power to decide how select tax law provisions can be used and who can use them.[121]

Tax professionals have also expressed concerns over the impact of tax strategy patents upon their own practices, as well as taxpayers in general.

Some observers believe that the burdens of investigating whether a taxpayer's planned course of action is covered by a tax strategy patent, determining whether the patent was providently granted by the USPTO, and potentially negotiating with the patent proprietor in order to employ the strategy, will be costly and impractical for many taxpayers.[122] Further, because compliance with the tax laws and its self-assessment system is obligatory for all citizens of the United States, the scope of this burden could be considerable.[123]

Several additional objections have arisen to patenting the inventions of genetic materials. Some individuals believe that patenting genetic materials devalues the worth and dignity of living beings. These commentators believe that such patents would allow individuals to obtain an ownership right in another sentient being. From this perspective, such a patent right is akin to slavery and morally wrong. Human genetic materials in particular are instead deemed to be the common heritage of humanity and therefore should be the subject of shared public ownership, rather than proprietary rights.[124]

Patents on genetic materials have also been said to lead to possible deleterious effects on healthcare and research related to healthcare. For example, some patents claim human genes that indicate susceptibility to a particular disease and diagnostic tests for detecting that gene. Observers question whether having only one proprietary diagnostic test for a particular disease lies in the public interest. They also suggest that patent rights over a gene that is linked to a particular disease might inhibit further research concerning that disease.[125]

Professors Heller and Eisenberg have also expressed the concern that the "tragedy of the anticommons" may lead to the underuse of patented genetic resources. In their view, too many overlapping intellectual property rights with respect to genetic materials may hinder research and development, and ultimately the exploitation of potential future products. For example, one enterprise might own a patent on a genomic DNA fragment, another on the corresponding protein, and yet another on a diagnostic test for a genetic disease. In this circumstance, multiple owners each have the right to exclude others and no one has an effective privilege of use. Development of a commercial product in this situation may prove difficult or impossible.[126]

Additional assertions have been made both in support of a broad scope of patentable subject matter, as well as in favor of restricting the scope of patenting. Unfortunately, no rigorous analytical method allows for study of the role the patent system plays in promoting innovation, investment, and competition. As a result, arguments for and against a broad scope of patentable subject matter are difficult to quantify. Determining the precise scope of

Current Issues in Patentable Subject Matter 167

patentable subject matter therefore remains a matter of legal reasoning, as informed by concerns over innovation and competition policy.

CONGRESSIONAL ISSUES AND OPTIONS

If Congress decides that the current rules with respect to patent eligibility are satisfactory, then no action need be taken. Should Congress choose to take action, however, a number of options exist. One possibility is an amendment to section 101 of the Patent Act stipulating that certain subject matter is not patentable. Legislation introduced in the 111th Congress would take this step with respect to tax shelters,[127] while legislation in the 110th Congress would have done so with respect to nucleotide sequences.[128]

Another option is to allow patents on particular inventions to issue, but to limit the remedies available to proprietors of such patents. The Patent Act currently stipulates that damages and injunctions are not available for patent infringement caused by "a medical practitioner's performance of a medical activity" under certain circumstances.[129] This provision could potentially be amended to include other categories of inventions.

Other legislative responses are also possible. Congress could choose to track USPTO practices with respect to patents on business methods, tax strategies, or genetic materials. In this respect, commentators have proposed several reforms, including the hiring of USPTO examiners with expertise in taxation or other sensitive areas.[130] Congress could also encourage continued cooperation between the USPTO and other federal agencies, such as the IRS, with expertise in particular disciplines.

If legislation is contemplated, one international agreement that deserves consideration is the World Trade Organization (WTO) Agreement on Trade-Related Aspects of Intellectual Property Rights, commonly known as the TRIPS Agreement.[131] As a WTO member, the United States has committed to "give effect to the provisions of [the TRIPS] Agreement."[132] The TRIPS Agreement provides that "patents shall be available for any inventions, whether products or processes, in all fields of technology."[133] It further states that "patents shall be available and patent rights enjoyable without discrimination as to ... the field of technology."[134] The TRIPS Agreement additionally stipulates that WTO member states may exclude from patentability certain inventions, in particular "diagnostic, therapeutic and surgical methods for the treatment of humans and animals" and "plants and animals other than micro-organisms, and essentially biological processes for the production of plants and animals other than non-biological and microbiological processes."[135] Compliance with the TRIPS Agreement may place some limits on the ability of WTO member states to legislate with respect to patentable subject matter.

CONCLUDING OBSERVATIONS

The topic of patentable subject matter has raised a surprisingly heated debate in many contexts, including business methods, tax strategies, and genetic materials. Many knowledgeable observers have voiced strong objections to patents in these fields on a number of grounds. However, other experts point to the lack of direct evidence that granting patents within these fields has persistently led to deleterious consequences, and instead believe that they potentially benefit society. Although the patenting of business methods, tax strategies, and genetic materials has generally been viewed on an individual basis, the policy issues raised in these debates share many common themes. Collectively, these debates may promote further inquiry into the sorts of inventions that may be appropriately patented.

ACKNOWLEDGMENTS

This report was funded in part by a grant from the John D. and Catherine T. MacArthur Foundation.

End Notes

[1] H.R. 1265, § 303; H.R. 2584, §1; S. 506, § 303.

[2] U.S. House of Representatives, Committee on the Judiciary, Hearing on H.R. 1260, the "Patent Reform Act of 2009," April 30, 2009.

[3] See, e.g., The Genomic Research and Accessibility Act, 110th Congress, H.R. 977. This legislation was not enacted.

[4] 35 U.S.C. § 101 (2006). If an invention is judged to fall within one of these four categories of patentable subject matter, then it must meet other standards in order to be subject to a patent. In particular, the invention must not have been obvious to a person of ordinary skill in the art at the time it was made. 35 U.S.C. § 103(a) (2006).

[5] See Ryan Hagglund, "Patentability of Human-Animal Chimeras," 25 *Santa Clara Computer & High Technology Law Journal* (2008-2009), 51.

Current Issues in Patentable Subject Matter

[6] See Dana Remus Irwin, "Paradise Lost in the Patent Law? Changing Visions of Technology in the Subject Matter Inquiry," 60 *Florida Law Review* (2008), 775.

[7] See Scott D. Locke & William D. Schmidt, "Business Method Patents: The Challenge of Coping with An Ever Changing Standard of Patentability," 18 *Fordham Intellectual Property, Media and Entertainment Law Journal* (2008), 1079.

[8] See Leo J. Raskind, "The *State Street Bank* Decision: The Bad Business of Unlimited Patent Protection for Methods of Doing Business," 10 *Fordham Intellectual Property, Media & Entertainment Law Journal* (1999), 61.

[9] See Tinna C. Otero, "Banning Tax Strategy Patents—Should We Listen to the Tax Practitioners?," 48 *Jurimetrics Journal* (2008), 309.

[10] See Michele Westhoff, "Gene Patents: Ethical Dilemmas and Possible Solutions," 20 *Health Lawyer* no. 4 (2008), 1.

[11] See Christopher A. Harkins, "Throwing Judge Bryson's Curveball: A Pro Patent View of Process Claims as Patent-Eligible Subject Matter," 7 *John Marshall Review of Intellectual Property Law* (2008), 701.

[12] See Kevin Schubert, "Should *State Street* Be Overruled? Continuing Controversy Over Business Method Patents," 90 *Journal of the Patent and Trademark Office Society* (2008), 461.

[13] Article I, Section 8, Clause 8.

[14] P.L. 82-593, 66 Stat. 792 (codified at Title 35 of the United States Code).

[15] 35 U.S.C. § 131 (2006).

[16] 35 U.S.C. § 102 (2006).

[17] 35 U.S.C. § 103(a) (2006).

[18] See KSR International Co. v. Teleflex Inc., 550 U.S. 398 (2007).

[19] See In re Fischer, 421 F.3d 1365, 1371 (Fed. Cir. 2005).

[20] 35 U.S.C. § 101 (2006).

[21] In re Comiskey, 554 F.3d 967 (Fed. Cir. 2009).

[22] See In re Bilski, 545 F.3d 943 (Fed. Cir. 2008) (*en banc*).

[23] 35 U.S.C. § 112 (2006).

[24] See Invitrogen Corp. v. Clontech Labs., Inc., 429 F.3d 1052, 1070-71 (Fed. Cir. 2005).

[25] See High Concrete Structures, Inc. v. New Enterprise Stone and Lime Co., 377 F.3d 1379, 1382 (Fed. Cir. 2004).

[26] 35 U.S.C. § 271(a) (2006).

[27] 35 U.S.C. § 283 (2006). *See* eBay Inc. v. MercExchange L.L.C., 126 S.Ct. 1837 (2006).

[28] 35 U.S.C. § 284 (2006).

[29] 35 U.S.C. § 154(a)(2) (2006). Although the patent term is based upon the filing date, the patentee obtains no enforceable legal rights until the USPTO allows the application to issue as a granted patent. A number of Patent Act provisions may modify the basic 20-year term, including examination delays at the USPTO and delays in obtaining marketing approval for the patented invention from other federal agencies.

[30] 28 U.S.C. § 1295(a)(1) (2006).

[31] 28 U.S.C. § 1254(1) (2006).

[32] 35 U.S.C. § 100(b) (2006).

[33] See In re Pleuddemann, 910 F.2d 823, 826 (Fed. Cir. 1990).

[34] See Laboratory Corp. of America Holdings v. Metabolite Laboratories, Inc. 548 U.S. 124 (2006) (opinion of Justice Breyer, dissenting from dismissal of writ of certiorari as improvidently granted) (hereinafter "LabCorp.").

[35] Gottschalk v. Benson, 409 U.S. 63, 67 (1972).

[36] Funk Brothers Seed Co. v. Kalo Inoculant Co., 333 U.S. 127, 130 (1948).

[37] LabCorp., *supra*, at 128.

[38] Business Method Patent Improvement Act, H.R. 5364, 106th Cong., § 2 (2000). This legislation was not enacted.

[39] H.R. 1908, 110th Cong., § 10(b)(2)(A) (2008). In a portion of the definition not quoted above, the legislation expressly explained that "the use of tax preparation software or other tools used solely to perform or model mathematical calculations or prepare tax or information returns" was not considered a "tax planning method." This legislation was not enacted.

[40] Lowe's Drive-In Theaters, Inc. v. Park-In Theaters, Inc., 174 F.2d 547, 552 (1st Cir. 1949).

[41] 149 F.3d 1368 (Fed. Cir. 1998).

[42] See U.S. Patent No. 5,193,056.

[43] 149 F.3d at 1370.

[44] Id.

[45] 35 U.S.C. § 101 (2006) (identifying processes, machines, manufactures, and compositions of matter as patentable subject matter).

[46] 927 F. Supp. 502 (D. Mass. 1996).

[47] Id. at 515.

[48] Id.

[49] Id. at 516.

[50] Id.

[51] 149 F.3d at 1373.

[52] Id. at 1375.

[53] Id. at 1373.

[54] Id. at 1375.

[55] Id.

[56] See, e.g., John R. Allison & Emerson H. Tiller, "The Business Method Patent Myth," 18 *Berkeley Technology Law Journal* (2003), 987.

[57] Katherine J. Strandburg, "What If There Were a Business Method Use Exemption to Patent Infringement?," 2008 *Michigan State Law Review*, 245.

[58] See, e.g., Nicholas A. Smith, "Business Method Patents and Their Limits: Justifications, History, and the Emergence of a Claim Construction Jurisprudence," 9 *Michigan Telecommunications & Technology Law Review* (2002), 171.

[59] Thomas J. Scott, Jr. & Stephen T. Schreiner, "Planning for the Brave New World: Are Business Method Patents Going to Be Second Class Citizens?," 19 *Intellectual Property & Technology Law Journal* no. 6 (2007), 6.

[60] Andrew A. Schwartz, "The Patent Office Meets the Poison Pill: Why Legal Methods Cannot Be Patented," 90 *Journal of the Patent and Trademark Office* (2008), 194.

[61] P.L. 106-113, 113 Stat. 1536 (1999) (codified at 35 U.S.C. § 273(b) (2006)).

[62] See generally David H. Hollander, Jr., "The First Inventor Defense: A Limited Prior User Right Finds Its Way Into U.S. Patent Law," 30 *American Intellectual Property Law Association Quarterly Journal* (2002), 37.

[63] See Rochelle Cooper Dreyfuss, "Are Business Method Patents Bad for Business?," 16 *Santa Clara Computer and High Technology Law Journal* (2000), 263.

[64] John R. Allison & Starling D. Hunter, "On the Feasibility of Improving Patent Quality One Technology At a Time: The Case of Business Methods," 21 *Berkeley Technology Law Journal* (2006), 729.

[65] See, e.g., Paul E. Schaafsma, "A Gathering Storm in the Financial Industry," 9 *Stanford Journal of Law, Business and Finance* (2004), 176.

[66] Meyer, *supra*, at 187.

[67] H.R. 1908, 110th Cong., § 10(b)(2)(A) (2008).

[68] It should be appreciated that some observers have criticized the USPTO classification system as unreliable. *See, e.g.,* John R. Allison and Mark A. Lemley, "The Growing Complexity of the United States Patent System," 82 *Boston University Law Review* (2002), 77. As a result, it is possible that some patents arguably directed towards tax strategies may presently be classified under different categories.

[69] USPTO, U.S. Patent Statistics, Calendar Years 1963-2009 (available at http://www.uspto.gov/web/offices/ac/ido/ oeip/taf/us_stat.pdf).

Current Issues in Patentable Subject Matter 171

[70] Editorial, "Pay to Obey," *New York Times* (Oct. 31, 2006).

[71] David Nolte, "USPTO is Getting It Wrong on Tax Strategy Patents," (July 20, 2006) (available at http://www.expertclick.com/NewsReleaseWire/default.cfm?Action=ReleaseDetail&ID=13238).

[72] Melone, *supra*, at 438.

[73] H.R. 1265, § 303; H.R. 2584, §1; S. 506, § 303.

[74] H.R. 1265, § 303(a); S. 506, § 303(a).

[75] H.R. 2584, §1(a).

[76] H.R. 1265, § 303(b); H.R. 2584, §1(b); S. 506, § 303(b).

[77] 130 S.Ct. 3218 (2010).

[78] 545 F.3d 943, 949 (Fed. Cir. 2008).

[79] *Id.* at 954.

[80] *Id.* at 962.

[81] *Id.* at 965.

[82] 130 S.Ct. at 3227.

[83] 35 U.S.C. § 273.

[84] 130 S.Ct. at 3228.

[85] *Id.* at 3231.

[86] *Id.*

[87] *Id.* at 3258-59.

[88] Marvin Petry, "*Bilski v. Kappos: A New Chapter in Tax Strategy Patentability* ((Oct. 28, 2010) (available at http://www.lexisnexis.com/COMMUNITY/PATENTLAW/blogs/patentcommentary/archive/2010/10/28/bilski-v-kappos-a-new-chapter-in-tax-strategy-patentability.aspx).

[89] Ellen P. Aprill, "The Impact of *Bilski* on Tax Strategy Patents," TaxProfBlog (June 28, 2010) (available at http://taxprof.typepad.com/taxprof_blog/2010/06/aprill-bilski-.html).

[90] See Kevin T. Kelly, "Fragging the Patent Frags: Restricting Expressed Sequence Tag Patenting Using the Enablement-Commensurate-In-Scope-With-the-Claims Requirement," 17 *Texas Intellectual Property Law Journal* (2008), 49.

[91] See Eileen M. Kane, "Splitting the Gene: DNA Patents and the Genetic Code," 71 *Tennessee Law Review* (2004), 707.

[92] 447 U.S. 303 (1980).

[93] Id. at 308.

[94] Id. at 310.

[95] Roger Schechter & John Thomas, *Principles of Patent Law* (2d ed. 2004), 33.

[96] 702 F.Supp. 2d 181 (S.D.N.Y. 2010).

[97] See Miri Yoon, "Gene Patenting Debate: The Meaning of *Myriad*," 9 *John Marshall Journal of Intellectual Property Law* (2010), 953.

[98] See CRS Report RS22516, *Gene Patents: A Brief Overview of Intellectual Property Issues*, by Wendy H. Schacht.

[99] Nuffield Council on Bioethics, The Ethics of Patenting DNA—A Discussion Paper (2002).

[100] R. Stephen Crespi, "Patenting and Ethics—A Dubious Connection," 85 *Journal of the Patent and Trademark Office Society* (2003), 31.

[101] H.R. 977, § 2(a).

[102] Id. at § 2(c).

[103] H.R. 3967.

[104] See, e.g., Michael Moulton, "Effecting the Impossible: An Argument Against Tax Strategy Patents," 81 *Southern California Law Review* (2008), 631.

[105] See, e.g., Lucas Osbron, "Tax Strategy Patents: Why the Tax Community Should Not Exclude the Patent System," 18 *Albany Law Journal of Science and Technology* (2008), 325.

[106] See, e.g., Christopher A. Harkins, "Throwing Judge Bryson's Curveball: A Pro Patent View of Process Claims as Patent-Eligible Subject Matter," 7 *John Marshall Review of Intellectual Property Law* (2008), 701.

[107] 35 U.S.C. § 112 (2006).

[108] See Robert G. Bone, "A New Look at Trade Secret Law: Doctrine in Search of Justification," 86 *California Law Review* (1998), 241.

[109] See Fusco, *supra*.

[110] Paul J. Heald, "Optimal Remedies for Patent Infringement: A Transactional Model," 45 *Houston Law Review* (2008), 1165; Paul J. Heald, "A Transaction Costs Theory of Patent Law," 66 *Ohio State Law Journal* (2005), 473.

[111] Michael J. Meurer, "Inventors, Entrepreneurs, and Intellectual Property Law," 45 *Houston Law Review* (2008), 1201.

[112] See, e.g., Osbron, *supra*.

[113] Robert P. Merges, "Intellectual Property in Higher Life Forms: The Patent System and Controversial Technologies," 47 *Maryland Law Review* (1998), 1051.

[114] AICPA, "Analysis and Legislative Proposals Regarding Patents for Tax Strategies" (February 28, 2007) (available at http://tax.aicpa.org) (hereinafter "AICPA Analysis").

[115] David Kappos *et al.*, "A Technological Contribution Requirement for Patentable Subject Matter: Supreme Court Precedent and Policy," 6 *Northwestern Journal of Technology and Intellectual Property* 152 (2008) at *57.

[116] See Alexandra Wilson, "Business Method Patents Gone Wild: Narrowing *State Street Bank* and Shifting to a European Perspective," 12 *Journal of Technology Law and Policy* (2007), 71.

[117] Drennan, *supra*, at 280.

[118] Id.

[119] See Richard S. Marshall, "Tax Strategy Patents—Legislative, Judicial and Other Developments," 48 *Tax Management Memo* (2007), 243.

[120] Steve Seidenberg, "Taxation Innovation: Patent Office Receives Criticism for Issuing Patents on Tax Strategies," *Inside Counsel* (December 2006).

[121] AICPA Analysis, *supra*, at 5.

[122] Gary C. Bubb, "Patented Tax Strategies—Are You Serious?," *Rhode Island Lawyers Weekly* (August 20, 2007).

[123] Ellen P. Aprill, "Responding to Tax Strategy Patents," American Bar Association Annual Meeting (August 11, 2007), 7.

[124] Nuffield Council on Bioethics, "The Ethics of Patenting DNA: A Discussion Paper," 22 (2002).

[125] Id. at 40.

[126] Michael A. Heller and Rebecca S. Eisenberg, "Can Patents Deter Innovation? The Anticommons in Biomedical Research," 280 *Science* (May 1, 1998), 698.

[127] H.R. 1265, § 303; H.R. 2584, §1; S. 506, § 303.

[128] Genomic Research and Accessibility Act, H.R. 977, § 2.

[129] 35 U.S.C. § 287(c) (2006).

[130] Aprill, *supra*, at 21.

[131] See Agreement on Trade-Related Aspects of Intellectual Property Rights, Apr. 15, 1994, Marrakesh Agreement Establishing the World Trade Organization, Annex 1C, art. 66, para. 1, Legal Instruments—Results of the Uruguay Round vol. 31, 33 I.L.M. 81 (1994).

[132] Id. at Art. 1, § 1.

[133] Id. at Art. 27(1).

[134] Id.

[135] Id. at 27(3).

In: U.S. Patent System Reform ...
Editors: F. Parker and M. Lopez

ISBN: 978-1-61470-528-4
© 2011 Nova Science Publishers, Inc.

Chapter 8

GENE PATENTS: A BRIEF OVERVIEW OF INTELLECTUAL PROPERTY ISSUES

Wendy H. Schacht

SUMMARY

The courts have upheld gene patents that meet the criteria of patentability defined by the Patent Act However, the practice of awarding patents on genes has come under scrutiny by some scientists, legal scholars, politicians, and other experts. Gene patenting may raise ethical, legal, and economic issues; a short discussion of these issues follows.

PATENTS

The Patent Act of 1952, codified in Title 35 of the United States Code, defines current patent law According to section 101, one who "invents or discovers any new and useful process, machine, manufacture, or any composition of matter, or any new and useful improvement thereof, may obtain a patent therefore, subject to the conditions and requirements of this title." To be patentable, an invention must be useful, novel, and nonobvious The requirement of usefulness, or utility, is satisfied if the invention is operable and provides a tangible benefit To be judged novel, the invention must not be fully anticipated by a prior patent, publication, or other knowledge within the public domain A nonobvious invention must not have been readily within the ordinary skills of a competent artisan at the time the invention was made The invention must be fully described Once the United States Patent and Trademark Office (USPTO) issues a patent, the owner enjoys the right to exclude others from making, using, selling, offering to sell, or importing into the United States the patented invention Generally, the term of a patent is 20 years from the date the application was filed In the process of obtaining a patent, the information associated with the patent is published and made available to the public.

GENE PATENTS

Genes are chemical compounds and, as such, they qualify as compositions of matter with respect to patent criteria. Within the parameters of patentability delineated by the Patent Act, there are several exceptions as interpreted by the courts Products of nature (a preexisting substance that is found in the wild) may not be patented, *per se* However, the courts have also determined that such a product of nature may be patentable if significant artificial changes are made By purifying, isolating, or otherwise altering a naturally occurring product, an inventor may obtain a patent on the product in its altered form.[1] Thus, "one cannot patent a naturally occurring gene or protein as it exists in the body, but one can patent a gene or protein that has been isolated from the body and is useful in that form as a pharmaceutical drug, screening assay or other application."[2]

Research indicates that by 2005, 20% of human genes were claimed by patents in the United States.[3] According to the U.S. Patent and Trademark Office, as of the end of FY2007, over 49,000 patents issued relate to genes (including method of use) This practice of awarding patents on genes, while upheld by the courts, has come under scrutiny and criticism by some scientists, legal scholars, and politicians The subject of gene patenting involves various ethical, legal, and economic components While not mutually exclusive, a short discussion of several issues follows.

ETHICAL ISSUES

An often held belief is that gene patents permit outsiders ownership of another person's genetic makeup, often without their knowledge or consent.[4] This concern has led to complaints that patients no longer control their own bodies and doctors are being constrained from testing for various diseases.[5] Professor Lori Andrews argues that patents hinder access to testing procedures because "... gene-patent holders can control any use of 'their' gene; they can prevent a doctor from testing a patient's blood for a specific genetic mutation and can stop anyone from doing research to improve a genetic test or to develop a gene therapy based on that gene."[6] This perceived constraint on research and testing options is an issue to opponents of gene patents.[7] According to Dr. Debra Leonard, patents on "... specific genetic information limits the medical use of the information and impedes or prevents widespread research on the disease, the traditional pathway by which medical knowledge is advanced and shared."[8]

However, other experts disagree As noted by Dr. Jorge Goldstein and Attorney Elina Golod, the courts have consistently "... taken the position that a person does not own any tissues or cells once they are outside the person's body."[9] Attorneys Lee Bendekgey and Dr. Diana Hamlet-Cox found no evidence of patients unable to utilize existing genetic tests because of patents Instead, they maintain, it is a financial issue associated with the cost of health care and/or an issue of profits for the doctor or clinical geneticist wishing to administer tests patented by other inventors.[10] Similarly, Professor Iain Cockburn found "... there is little quantitative evidence thus far of a negative impact of patents on scientific research activity...."[11] From his perspective, the disclosure obligations of the patent system may better serve the objective of encouraging the diffusion of knowledge and raising social returns than the chief legal alternative, trade secret protection.[12]

LEGAL ISSUES

Some commentators argue that genes are products of nature — discoveries, not inventions — that do not meet the criteria necessary to obtain a patent.[13] As stated by Professor Andrews, "The useful properties of a gene's sequence ... are not ones that scientists have invented, but instead, are natural, inherent properties of the genes themselves."[14] The fact that the gene has been isolated is considered a "technicality" by experts who subscribe to this position.[15]

The courts have upheld gene patents if they meet the requirements of the Patent Act. According to some experts, the law allows for patents on discoveries:

> ... despite what is repeatedly asserted by the opponents of gene patenting, patent law applies equally to "discoveries" as to "inventions." In fact, Article 1, Section 8 of the U.S. Constitution ... explicitly refers to "discoveries," as does the Patent Statute: "Whoever invents or *discovers* any new and useful process, machine, manufacture, or composition of matter, or any new and useful improvement thereof, may obtain a patent therefor...." [Emphasis added.][16]

As Bendekgey and Hamlet-Cox point out, many biotechnology products are built upon compounds existing in nature including such therapies as interferons, interleukins, and insulin.[17] Similarly, a patent on penicillin was awarded to Alexander Flemming who isolated and purified the drug from mold, a "naturally occurring source."[18]

The quality of the gene patents awarded by the USPTO is a concern for some experts. A study by Professors Jordan Paradise, Lori Andrews, and Timothy Holbrook found that 38% of the claims contained in 74 patents on human genetic material were "problematic."[19] This research indicated that utility issues were identified as the most prevalent problem, followed by the required written description of the invention.[20] In another paper, Andrews also argues "... gene patents do not meet the criteria of non-obviousness, because, through *in silico* analysis, the function of human genes can now be predicted on the basis of their homology to other genes."[21]

This analysis is not without criticism, as questions have been raised regarding the authors' definition of "problematic" that is based upon the authors' perspectives rather than court decisions In addition, the data include patents issued in the early 1990s when gene patenting was in its infancy and there was little expertise and experience on which to grant these patents.[22] Such concerns over patent quality, however, are not limited to gene patents The debate over whether or not the USPTO is too lenient in awarding patents is on-going and is particularly intense as new industries develop and seek patents. The patent process is a "one size fits all" activity leading to claims that certain technologies are not amenable to patenting or that patents granted do not meet the requirements of the Patent Act However, as patent examiners

Gene Patents: A Brief Overview of Intellectual Property Issues   177

build up expertise in a new field and develop prior art, the quality of patents typically increase.[23]

ECONOMIC ISSUES

Biotechnology industry leaders perceive patents as critical to protecting innovation. Research by Professor Wesley Cohen and his colleagues found that patents were considered the most effective method to protect inventions in the drug industry, particularly when biotechnology is included.[24]   Other commentators note that patents are particularly important in this sector because of the relative ease of replicating the finished product. Costs associated with imitating a product "... are extremely low relative to the innovator's costs for discovering and developing a new compound."[25]

Opponents of gene patents argue that they restrain additional research because "... there are no alternatives to a patented gene in diagnosis, treatment, and research,"[26] and owners require licensing fees.[27] However, despite what some experts claim to be a negative result of financial considerations in the biomedical research community,[28] others maintain that, at most, gene patents "... prevent the doctors and clinical geneticists from performing these tests for profit, or in a way that competes with the patent holder, without reimbursement to the inventors of those tests."[29]

Some analysts assert that certain patents, particularly those on research tools[30] in biotechnology, hinder the innovation process Professors Rebecca Eisenberg and Richard Nelson state that ownership of research tools may "... impose significant transaction costs" that result in delayed innovation and possible future litigation.[31] They argue that patents also can stand in the way of research by others:

> Broad claims on early discoveries that are fundamental to emerging fields of knowledge are particularly worrisome in light of the great value, demonstrated time and again in the history of science and technology, of having many independent minds at work trying to advance a field Public science has flourished by permitting scientists to challenge and build upon the work of rivals.[32]

Professor Arti Rai argues that "the most important research tools are fundamental research platforms that open up new and uncharted areas of investigation" that need further development by researchers in the field.[33]

While acknowledging that patent protection on research tools has stimulated private investment in biotechnology and the development of new products and processes, Eisenberg writes that:

> Patents on research tools threaten to restrict access to discoveries that, according to the firm beliefs of scientists trained in the tradition of open science, are likely to have the greatest social value if they are widely disseminated to researchers who are taking different approaches to different problems.[34]

Other commentators dispute these assertions Professor F. Scott Kieff maintains that there was no such "norm" regarding open scientific access as opposed to intellectual property protection in the basic biological science community.[35] He notes that "... experience shows that patents on inputs generally do not prevent the production of outputs" and that the availability of intellectual property protection has expanded the resources available in the biotechnology community and led to its success.[36] Bendekgey and Hamlet-Cox agree that there is no evidence that gene patents have caused a decrease in research as a whole in the biomedical arena or in gene therapies.[37]

A study by Professors John Walsh, Ashish Arora, and Wesley Cohen found little evidence that work has been curtailed due to intellectual property issues associated with research tools.[38] Scientists are able to continue research by "... licensing, inventing around patents, going offshore, the development and use of public databases and research tools, court challenges, and simply using the technology without a license (i.e., infringement)." According to the authors, private sector owners of patents permitted such infringement in academia (with the exception of those associated with diagnostic tests in clinical trials) "... partly because it can increase the value of the patented technology."

A later analysis by Professors Walsh, Cohen, and Charlene Cho concluded that patents do not have a "substantial" impact upon basic biomedical research and that "... none of [their] random sample of academics reported stopping a research project due to another's patent on a research input, and only about 1% of the random sample of academics reported experiencing a delay or modification in their research due to patents."[39] However, obtaining "tangible" research inputs (e.g., actual materials) appear to be more difficult because of competition, cost, and time issues.[40]

Gene Patents: A Brief Overview of Intellectual Property Issues   179

As genes continue to be patented and research in the field of biotechnology proceeds, the discussion surrounding the ethical, legal, and economic issues of gene patenting remains on-going in the public policy arena.

End Notes

[1] Scripps Clinic and Research Foundation v. Genentech, Inc., 927 F.2d 1565 (Fed. Cir. 1991).

[2] Biotechnology Industry Organization, *Primer: Genome and Genetic Research, Patent Protection and 21st Century Medicine*, available at [http://www.bio.org/ip/primer].

[3] Kyle Jensen and Fiona Murray, "Intellectual Property Landscape of the Human Genome," *Science*, October 14, 2005, 239-240.

[4] Michael Crowley, "They Own Your Body," *Readers Digest*, August 2006, available at [http://www.rd.com]

[5] Debra G.B. Leonard, "Medical Practice and Gene Patents: A Personal Perspective," *Academic Medicine*, December 2002, 1388.

[6] Lori B. Andrews, "Genes and Patent Policy: Rethinking Intellectual Property Rights," *Nature Reviews*, October 2002, 804.

[7] John F. Merz, "Disease Gene Patents: Overcoming Unethical Constraints on Clinical Laboratory Medicine," *Clinical Chemistry*, 45:3, 1999, 324.

[8] *Medical Practice and Gene Patents: A Personal Perspective*, 1388.

[9] Jorge A. Goldstein and Elina Golod, "Human Gene Patents," *Academic Medicine*, December 2002, Part 2, 1321.

[10] Lee Bendekgey and Diana Hamlet-Cox, "Gene Patents and Innovation," *Academic Medicine*, December 2002, Part 2, 1378.

[11] Iain M. Cockburn, "Blurred Boundaries: Tensions Between Open Scientific Resources and Commercial Exploitation of Knowledge in Biomedical Research," April 30, 2005, 15, available at [http://people.bu.edu/cockburn/cockburn-blurred-boundaries.pdf].

[12] *Ibid.*, 11.

[13] "Owning the Body and the Soul," *The Economist*, March 12, 2005, 77, and *They Own Your Body*.

[14] *Genes and Patent Policy: Rethinking Intellectual Property Rights*, 803.

[15] *They Own Your Body*.

[16] *Gene Patents and Innovation*, 1374.

[17] Lee Bendekgey and Diana Hamlet-Cox, "Rebuttal: Why We Need Gene Patents," *Law.com* [web journal], December 30, 2002

[18] Q. Todd Dickinson statement in "The Human Genome Project, DNA Science and the Law: The American Legal System's Response to Breakthroughs in Genetic Science," *American University Law Review*, 2001-2002, 380.

[19] Jordan Paradise, Lori Andrews, and Timothy Holbrook, "Patents on Human Genes: An Analysis of Scope and Claims," *Science*, 11 March 2006, 1566-1567.

[20] *Patents on Human Genes: An Analysis of Scope and Claims*, 1567.

[21] *Genes and Patent Policy: Rethinking Intellectual Property Rights*, 803.

[22] *Owning the Body and the Soul*, 77.

[23] See CRS Report RL31281, *Patent Quality and Public Policy: Issues for Innovative Firms in Domestic Markets*, by John R. Thomas.

[24] Wesley M. Cohen, Richard R. Nelson, and John P. Walsh, *Protecting Their Intellectual Assets: Appropriability Conditions and Why U.S. Manufacturing Firms Patent (or Not)*, NBER Working Paper 7552, Cambridge, National Bureau of Economic Research, February 2000, available at [http://www.nber.org/papers/w7552].

180 Wendy H. Schacht

[25] Henry Grabowski, "Patents and New Product Development in the Pharmaceutical and Biotechnology Industries," *Duke University Economics Working Paper*, July 2002, available at [http://www.econ.duke.edu/Papers/Other/Grabowski/Patents.pdf], 4.

[26] *Patents on Human Genes: An Analysis of Scope and Claims*, 1566.

[27] *They Own Your Body.*

[28] *Medical Practice and Gene Patents: A Personal Perspective*, 1390.

[29] *Gene Patents and Innovation*, 1378.

[30] A biotechnology research tool is a cell line, reagent, or antibody used in research.

[31] Rebecca S. Eisenberg and Richard R. Nelson, "Public vs. Proprietary Science: A Fruitful Tension?," *Daedalus*, Spring 2002.

[32] *Ibid.*

[33] Arti Rai, "Genome Patents: A Case Study in Patenting Research Tools," *Academic Medicine*, December 2002, Part 2, 1369.

[34] Rebecca Eisenberg, "Why the Gene Patenting Controversy Persists," *Academic Medicine*, December 2002, Part 2, 1383.

[35] F. Scott Kieff, "Facilitating Scientific Research: Intellectual Property Rights and the Norms of Science – A Response to Rai and Heisenberg," *Northwestern University Law Review*, Winter 2001, 694.

[36] *Ibid.*, 704.

[37] *Gene Patents and Innovation*, 1377, 1378.

[38] John P. Walsh, Ashish Arora, Wesley M. Cohen, "Working Through the Patent Problem," *Science*, February 14, 2003, 1021.

[39] John P. Walsh, Charlene Cho, and Wesley Cohen, "Patents, Material Transfers and Access to Research Inputs in Biomedical Research," September 20, 2005, 37, available at [http://tigger.uic.edu/~jwalsh/WalshChoCohenFinal050922.pdf].

[40] *Ibid.*, 2.

CHAPTER SOURCES

Chapter 1 – This is an edited, reformatted and augmented version of Congressional Research Service Report R41638, dated April 21, 2011.

Chapter 2 – This is an edited, reformatted and augmented version of Congressional Research Service Report R41090, dated January 5, 2011.

Chapter 3 – This is an edited, reformatted and augmented version of Congressional Research Service Report RL33367, dated January 12, 2011.

Chapter 4 – This is an edited, reformatted and augmented version of Congressional Research Service Report R41261, dated May 27, 2010.

Chapter 5 – This is an edited, reformatted and augmented version of Congressional Research Service Report R41418, dated January 6, 2011

Chapter 6 – This is an edited, reformatted and augmented version of Congressional Research Service Report R40378, dated January 14, 2010.

Chapter 7 – This is an edited, reformatted and augmented version of Congressional Research Service Report R40681, dated January 13, 2011.

Chapter 8 – This is an edited, reformatted and augmented version of Congressional Research Service Report RS22516, updated January 7, 2008.

INDEX

#

21st century, 163

A

agencies, 38, 42, 69, 95, 145, 167, 169
antibody, 88, 180
antitrust, 84
assessment, 40, 47, 50, 53, 81, 83, 84
assets, 6, 128, 154, 164
asymmetry, 37
AT&T, 50, 64, 65, 71
awarding patents on genes, viii, 173, 174
awareness, 51, 67, 68

B

basic research, 80
benefits, 5, 76, 77, 80, 99, 100, 113
biological processes, 168
biotechnology, 37, 39, 78, 80, 85, 88, 150, 160, 176, 177, 178, 179, 180
blogs, 171
business model, 39

C

candidates, 79
case law, 59, 66
certificate, 19, 124, 131, 132, 133
certification, 25
challenges, 20, 30, 81, 93, 132, 136, 142, 143, 146, 178
Chief Justice, 70, 161
civil action, 13, 58, 112, 139
classification, 157, 170
clinical trials, 79, 80, 81, 178
commercial, viii, 2, 5, 14, 34, 35, 61, 76, 80, 123, 131, 141, 166
commodity, 158
communication, 54
community, 2, 9, 33, 39, 84, 85, 100, 133, 135, 177, 178
compensation, 6, 35, 128, 164
competition, 37, 81, 112, 113, 116, 150, 156, 163, 165, 166, 178
competition policy, 167
competitiveness, 33, 77
competitors, 7, 10, 21, 25, 34, 38, 74, 75, 77, 85, 92, 101, 102, 112, 116, 129, 132, 134
complexity, 9, 30, 33, 101, 131, 134
compliance, 29, 158, 166
composition, 4, 51, 75, 85, 94, 126, 149, 151, 152, 160, 173, 176

184   Index

computer, 29, 40, 60, 81, 82, 83, 85
computer software, 81, 85
Congressional interest in patent reform, vii, 1, 2
Congressional recognition, viii, 123
consent, 22, 75, 113, 120, 175
Consolidated Appropriations Act, 41, 44
Copyright, iv, 31, 45, 121
copyright law, 31
cost, viii, 5, 21, 24, 34, 35, 36, 39, 58, 79, 80, 86, 87, 123, 124, 127, 140, 141, 143, 175, 178
counsel, 18, 19, 63, 100, 102, 117, 118
counterfeiting, 120
Court of Appeals, 2, 3, 5, 12, 18, 50, 52, 72, 95, 111, 114, 127, 153, 154, 159

D

damages, viii, 5, 12, 13, 17, 18, 19, 34, 35, 40, 50, 52, 53, 55, 59, 60, 61, 62, 63, 66, 95, 111, 112, 113, 120, 127, 153, 167
data processing, 24, 31
decision-making process, 68
defendants, 56, 57, 112, 116
deficiencies, vii, 1, 3, 124
denial, 55, 130
deoxyribonucleic acid, 160
Department of Justice, 119
district courts, 5, 52, 57, 61, 67, 95, 114, 115, 116, 119, 127, 153
documentary evidence, 58
draft, 163

E

economic downturn, 96
economic growth, vii, viii, 1, 5, 38, 73, 74, 75, 123, 124, 127
economics, 87
economies of scale, 154
enforcement, 5, 31, 32, 34, 35, 37, 52, 53, 76, 84, 95, 116, 127, 153
entrepreneurs, 34, 38, 96, 164

F

facilitators, 164
FAS, 44
FDA, 75, 79, 80, 100, 148
FDA approval, 79, 100
federal courts, 5, 52, 67, 95, 111, 113, 125, 127, 129, 142, 153, 156
federal government, 26, 86, 112
federal law, 159
Federal Register, 107
Federal Trade Commission, vii, 1, 3, 41, 74, 79, 86, 87
funding, 8, 15, 38, 81, 99, 143
funds, 154

G

gene patenting, 174, 176, 179
gene therapy, 175
genes, viii, 161, 166, 173, 174, 175, 176, 179
genetic disease, 166
genetic information, 175
genetic materials, viii, 149, 150, 151, 160, 161, 162, 163, 164, 166, 167, 168
genetic mutations, 150, 160
genetics, 161
genomics, 161
goods and services, 5, 34, 47
grants, viii, 2, 14, 17, 73, 74, 75, 126
growth, 6, 38, 47, 76, 128

H

House of Representatives, 69, 168

I

incentive effect, 153
income, 25, 102, 154
individual inventors, viii, 10, 33, 38, 123, 164

Index

185

intellectual property, vii, viii, 36, 37, 57, 73, 74, 75, 80, 81, 82, 83, 84, 93, 105, 113, 117, 141, 142, 143, 149, 162, 166, 178

intellectual property rights, 143, 162, 166

inventions, viii, 5, 9, 11, 14, 17, 24, 30, 31, 34, 35, 38, 39, 40, 54, 66, 73, 74, 76, 78, 82, 83, 85, 98, 127, 149, 151, 153, 162, 163, 164, 166, 167, 168, 175, 176, 177

inventors, viii, 6, 7, 9, 10, 11, 14, 16, 23, 29, 30, 31, 33, 36, 38, 39, 73, 76, 77, 85, 91, 93, 96, 98, 99, 102, 123, 126, 128, 163, 164, 175, 177

investment(s), 5, 7, 28, 35, 38, 39, 75, 76, 77, 79, 80, 82, 84, 87, 129, 132, 143, 150, 154, 155, 157, 166

investors, 34, 83, 84, 129, 143

IPO, 71, 83

J

judicial branch, 135

judiciary, 49, 50, 54, 68, 88

Judiciary Committee, 58, 60

jurisdiction, 5, 8, 28, 31, 36, 52, 56, 57, 67, 95, 127, 129, 153

K

knowledge-based economy, 2

L

laws, 3, 7, 24, 31, 33, 34, 36, 40, 57, 66, 68, 73, 74, 75, 85, 93, 124, 149, 152, 158, 159, 161, 165, 166

lawyers, 57, 163

legal scholars, viii, 173, 174

legislation, vii, viii, 2, 3, 4, 13, 31, 33, 34, 43, 49, 50, 51, 53, 54, 56, 58, 59, 67, 74, 92, 104, 112, 114, 123, 125, 132, 146, 151, 158, 160, 162, 167, 168, 169, 170

Legislative interest, vii, 49, 50, 135

legislative proposals, 34, 54, 124, 135

legislative responses, 167

litigation, vii, 4, 5, 13, 26, 27, 30, 31, 32, 33, 35, 36, 37, 52, 54, 56, 57, 58, 59, 60, 62, 65, 80, 95, 112, 114, 116, 121, 125, 127, 131, 132, 134, 139, 140, 142, 143, 150, 153, 156, 162, 177

local government, 165

M

modifications, 40, 50, 53

molecular biology, 161

monopoly, 5, 75, 76

motivation, 116

N

National Academy of Sciences, vii, 1, 3, 41, 74, 86

National Institutes of Health, 80

National Research Council, 41, 44, 86

negative consequences, 17, 92, 93, 99

nucleic acid, 160

nucleotide sequence, 162, 167

O

officials, 4, 51, 94, 126, 152

opportunities, 21, 23, 30, 47, 67

organize, 10

outreach, 32

ownership, vii, 1, 5, 40, 73, 74, 75, 80, 82, 83, 84, 142, 166, 175, 177

P

Patent Act, viii, 4, 11, 12, 13, 16, 42, 51, 53, 54, 55, 59, 64, 68, 69, 72, 75, 94, 95, 97, 104, 111, 112, 113, 114, 120, 121, 126, 131, 144, 150, 152, 153, 154, 156, 161, 163, 167, 169, 173, 174, 176

Patent ownership, vii, 1, 73, 74, 75

patent policy, vii, 73, 74, 113

186 Index

permission, 5, 33, 52, 95, 126, 143, 153
permit, 5, 10, 17, 27, 67, 76, 77, 175
police, 6, 10, 128, 164
policy, vii, 2, 3, 7, 14, 18, 23, 27, 30, 41, 77,
103, 105, 112, 115, 116, 117, 124, 125,
129, 136, 141, 142, 151, 168
policy issues, 2, 41, 168
policy makers, 151
potential benefits, 91, 92, 93
precedent, 63, 67, 115
preparation, iv, 65, 140, 158, 170
private investment, 178
procedural rule, 105, 109, 140
process innovation, 78
producers, 59
professionals, 29, 99, 157, 165
project, 81, 178
proliferation, 112, 120
promote innovation, 127, 151, 156
protection, 4, 5, 6, 10, 14, 15, 31, 33, 36, 39,
40, 50, 52, 64, 66, 74, 75, 76, 78, 80, 82,
85, 94, 95, 126, 128, 132, 134, 153, 163,
164, 175, 178
public domain, 6, 76, 100, 113, 118, 128,
142, 174
public goods, 127
public health, 162
public interest, 55, 113, 166
public policy, 116, 151, 179

Q

qualifications, 43

R

R&D investments, 40
regulations, 24, 44, 104, 105
rejection, 23, 31, 56, 155
relevance, 21, 22, 23, 130
requirements, 29, 34, 37, 39, 40, 52, 73, 75,
76, 77, 85, 94, 119, 126, 151, 152, 163,
173, 176
researchers, 81, 129, 177, 178

resources, 5, 10, 32, 33, 37, 68, 84, 92, 93,
95, 97, 99, 100, 105, 136, 141, 142, 143,
166, 178
restrictions, 3, 81, 143, 151, 155
royalty, 5, 52, 59, 60, 61, 62, 95, 127, 153
rules, 9, 16, 33, 55, 56, 58, 97, 103, 131,
150, 167

S

science, 77, 79, 80, 88, 177, 178
scope, 5, 22, 39, 40, 50, 68, 76, 77, 96, 102,
131, 134, 136, 137, 143, 151, 157, 159,
161, 164, 165, 166
Secretary of Commerce, 43
security, 6, 76, 128, 163
Senate, 3, 19, 24, 25, 29, 58, 60, 69, 112,
120
small businesses, 39, 47, 83
small firms, viii, 10, 33, 38, 47, 82, 83, 123,
164
social welfare, 28
society, 6, 35, 76, 128, 163, 168
software, 39, 40, 60, 61, 64, 65, 74, 75, 78,
80, 81, 82, 83, 84, 85, 88, 158, 164, 170
stakeholders, 68
startup firm, 84
statutes, 143
storage, 121, 122
structure, vii, 3, 92, 103, 154
subscribers, 54
Supreme Court, 5, 49, 50, 51, 52, 54, 55, 56,
57, 64, 65, 66, 67, 71, 72, 95, 113, 121,
127, 150, 153, 158, 159, 160, 172

T

tax planning methods, viii, 53, 65, 149, 150,
151, 160, 164
tax policy, 165
tax system, 165
taxation, 167
taxes, 28, 150, 157, 165
taxpayers, 28, 29, 165

Index

technological advancement, vii, 1, 5, 38, 73, 74, 75
technological change, 47
technological progress, vii, 1, 3, 73, 74, 77
technologies, 6, 33, 83, 128, 134, 150, 160, 163, 176
technology, 2, 6, 14, 16, 21, 29, 30, 34, 36, 38, 47, 54, 59, 60, 77, 80, 81, 83, 86, 92, 93, 96, 103, 128, 150, 164, 167, 177, 178
technology transfer, 16, 34, 38
telecommunications, 163
testing, 87, 150, 160, 162, 175
textbook, 11, 43
time constraints, 81
time frame, 20, 143
Title I, 144, 146
Title IV, 144, 146
trade, 6, 14, 15, 30, 38, 76, 128, 156, 163, 164, 175
trademarks, 24
trading partners, 2, 33, 36, 41, 98
transaction costs, 6, 80, 128, 164, 177
transactions, 2, 6, 34, 128, 157, 158, 164
Treasury, 24, 165

U

U.S. economy, 2, 7, 41, 47
U.S. Patent and Trademark Office (USPTO), viii, 1, 2, 3, 4, 8, 9, 10, 11, 14, 15, 17, 19, 20, 21, 22, 23, 24, 25, 26, 27, 28, 31, 32, 33, 34, 35, 38, 41, 42, 44, 46, 47, 51, 52, 68, 69, 74, 75, 86, 88, 91, 92, 93, 94, 95, 96, 97, 99, 101, 103, 104, 105, 106, 107, 108, 109, 123, 124, 125, 126, 127, 129, 130, 131, 132, 133, 134, 135, 136, 137, 138, 140, 141, 142, 143, 144, 145, 146, 147, 150, 151, 152, 153, 156, 157, 158, 159, 161, 166, 167, 169, 170, 171, 174, 176
unexamined applications, viii, 91, 93, 101
universities, viii, 10, 33, 38, 39, 81, 123
USPTO patent-granting process, viii, 91

V

valuation, 40
venture capital, 83, 100, 148
venue, 23, 50, 53, 56, 57, 58, 66, 69

W

World Trade Organization (WTO), 150, 167, 172

Y

Yale University, 77